Happiness
on the Blue Dot

warm wishes!

Lisa M

Happiness on the Blue Dot

INTIMATE CONVERSATIONS IN FARAWAY PLACES ABOUT LIFE, DEATH, LOVE, AND JOY

Lisa Marranzino

Palmetto Publishing Group
Charleston, SC

Happiness on the Blue Dot
Copyright © 2019 by Lisa Marranzino
All rights reserved

First Edition
Printed in the United States

ISBN-13: 978-1-64111-193-5
ISBN-10: 1-64111-193-3

CONTENTS

Introduction: Happiness-on-the-Blue-Dot Roadmap   vii

Part I: Southeast Asia: The Jewel in the Lotus   **1**

   1. Thailand: Siamese Rubies   3

   2. Vietnam and Cambodia: Pink Sapphires   37

Part II: Europe: Inner Summer, Fairytales, and Blue Lights   **69**

   3. Norway: The Happiest Place on Earth   71

   4. Denmark and Sweden: Hippies and Fairytales   93

   5. The Netherlands: Windmills and Blue Lights   113

Part III: Latin America: Hardship and Happiness   **125**

   6. Mexico: Land of Enchantment   127

   7. Argentina: Simplicity and Seduction   147

   8. Peru: Mysterious Land of the Incas   165

Part IV: Africa: Natural Rhythms   **181**

   9. South Africa: The Natural Order   183

   10. Zambia and Zimbabwe: Angels in Flight   198

Part V: The Middle East: Finding God   **215**

   11. Qatar: Land of Abundance   217

   12. Israel: Holy Kindness   231

   13. Egypt: Larger than Life   244

Epilogue: Insights on Happiness   **265**

Acknowledgments   **271**

Appendices

   Appendix A: Happiness Discoveries Checklist   273

   Appendix B: How to Change Your Beliefs   277

   Appendix C: How to Converse with a Stranger   281

Suggested Readings   **285**

About the Author   **287**

Introduction

HAPPINESS-ON-THE-BLUE-DOT ROADMAP

On Valentine's Day in 1990, a photograph of planet Earth was captured by the Voyager 1 space probe as it was leaving the solar system. From about 3.7 billion miles away, the Earth appeared as a tiny blue dot against the vastness of black space. Billions of people with infinite ideas about life and happiness reside on this tiny dot, the Earth, our home.

Happiness on the Blue Dot is a dialogue with exotic people from around the world who share their ideas about how to live a happy, satisfying life. This collection of colorful conversations from Asia, Europe, South America, Africa, and the Middle East took place during my four-year journey to discover what lies at the heart of happiness; global trips that helped me overcome a midlife malaise. It is my hope that these rich and fascinating stories will help you escape your everyday, while opening your heart and mind to new ways of thinking about life's possibilities.

A passionate tango-dancing couple in Buenos Aires. A healthy and happy prostitute in Amsterdam. A tracker in the wilderness of South Africa. A survivor of the Killing Fields in Cambodia. A man who made peace with his kidnappers in Egypt during the Arab Spring. These amazing people and others I met on my journey shared their stories and philosophies developed in times of prosperity and despair. Their life stories inspired me, and I hope they inspire you, too.

I wanted to live a happier life. Now I am doing just that. But in order to make the necessary changes, I had to take a long hard look at my belief system. I needed to invite happiness into my life. The world taught me how.

Welcome to the happiness adventure on the blue dot.

DIAMONDS IN THE ROUGH

As a licensed psychotherapist in private practice for many years, conversing with strangers comes easily to me. But connecting with people in faraway places—strangers with customs, cultures, and languages so different from my own—tested my confidence. Sitting down with people I did not know in coffee shops, bars, restaurants, and markets took all of my courage and humility—especially since these conversations took place in new, often boisterous, locations, rather than the comfort zone of my peaceful office.

Surprisingly, everyone I approached chose to speak with me about their lives. This book would not be possible without the kind, trusting people profiled here. I am humbled by their courage and openness, their ability to overlook my inadvertent cultural faux pas. I've included examples throughout the book for how to approach and converse with strangers. In this way, I hope to breathe life back into the art of conversation. I see the art of conversation as a sorely needed skill, now that our connectedness through technology has left most of us feeling more disconnected than ever before.

Many of my clients seek my help when they experience this type of emptiness, which creates a deep-seated need for change. Restlessness, boredom, longing, and itchy agitation all reach out and grip them as they move through their everyday routines. My clients complain of feeling like they are just going through the motions. I call this becoming the "real walking dead." Sometimes the reasons for this numbness are obvious—job loss, divorce, illness, loss of a loved one—but many times symptoms emerge for no apparent reason.

In 2013, I realized I had somehow joined their ranks. For me, the feeling seemed like the classic void of a midlife crisis. Yet my midlife crisis came during the absence of a crisis. Sure, I had experienced significant loss in the past, but when I looked at my life now, it appeared I had it all. (What I didn't realize back then was how quickly my life would change when a little-known syndrome robbed me of my health and left me fighting for my happiness in ways I never had before.) I had a supportive husband, and his endearing quirkiness made me laugh every day. Our kids were grown, and miraculously sought our advice on important issues. My work as a psychotherapist—a career where the more you know, the more you know you don't know—was always interesting and usually rewarding. Yet there I was, walking around like a zombie.

Even though I intentionally reminded myself every day of how fortunate I was, and consciously practiced gratitude and kindness, the gray cloud of discontent refused to dissipate. Waves of loneliness and despair washed over me in the most random moments, my life shifting from living color to a dismal black and white. I knew something had to give, as the gloomy sensation was relentless.

In my professional experience, ignoring emotions like these can lead to what I call "risky and frisky" behaviors; affairs, shopping sprees, overuse of alcohol, drugs, or food. I was determined not to go down any of those paths.

I needed to find a new path to a richer emotional life. But I wasn't sure where to begin.

One morning in the spring of 2014, I had back-to-back sessions with two clients I affectionately called my "diamonds in the rough." To say these two men came from challenging backgrounds would be a gross understatement. Despite a raft of troubles—physical and sexual abuse, neglect, drug addiction, and prison time—both men exhibited a rousing resolve and the ability to see the best in the world around them, in others, and within themselves. Closing down and contracting inward would be a natural reaction to the kind of psychological obstacles they faced. Instead, they expanded the very best of themselves outward into the world, providing hope and inspiration to others—a rare form of courage.

I realized these two men had each found a key to happiness.

I had always been fascinated by what makes one person able to get over intense trauma and hardship while another caves in to despair. So much depends on how they spin the stories of their own lives. Every day at work, my clients share their belief systems with me. They tell me what they think about the meaning of life, love, success, purpose, and death. Part of my job is to encourage them to examine their thoughts and beliefs, to make sure they are healthy and working well for them.

After the two troubled but happy clients left my office that day, I began to wonder about all the ways of thinking about life *I* had not yet considered. Surely there were new belief systems out there, ways of looking at life that were different from my own. Perhaps there were belief systems that would better suit my nature and make me happier. Maybe I could change myself and shake off the gloom that had darkened my life.

The usual modes of transition would not work for me. I needed something big, something dramatic that would engage all my senses. And that's when the idea hit me: I would venture out of my comfort zone, tap into our hard-earned savings, and search the world for more diamonds in the rough like my two clients. I would interview strangers in other lands and discover their secrets to living happy, satisfying lives.

But why limit my adventure to just diamonds? After all, the world is full of wondrous variety. As I booked my first trip to Thailand, I opened myself to whatever I would find. I would not limit myself to preconceived notions, but allow the world to share its gems, its beauty, and variety.

There's nothing quite as liberating, invigorating, or humbling as jumping on a plane and meeting the world of the unknown with an open mind.

A NOTE ON BELIEF SYSTEMS

Before we take off, a note about the relationship between beliefs and happiness: Maybe you've had a difficult life like my diamond-in-the-rough clients; or maybe you are one of the lucky ones who had a head start on happiness—good parents, a good education, and a good family. There's no one path to happiness and life satisfaction. Because it's not just the circumstances of our lives that create enduring happiness; there are other factors.

Research shows that about 50 percent of our enduring levels of happiness are due to our genes. Only around 10 percent of the influence on our happiness involves external circumstances, while the remaining 40 percent can be accounted for by how we think and feel about our past, present, and future. This is the part we have the most control over.

Our belief systems are based on the stories we tell ourselves about our lives. In our minds, we go over life experiences and current events, evaluating ourselves and how well we're doing, examining how others feel about us, and determining how we feel about ourselves. These stories are the way we make sense of the past and face unknowns in the future.

When we are young, our minds are untainted and our brains are like sponges. As time passes, however, we begin to interpret the world ourselves. These interpretations are influenced by our exposure to life and to the teachings of others, and they become the way we make sense of life. We hold tight to our life stories, which serve as our own personal reality.

The critical challenge is to recognize those beliefs that pilot our lives. These beliefs have tremendous power and can propel us into happiness and success, or keep us stuck in failure and despair. They can stifle us, free us, whip us into chaos, or calm us. They can hold us back in depressive rumination, or push us forward to realize our wildest dreams.

This is why we need to challenge old beliefs and open our minds to fresh ways of looking at life. I had to do this in order to push my way out of a stultifying malaise. As a result, I found a happier, more satisfying life. I hope this book will help you to rejuvenate your own approach to life and find greater happiness, too.

Part I

SOUTHEAST ASIA: THE JEWEL IN THE LOTUS

Chapter 1

THAILAND: SIAMESE RUBIES

With an open heart, an open mind, and a ravenous appetite for exploring new cultures, I set my sights on destination number one. I would begin my journey in a country at the center of Mainland Southeast Asia. I imagined Thailand as an enchanting land full of gleaming temples, majestic elephants, exotic beaches, and strikingly beautiful people.

I planned to talk to these people about their views on life, and this excited me. However, I didn't quite know how to go about it, especially since I don't speak Thai. In my research, I learned that Thailand is known as the Land of Smiles. So I thought that if I could smile and be warm, then the Thai people might warm to me, too.

Thailand seemed the perfect place to begin my adventures in happiness on the blue dot.

So I went. My husband Pocky came with me for moral support, and to enjoy the adventure. I was pleased to have him there. But as the plane touched down in Bangkok, I grew anxious. The largest commercial city, as well as the political and cultural hub of the country, Bangkok teemed with people. How would I ever be able to chat with any of these strangers about the most essential and personal aspects of life?

WISDOM OF THE *WAI*

Alive with thousands of bicycles, motors, and tuk-tuks driving every which way, Bangkok heaved with people and steamy food carts. Exhaust fumes intermingled with wafts of sweet and spicy air. As I made my way past chickens and children, street vendors and pedestrians, I focused on not getting run over. Finally, I stood on the street corner, frozen, afraid to step off the curb. I needed to cross the street, but that would mean entering into the teeming throngs of people and vehicles.

My husband, standing next to me, seemed equally at a loss.

A short, thin man in loose trousers noticed our hesitation. He smiled at me, indicating with his hand that I should go ahead, move forward—*walk.*

I stared at him. So I was supposed to ignore everything around me and stride into the street? No way!

To my surprise, the man spoke English. "Do not worry. Drivers know how to avoid hitting us. Everyone will allow you to pass," he said, channeling his inner Yoda.

Right.

I smiled at him, but didn't buy it. The kind of sheer will and foolish trust it would take to cross that crazy street made me hesitant to believe him. He continued to smile at me, waiting for me to follow his advice.

This is how I began to learn that adventures in happiness can be counterintuitive. I realized that I would have to trust whatever culture I had immersed myself in and become enveloped by it. I would have to let go of my old ways of being.

This would not be easy for me. I couldn't even begin to count the number of times in my life I had let opportunities slip away by waiting too long for things to line up in a way that minimized risk. How often I had waited for the perfect time in order to avoid the chaos. Looking back on the laundry list of situations where I could have jumped in and didn't, I understood how my cautious nature contributed to my feelings of discontent.

I had to learn to jump in and go. Do the counterintuitive thing.

But how? I couldn't get my beating heart out of my throat. I was frozen on the curb of the insanely busy street in Bangkok, just like I'd been frozen in my life. I was also battling jet lag heavily seasoned with sensory overload which gave the whole experience a kind of the-force-will-be-with-you vibe.

I moved forward: Step. Trusting. Step. Hoping. Step. Praying.

My husband has a square jaw and steely blue eyes. He shot me a familiar look, his smile wry, his bushy eyebrows raised. But Pocky stayed at my side, choking back laughter while I inched along. "Remind me why we're here again?!" he yelled as we approached the middle of the traffic-clogged mess.

His question shattered what little zen I'd mustered. "We're trying to find out how to be happy!" I shouted above the clamor.

On the far side of the busy street, we laughed and linked arms. Chickens ran by squawking. Kids chased each other around gaggles of people and rickety food carts. The noise was deafening.

Pocky leaned in close and said, "We didn't have to come all the way to Thailand. You know what makes me happy."

The very first step I took onto that busy street began my adventure of coming home to a happier self. Meeting her in the situations, places, and people I hardly knew. And, like crossing that chaotic street, the courage to discover happiness came through sheer will combined with trust in my own instincts. I would learn all this from the amazing people I was privileged to meet along the way.

The love and connection I experienced through these adventures in happiness would create bonds and understanding that healed me. The infusion of fresh thoughts and endless possibilities filled me up and chased away the overwhelming emptiness I had been feeling. This gave me a window into what it means to be truly happy.

But first I had to learn how to jump in.

Once Pocky and I had made our way across the street, the heavens opened with what we would discover was an everyday occurrence in Thailand, the afternoon tropical rainstorm. We took shelter under a food cart umbrella before hailing a cab. Once inside, we quickly became caught in a current of vehicles.

The chaotic atmosphere shifted quickly as we drove up a grand circular drive to the entrance of our hotel. This gorgeous oasis was lined with stone elephants, bright yellow golden shower trees, and beautiful ponds filled with lotus flowers in full bloom. We left the cab for an opulent lobby reflecting legendary Thai hospitality, paved in white marble and filled with the fragrance of frangipani. Once again, my senses reeled.

Amidst the splendor of high ceilings, arched walls, and extravagant orchid arrangements, a strikingly beautiful Thai woman approached. Her shiny jet-black hair was pulled back in a tight bun, accenting her pristine skin and accentuating her lavish eye makeup. Wrapped in an intricately patterned sari, her bright red lipstick matched the fabric, as did the plumeria flower tucked behind her ear. She emitted an intense, radiant joy—just the kind of person I had dreamed of interviewing.

She nodded at me with a friendly smile. I looked down at my sweaty traveling skirt and loose-fitting T-shirt. I had to speak to her, but I couldn't speak. *Say something*, I told myself. But I didn't know what to say.

Finally, I extended my hand. Instead of shaking it, however, the gorgeous woman pressed her palms together, bowing her head slightly. She gave me the Thai greeting called the *wai*; the sweetest of ancient Thai practices. Her gaze communicated so much more than words of welcome. Her countenance and manner oozed peace and tranquility, making me feel calm—quite the change from the chaos I'd experienced in the sea of humanity and machinery I had just learned to navigate.

I smiled back; my version of the wai.

Her face lit up. And just like that, I'd made my first real connection in the Kingdom of Thailand. In this moment, I saw how a smile could break language barriers.

Such a simple lesson: Smile more. Simple but important, a lesson I would take with me all over the world. As I smiled throughout my adventures in happiness, it seemed like 95 percent of the time, other people smiled back. The definitive ice breaker, a smile opened my heart, and many other hearts all over the globe.

There is a form of therapy called "smile therapy," which is based on the idea that facial expressions have a direct impact on the emotional centers in the brain. Scientific research shows that you can fake a smile and feel happier. This seems weird, but it works.

A smile is such a simple gesture, yet it can warm the heart, create peace, and communicate to others. A smile is the simplest way I can think of to create instant comfort between two people, and yet it seems such a rarity.

So many of the people I encounter in my everyday life have a dullness to them. The real walking dead have forgotten how to smile, and most have developed the ability to avoid eye contact. What a difference it would make if the wai were practiced everywhere. What joy we would experience if we offered a smile and acknowledged everyone we came into contact with.

I made a note to myself to smile more—and to jump in more often.

KARMA ON A CAR RIDE

Our guide greeted us at our hotel early the next morning. His ample pear-shaped face framed a confident smile that lit up his dark eyes. Gan, a history teacher, had a lively and engaging spirit.

Pocky and I stood before him in the gleaming lobby. He ushered us in close. "Can I share with you a little secret?"

We nodded.

"I've been informed by a senior monk that in a past life I, too, was a monk, but chose to have a love affair with a nun. So karma dictates that I am demoted to my current status for several more lifetimes." His smile was quick, infectious.

I wasn't sure if he was kidding, but we all laughed. Just the kind of guide we needed for Bangkok, he provided the perfect beginning to a day of adventures in happiness.

As a way of introducing himself, Gan told us about his family. The youngest of seven siblings, he had been a teacher for twenty years. He said he was married, and that his Chinese father and Thai mother had been married for fifty-five years.

I shared with Gan that I wanted to learn all I could about the Thai people and their beliefs about life and happiness. I asked if there were other customs besides the wai I should be aware of, because I wanted approach the Thai people with utmost respect.

Gan indicated that we should sit for a moment to talk more. We seated ourselves in plush armchairs in a sunny corner of the lobby to continue the conversation.

"Let's start with the feet," he said, pointing down at his sturdy walking shoes. "You in the West think of feet as the lowest, dirtiest part of the body, no?"

I couldn't deny it.

"While you are in Thailand, it is very important that you never show someone the bottoms of your feet."

I waited for his boisterous laugh, but he became serious instead.

"Do not point with your feet, or have them higher than the level of someone's head."

Pocky glanced at me with a playful look in his eye. I had to suppress the urge to giggle. Why would I be raising my feet higher than someone's head?

"Keeping face also plays a big role here. You lose face if you have a temper tantrum. Also, you should never touch someone's head. Or give public displays of affection."

Pocky and I glanced at each other. No hugging or kissing in Thailand. Not in the streets, anyway.

Gan rattled off more items for my checklist. I rummaged through my purse and pulled out a pen and a small notebook to write down Gan's words of wisdom. The student ready, he proved a generous master.

"You might notice that the Thai national anthem is played every day at 0800 and 1800 hours. It's considered good etiquette to stop and pay your respects at these times."

I hadn't noticed. I asked, "How do I do that?"

"A simple bow of the head, and a moment of silence."

"Got it."

He sat forward in his chair. "Also, show respect for the royal family by never saying anything bad about the king. And don't be offended if a Thai talks to you in a way that seems too direct." He sat back in the chair. His eyes twinkled with good humor. "It is considered rude to lie. Direct honesty is normal in Thailand."

Directness would be good for my research. I took more notes.

The Thai intolerance for lies intrigued me. I wondered about white lies. Did they help avoid hurt feelings, or muddle up the truth?

The way we see the world is filtered by our customs and assumptions. So many of Thailand's customs were different than mine. However, it's not our differences that divide us, it's our unwillingness to open our minds to, and find value in, those differences. The truth is, humans are far too complicated to understand each other completely. So we can either choose to judge our fellow humans with suspicion, or approach them with open minds.

We strolled out of the hotel into the heavy, humid air. My dry skin soaked in the welcome hydration. As we followed Gan to the parking lot, I said to him, "You seem like such an enthusiastic person. What makes you so happy?"

"I'm happy because I do good karma," he answered without hesitation.

I would think about the concept of karma when I was in Thailand, as it became part of almost every discussion I had with the people there. The Thai people I met focused on karma every day. My psychotherapy practice has taught me that what we focus on has a tendency to grow. It became apparent to me that because Thais focused so much on karma, it gave them some kind of edge in the goodness and happiness departments.

"You're glowing, honey," Pocky said, giving me a sideways hug. Remembering this was inappropriate, he quickly backed off.

We both laughed.

"You're learning," Gan said with a smile.

He opened the door to the back seat of his car, and Pocky and I slid inside. Peeking through our window, Gan said, "Since I had that affair with a nun in my previous life, I have much to make up for." He winked.

After he settled in the front seat, he turned around to face us.

"Teaching kids and helping to support my parents and some of my nieces and nephews is how I do good karma. I would never hurt a living thing, and would even feel guilty killing a crab. But I am not discouraged because I accept the ways of karma. If you send out goodness and happiness from yourself, it will come back to you a thousand times over. Now, are you ready to see the most beautiful temple in all of Bangkok?"

We nodded. He hit the gas and gave a belly laugh. Our car took its place in the river of vehicles battling Bangkok traffic.

As we jostled through the busy streets, I realized I was immersed in the reality of East meets West, and felt eager to open my mind to worldviews I hadn't considered before. I wanted to be exposed to new ideas regarding the pursuit of happiness. But I knew I would have to wrestle with my own beliefs.

The car wound around a crazy roundabout and I slid into Pocky. He slipped his arm around my waist and I smiled.

Happiness research indicates that when you send kindness into the world, it comes back to you. This is the major benefit of the concept of karma, as well as the Golden Rule—do unto others as you would have them do unto you. And doing good deeds helps to make us happy for a few physiological reasons. When we do good deeds, serotonin is released in the body. This hormone reduces the levels of the stress hormone cortisol. Participation in good works helps to get our bodies and our lives back in balance.

When my clients are unhappy, they are out of balance in a way that causes them to focus on the self. Good deeds help to frame our place in the world in a broader context, getting us out of our own heads. Good works help us to understand our life experiences in a richer way.

But nothing was richer than the mental picture I had of Gan as a monk. I smiled at the image in my mind. Judging by all the amazing karma he was engaged in, I figured he'd be back to monk life the next time around.

After what could be best described as a vehicle ballet, we arrived at Wat Pho. The temple had exotic, extravagant architecture, including a roof that seemed to be in flames. Home of the largest collection of Buddha images in Thailand, Wat Pho also housed an enormous, gold reclining Buddha.

"This way, my new friends," Gan urged.

The temple compound was dotted with lavishly decorated doorways and gorgeous mosaic *stupas*. A stupa is a holy Buddhist monument that houses sacred remains and objects.

Pocky nodded toward a small sign: Traditional Thai Massage. "I think we should find out if this will make us happy," he said with a grin.

I was blown away that a temple offered Thai massage. Talk about karma. Then Gan explained that the site of the temple had originally housed a school of traditional Thai medicine, which later became a massage school.

We walked past a booth that rented clothing to tourists to cover bare shoulders and knees. They had plenty of customers. Busloads of schoolchildren swarmed past us. One by one, the small children would look back at me with gorgeous smiles. I couldn't help smiling back.

The sound of the beautiful Thai language swirled around us, and an intense heat seemed to rise with every step we took. Wat Pho provided the most exquisite, fitting setting to process all that Gan had to share with us about karma. The presence of noble, elegant representations of the Buddha made our earlier discussion come alive in my mind. It occurred to me that every deed has a ripple effect on the world.

Once inside the temple of the reclining Buddha, the darkness cooled us. The roar of the city outside quieted, and we were enveloped in the silence of people gathered in prayer. The huge Buddha gleamed. It was so massive that even the toes were taller than Pocky.

Gan whispered, "If you do good karma, when you are reincarnated, your next life will be even better!"

I smiled at him with deep gratitude.

On our way back to the car, we passed a tiny raised garden with a Bodhi tree at the center. Gan said, "This is believed to have arisen from the very Bodhi tree in India where our holy Buddha sat as he awaited enlightenment."

I stared at the well-manicured garden. "Is enlightenment like heaven for Buddhists? Is enlightenment what happens when people die?"

Gan smiled. "Ah, life and death, death and life. Enlightenment or heaven? My dear, they are one and the same."

After leaving the temple grounds, we got back in the car and wound through the snake-like crawl of Bangkok traffic to the outskirts of town, heading toward the river. We passed many little model houses on pedestals, each with an odd assortment of food and flowers inside. I asked Gan about them.

He spoke over his shoulder. "Those are spirit houses. Buddhist Thai believe they serve as the home of ancestral spirits. We make various offerings to them. Sometimes we also give offerings to large trees, which are also the homes of spirits."

Out of the city now, the forest of massive banyan trees suddenly became more mystical.

"The older the tree, the more likely it is to house a spirit," he added.

This gave me a feeling that anything was possible—the good and the bad, things I hadn't anticipated. "Because of your belief in karma and spirits, do you fear death?" I asked Gan.

His eyes caught mine in the rearview mirror. "I do fear death, but contemplating it helps me come to terms with its reality and inevitability. Buddhists don't see death as the end, nor birth as the beginning. We see them as a cycle. Something natural, like dead leaves falling, decaying to make the soil stronger and to build up new growth."

I scanned the thickening forest and caught my first sight of the river. "What happens when one of your loved ones is dying?"

Gan said, "Sometimes Buddhist monks will come to the room and say a few soothing words to the dying person and their friends and relatives. Symbols like Buddhist statues are sometimes brought in. We try to make the atmosphere peaceful for the person, and we try not to have a lot of wailing and screaming."

I reflected on how so often in our own culture, fueled by a fear of death and loss, we go to extremes to avoid the subject. This can be at the expense of the dying. Gan's way of approaching death appealed to me. After all, like birth, death is a natural process. If we can accept that, we may be able to transcend our fear.

Gan pulled the cab up to the riverbank and opened my door. The three of us walked to the river's edge. Boats made of wood painted bright reds, greens, blues, and yellows, each with a long tail, waited for us at the end of a wooden dock.

As we made our way down the dock, my mind whirled. If so many religious belief systems in the world allowed for an acceptance of death, why did people prolong their lives? How much did the fear of death get in the way of their enjoyment of life? Would contemplating death help us live our lives with more appreciation, joy, and gratitude? If we didn't fear death, would we take life for granted? Or would we live life to the fullest?

I stared into the murky brownish-green water surrounding the boat. My heart opened and warmed at the thought of loved ones gathered around a dying person, reassuring them that they were loved and free to leave this world. The beautiful image Gan had painted for me of peaceful death honored the transition between worlds in a profound, respectful way.

The quality of life and death is determined by how we learn to master our thoughts on the battleground of our minds. If we try to make too much sense of what happens after we die, what we may see as concrete conclusions are in effect only flimsy assumptions. We may be better able to fully enjoy life if we allow that death will come, that it's natural and not to be feared—or postponed.

I decided I would try not to waste any more precious time worrying about how much time I had left, or fearing death. Instead, I would think of my eventual death as a great adventure into the unknown. Doing this would allow me to feel the freedom of not leaning on my own limited understanding.

SANUK AT THE FLOATING MARKET

Pocky steadied me as we took our seats in one of the boats. The long tail allowed for a funky outboard motor. Its long shaft and tiny propeller acted like a tiller, enabling the captain to navigate down the narrow waterways. Our boat was painted a deep blue with gold Thai lettering. It could fit a dozen people including the captain, but it was just the three of us.

Gan stood on the bank and waved goodbye. I lost sight of him as we slowly sailed downriver. We could see the roadways clogged with slow-moving traffic on the outskirts of Bangkok. Eventually we moved away from the road and deep into a network of waterways. Other boats joined us as we left the city, floating past quaint villages with teakwood houses, vegetable gardens, and simple temples.

We rounded a bend in the canal and came upon a floating market. A tradition left over from the days before roads, such markets once served as the place for local trade. Farmers would paddle their produce to an established gathering spot on the bank of a waterway. Merchants would dock boats loaded with dried staples and hardware, with buyers arriving by water to bargain for food and other necessities. Visiting a floating market is a good way to immerse yourself in the traditional Thai lifestyle. I became entranced with how they lived and worked on the water.

Boats were heaped with fresh tropical fruit and vegetables. Meats and seafood were grilled to perfection on the wooden vessels. The locals wore big straw hats and colorful garments. They chatted with one another, laughing and sharing drinks, merging work with pleasure.

Pocky and I disembarked, and we walked from stall to stall along the waterfront. Vendors peddled authentic Thai street food, local produce, and handicrafts. The villagers were completely engaged with what they were doing right there in the moment. They seemed to take pride in their work, perfecting their displays, offerings, and selections. Locals slid their boats along the banks to offer us rambutan, durian, fresh coconuts, bananas, kaffir limes, and homemade desserts. The scene and selections made us giddy. The food came to us!

We slurped noodles and ate charcoal-grilled snakehead fish. Tasting the local food, exchanging money for goods, and negotiating at the market proved to be great fun; a dash of flirtation here, a smile there. Even though the vendors were in competition for our business, an enjoyable sort of camaraderie infused their spirit. The social aspect of the market seemed every bit as important as the selling of goods. The market brimmed with the attitude that anything worthwhile had an element of fun. There is a word in Thai that describes this sense of fun: *sanuk*.

Pocky and I stopped to chat with an older woman with the most fascinating pattern of lines etched in her happy, weathered face. She was cooking onboard her little boat next to the pier.

"This is her version of Chipotle," Pocky said.

Her food was fresh, fragrant, and unbelievably inexpensive. As she tenderly served us stuffed banana peels, her sweet manner reminded me that feeding people is a form of loving them.

I said to Pocky, "This market feels like a perfect, happy community."

After all, happiness *is* community; relying on others, sharing our burdens and our blessings, and being engaged in something bigger than ourselves.

"Happiness is eating. Put that in your book," Pocky said, handing me a fresh coconut with a straw in it. "Eating, and staying properly hydrated."

The chilled coconut milk refreshed me, a lovely reprieve from the intense heat of the late afternoon.

Pocky looked up at the sky. "Three, two, one . . . ," he said in an ominous voice.

The deluge arrived right on cue. The rain felt cool and soft on my sweaty skin.

Pocky grabbed my empty coconut and set it on the riverbank. Laughing, we stepped into our boat and lay back in our seats, sprawling our arms over the sides. Our faces to the heavens, we let the downpour soak our hot bodies.

When the sun came out a few minutes later, I watched the marketplace come back to life. People from different parts of the world mingled with locals around booths and boats. This was a virtual United Nations of eating. And no matter where in the world everyone came from, appreciation of the art of food was at the heart of the scene. Food is a universal language that is easy to understand.

Satiated and soaked, I vowed to add to the deliciousness of my life. I would begin by considering the food I prepared as a form of loving my family. I would give thanks for my community of friends and colleagues when the opportunity arose to share dishes and meals at events and holidays. I would build happiness that way.

Smiling, I held Pocky's large, warm hand as our boat floated away from the market.

NUT AND NATCHA

Our clothes dried in the sinking sun as the boat meandered the canals. Sailing was not nearly as hot as standing on the riverbank, but the night's steamy air didn't cool much, even after the sun went down. As we approached a waterfront restaurant filled with candlelit lanterns, I let out a huge sigh. The romantic arrival took my breath away.

We left the boat behind and crossed the dock. As we stepped onto the riverfront deck of the restaurant, we were greeted by a gorgeous young couple. Both were short with dark eyes and shiny black hair. They wore matching rose-colored attire, she in a long skirt, and he, a loose shirt. They greeted us with sweet, shy smiles and offered the wai.

The smiles they shared gave a window into their love. Because the energy they emitted was almost palpable, I instantly felt as if I stood in the presence of true love. Their gentle regard, illustrated by their body language, displayed a love so deep and sure that I knew they had love left over, enough to share with others—including two damp and sweaty foreigners who smiled at them but did not speak their language.

Still smiling, they shepherded us to a wide veranda filled with low tables. The rich decor was done in red and gold, with charming details, such as intricately folded napkins in the shape of swans and seat cushions embroidered with temple scenes. The indoor-outdoor dining space overlooked the river. The many paper lanterns and wooden wind chimes added to the romantic ambiance. There were several other tables with diners. The serene atmosphere was interrupted only occasionally by the sound of a long-tail boat motor.

A waiter joined us. The young man spoke English, so he interpreted while the couple advised us on what to order. Pocky and I sampled a variety of traditional Thai food, including green papaya salad, chicken curry, and Thai-style fried noodles. Everything was delicious.

As we finished the main course, I asked our interpreter to see if the couple would agree to a brief interview. The woman placed a hand on her heart and looked at us as if to say, *Who, us?* When I nodded enthusiastically, she offered the wai, and sent the waiter back to tell us they would wait until we had the opportunity to finish our meal.

While we lingered over jasmine tea, the couple approached our table. They sat down across from us and huddled close together, looking shy and uncomfortable. Still, I knew I had to be direct and open if I wanted to learn from them. There was an electricity between Nut and his wife Natcha; something energetic about their love for each other that I had to know more about.

With our waiter interpreting, I began asking questions about the restaurant. Nut was a straight shooter, answering me in short, succinct responses. His wife continued to smile but said little. Because of their private nature, my questions set off reactions I hadn't anticipated. I knew I had to be careful, but I was surprised at how intimate we became in just a few minutes.

Seeing that they had become comfortable with me, I asked Natcha, "What do you love about him?"

Tears welled up in her eyes.

I sat back in my seat. I didn't know what to do. It seemed as if I'd offended her. Pocky took my hand under the table, his presence reassuring.

Our translator quieted my fears, telling us that her tears were tears of happiness. We sat quietly and gave her a minute to compose herself.

Natcha explained that she had never been asked that question in such a direct manner, and it deeply moved her. "I love his generosity and kindness," she said, staring into her husband's eyes. She then told us that Nut took care of her mother and her child from a previous marriage. He had brought them into their home so that she could be with her family.

As she spoke, Natcha never took her eyes off her husband. When she became so overwhelmed with emotion that she could no longer speak, he took over.

"She encourages me to spend time with friends," he said, smiling at his wife. "I show her love by listening to her, which is easy, as I am a quiet man and she loves to talk."

"There will be no living with you after this," Pocky said to me in a low voice. I tried not to smile.

Natcha said, "I show him love by taking care of him like a baby. I enjoy bathing him daily to show my appreciation for his generous and kind spirit."

The interpreter added, "They are quite overcome by saying their feelings out loud. They don't typically speak of such things so openly. Not even to each other."

I nodded thoughtfully. Answering my questions had given them ways to voice what they had never before put into words. They loved each other without thought. They were second nature to each other, so pleasing each other came as naturally to them as breathing.

This discovery gave me pause. Nut and his wife were other-focused in a way many couples are not. They gave with all their hearts. It was beautiful how they made each other happy; how they made each other a priority.

"They are enjoying this process," the interpreter told us.

This made me smile. They made me happy, too. In fact, their deep affection and regard for each other bowled me over.

Nut said that in Thailand the main goal of marriage is to strive to be gentle, calm, and generous. He added that showing annoyance, and shouting or raising the voice, is frowned upon, no matter the situation. Such displays showed a lack of self-control, discipline, and respect.

The interpreter added, "What Nut speaks of is known as 'jai yen' in Thai. Which means 'cool heart.'"

I loved the imagery this phrase brought to mind. Some of the people I saw in my practice who suffered from heartache allowed their hearts to become hard, either overheated or cold. So I liked the idea of a cool heart. I could see how this would lead to happiness.

Nut told us the Thai husband was normally the head of the household, but the wife had considerable authority.

Natcha explained that the women in the household were responsible for most of the domestic chores. "But," she added, "Nut helps, and is great with our child."

Their give-and-take partnership appeared to enrich their relationship through their generosity and dedication. They complemented each other, freeing the relationship from power struggles that could take energy away from the love they shared.

Nut stated that he believed married couples should establish their own household as soon as possible. However, residence with the parents of the husband or wife was common in Thailand, especially among poorer couples. Although the nuclear family made up the core of any home, a household often included members of the extended family. This might be unmarried siblings, widowed parents, and unmarried or widowed distant relatives.

This made me think about life and family back in America. Granted, distance from toxic extended family members can be a good thing. But how much added support are we missing out on by not leveraging our extended family relationships like they do in Thailand? Valuing the unique contributions made by both young and old in a family can increase joy and diminish the isolation so many people feel these days.

When our discussion drew to a close, I thanked our hosts for the delicious food and for the time they spent sharing their feelings about marriage and happiness with us.

As Pocky and I crossed the dock to the boat, I kept thinking about Natcha giving her husband a bath. What an excellent way to show appreciation for a beloved. And showing one's appreciation is one of the most important aspects of a relationship. Too often, instead of showing our gratitude for what is good, we focus on what is bad in our relationships because those things need to be fixed. However, what we focus on has a tendency to grow, so this leaves us with the feeling that there is more bad than good in the relationship.

One of the cures to an unhappy marriage lies in making an effort to look for the positive in the other person; to be grateful for the little things they do every day. Natcha and Nut made me think about my own marriage and the things I love about Pocky—his good deeds, his selfless support, his mischievous smile, his wonderful sense of humor. I vowed I would focus more on these things, and less on the everyday irritations I tended to overemphasize in my mind.

When we reached the boat, Pocky asked me what I was thinking about. I admitted, "How Natcha bathes her husband. I find that amazing."

Pocky got that impish look in his eye. "I like my bathwater really warm, and scented with the fragrance of frangipani."

I laughed.

A BUDDHIST MONK CHAT

Our second stop in Thailand, Chiang Mai, had a residential feel, yet the city housed an elephant sanctuary and some elaborate Buddhist temples. Located near a mountainous area of northern Thailand, there were modern Thai homes surrounding the walled part of the city. Everything seemed to be made of teak. In medieval times, elephants brought teak-wood from the surrounding forests.

We hired a cab and ventured into the lush countryside. The ride was filled with glimpses of incredible waterfalls, thickets of forest, and enchanting villages dotted with elaborate fourteenth- and fifteenth-century Buddhist temples. We stopped at Wat Chedi Luang, which means "temple of the big stupa."

Buddhists circumnavigate stupas on foot in a clockwise direction while meditating. They do this in order to purify negativity and accumulate virtue. Some people prostrate themselves, praying in front of a stupa. It is said the statues represent Buddha's holy body, while the stupas represent Buddha's holy spirit. The spiritual texts represent Buddha's holy speech.

At Wat Chedi Luang, large staircases flanked all four sides, and were guarded by statues of the mythical Naga that looked like supernatural snakes. The statues were so lifelike they took my breath away, the stunning features crafted in exquisite detail. The Naga had retained their dramatic effect, even after centuries of guarding and protecting the temple.

Pocky led the way up the steep steps of the temple. I followed behind him as we climbed higher and higher, feeling like we were characters in *Raiders of the Lost Ark*.

I was grateful for my husband's fun-loving company. We had originally planned to travel after retirement, but Pocky had supported me in finding a way to begin the adventures right away. He had even planned our itineraries. At the beginning of our adventures, Pocky hesitated to approach strangers to talk about their lives and happiness. He wanted to leave that part to me. Most of the time, I spoke to people one on one, but as time went on, curiosity got the best of him. So, when appropriate, he would join in the conversations. His participation became one of the best parts of the trip for both of us. The adventures in happiness brought us closer, and helped us discover our own happiness.

At the top of the stairs, we entered the sanctuary, or *chedi*. Once inside, we joined a tour group, where our guide explained that the sacred monument was originally commissioned by King Saen Muang Ma to serve as the final resting place for his father's ashes.

Construction of the chedi began in 1391, and lasted almost a century. The sanctuary reached a height of eighty-five meters, becoming the largest structure in Chiang Mai, famous for housing the most revered Buddha image in Thailand. The emerald Buddha is now on display in a temple in Bangkok. A devastating earthquake destroyed the chedi in 1545, shaking sixty meters off the top. We viewed the partial restoration completed within the last twenty years, and strolled by a stunning likeness of the emerald Buddha at the end of the tour.

On the temple grounds, I approached the guide to see if he would be able to arrange for me to have what they call a "monk chat," a brief sit-down with one of the Buddhist monks who made their home at the temple. The guide set this up for me.

My interview took place outside the temple. The guide led me to a picnic-style table where a young monk sat. He was stiff, unsmiling. I received instructions to sit perpendicular to the monk, rather than beside him. When I asked why, the guide, who would serve as my interpreter, explained that the rule enabled monks to avoid temptation.

There would be more rules along those lines.

The monk was probably in his early twenties, with a slim build and a shaved head. He had commendably good posture, and was dressed in a vibrant saffron-colored robe. He did not smile at me, but appeared calm and centered. I knew I should limit the banter and keep my tone serious.

It was awkward at first. I wasn't sure what to ask. The monk seemed too young to hold much wisdom. I tried to hand him a water bottle as a gesture of gratitude, but he ignored me. I offered the bottled water again, holding it toward him. The young monk simply sat there.

The guide intervened, explaining that monks were not allowed to touch anything a woman held in her hands. So I set the bottle down on the table and let go of it, and put my hands in my lap. The monk then picked up the bottle and bowed to me in gratitude.

Wow. I was impressed and a bit surprised by his level of dedication to the practice of avoiding temptation. I made a note to watch myself so I wouldn't offend him in any way. But I decided since our chat would be brief, I should just ask whatever was on my mind. So I launched in. "What makes people happy?"

The monk stared out into the distance at leafy green trees. He seemed full of confidence. He said in perfect English, "In life, there is suffering. Our bodies have pain and disease, and we get old. We also have psychological suffering, like loneliness, frustration, fear, disappointment, and anger. These truths can't be denied. But much suffering is caused by craving and aversion. We will suffer more if we expect other people to conform to our expectations. For example, if we want people to like us, or if we don't get what we want. Getting what you want does not guarantee happiness."

Everything he said made sense. His words washed over me like a kind of tonic. I drank them in.

I asked, "What are practical ways to avoid such cravings?"

His voice was low and clear. "Rather than struggling to get what you want, it is better to tone down your wanting. Wanting deprives us of contentment and happiness. It is best to not get attached to anything, because attachment adds to suffering. Learn to let go of your expectations and attachments and you will begin a journey to greater happiness."

I asked, "So how do we begin to let go of expectations and attachments?"

He did not look at me. "You must move away from cravings and learn to live in the present, which will allow you to find happiness and provide the energy to do good things for others. The spiritual development of a person is more important to happiness than material welfare.

We cannot expect to gain both worldly happiness and everlasting happiness at the same time. Buddhism is not meant to entertain the mind or satisfy human emotion, it is a method for those who wish to understand and experience the reality of life."

I nodded. I liked the emphasis he placed on taking accountability for our own happiness. So often we look to outside situations and other people, expecting them to make us happy. I appreciated how the monk pointed out that if we rely on external sources, our happiness becomes vulnerable to them.

I sat forward. "So how can we attain everlasting happiness?"

He did not change his serene expression. "We experience peace and happiness when we do good deeds. Happiness means cultivating the mind and leading a noble life. Not by traditional customs, but by experiencing and understanding truth and reality with an open and objective mind. This process takes compassion, courage, patience, and intelligence. Nirvana is the ultimate form of happiness. It is reached through letting go of attachments, aversions, and unhealthy desires in order to lead a noble life."

Everything he said seemed like it would be easier said than done, yet his words were so right on. I couldn't get enough of his wisdom. "What happens when we die?" I asked.

"Buddhists believe we are reborn to a life that is equivalent to the merit earned in the past life. According to the teachings of the Buddha, if people realize what they are doing is wrong, and mend their ways to do good, they can change the outcome—for this life and the next. A dying man's destiny in his next life depends on the last thoughts he may have. His next life depends on the good and bad karma he has accumulated during his current life."

This made sense to me. "What is the best way to lead a good life?" I asked.

He answered without hesitation. "Be moral in what you say and do. Focus your mind. Be aware of your thoughts and actions, and develop compassion for others. Don't take the life of anything living, and don't take anything not freely given. Abstain from sensual overindulgence, intoxication, and untrue words."

His wisdom came fast and sure. I liked how sure he was of the worthiness of his words.

I said, "I've been hearing so much about karma here in Thailand. Any advice on that?"

He shifted slightly on the bench. "Our actions have results. We are all responsible for our past and present actions. This is karma. Your karma depends on the decisions you make about the actions you will take. Look at the intention behind any action you may take. Consider the effects of the action on yourself and others before making any decision."

With that, the guide indicated I'd used my allotted time. My monk chat over, I held out some money, but the monk did not take it. He stood up. I felt embarrassed and awkward until I remembered the rules, and placed the cash on the table between us. He picked up the money and walked off, his saffron-colored robe gleaming in the afternoon sun.

I stood up, looking around the grounds for Pocky. I thought about how Buddhists are able to exhibit a profound sense of dignity and the wisdom of great responsibility. Too many people avoid responsibility and believe they are victims of their circumstances. Buddhists don't put the blame on others when bad things happen. Instead, through doing good deeds and living a noble life, they are reassured their suffering will not be carried into the next life.

The key to developing dignity and wisdom is the cultivation of peace. Buddhists use mantras while meditating to cultivate peace, as well as inner strength and greater self-awareness. One of their mantras is *Om mani padme hum*, which translates to "the jewel in the center of the lotus flower, the spirit of enlightenment." The lotus flower blooms over muddy water, serving as an apt metaphor for overcoming obstacles.

I spotted Pocky at the exit to the temple and headed over to join him. He handed me some lovely prayer beads he had purchased. I held the smooth beads in my hands as we walked away from the temple, passing by elaborate Naga decorations made of flowers and seaweed, gorgeous in both scale and intricacy.

FLOWERS, NOT OPIUM

Spending time with an elephant is a must when you're visiting Thailand. So, one morning our guide picked us up to take us to one of the animal sanctuaries devoted to the rescue and rehabilitation of Thailand's working elephants. We were met by the sanctuary guide, a lean young man who greeted us with a big smile and a small bow before showing us around the grounds.

The air was hot and still as we followed our guide along a path that led to the elephants. He said, "Elephants play an important role in Thailand's history and culture. Due to a past association with Thai royalty, the white elephant is a symbol of wealth and power. It also has spiritual significance in the Buddhist and Hindu belief systems."

In fact, Buddhists believe a white elephant was one of the many incarnations of the Buddha. And spotting a white elephant in Thailand is believed to impart wisdom. This is because the Hindu god Ganesh—the god of wisdom and learning—has the head of an elephant. Ganesh is also considered to be the remover of obstacles.

The elephant sanctuary smelled of hay and manure. We stood under a tall palm tree as our guide told us about the elephants. "The Thai word for elephant is 'chang,' just an *i* away from 'Chiang Mai.' I will teach you how to care for our elephants as if you were their mahouts— the trainers who dedicate their lives to the animals. A mahout may even sleep with his elephant, staying by the animal's side night and day, year round. They form a special bond. The elephant will obey the trainer and respond to the mahout's voice."

As he spoke, a baby elephant snuggled up right next to me. He was about my height and he looked me right in the eyes as he reached around me, drawing me close and hugging me with his trunk. I froze, then relaxed in his gentle embrace. His gray skin felt rough, but he was gentle.

Pocky handed me a banana, which I started to unpeel. But the impatient elephant snatched it out of my hand and ate it, peel and all! To my surprise, his trunk worked more like a hand than a nose. I stood there grinning, completely charmed.

After the baby elephant wandered off, our guide led us to the area where we could ride on an elephant. The animal was enormous, with kind eyes.

"His name is Babar," the guide told us, and we laughed, immediately recognizing the name of the elephant from the popular children's books. Then he instructed us on how to feed the elephant, and made sure we knew how to give several commands: *goy*, which meant "slow down"; *bai*, to indicate "go"; and *nung long*, if we wanted the animal to lie down.

Our guide helped me mount Babar, then Pocky climbed up behind me. He hugged my waist and off we went. I couldn't believe I was actually riding an elephant, the animal's tremendous floppy ears rubbing against my legs. When Babar decided to speed up, his gentle-giant steps tossed us side to side, requiring us to surf elephant waves full of twists and turns.

University of Virginia psychologist Jonathan Haidt wrote about riding elephants in *The Happiness Hypothesis: Finding Modern Truth in Ancient Wisdom*. He claims the elephant can serve as a metaphor for our emotional side, while the rider represents our rational side. Atop the elephant, the rider holds the reins and seems to be in charge, but control is precarious because the rider is so small relative to the elephant. Anytime elephant and rider are at odds about which direction to go in, the rider will lose that semblance of control.

Riding the elephant, my happiness was pure and uncomplicated. When we returned to the spot where we'd begun, my heart sank. Reluctantly, I climbed down, then Pocky dismounted. We both said goodbye to our sweet and gentle friend, Babar.

After leaving the elephant sanctuary, we drove for a while on a dusty road until we came upon a tiny village. I was curious to see how the village people lived, so we stopped at a food stall and bought a cold drink. Then we toured the tree-lined village. The homes were small tin huts, and loose electric wires dangled everywhere. Outhouses served as the bathrooms for this village with no indoor plumbing. The road was rutted and rocky. Children in dirty shorts ran about, giggling and yelling to one another. Birds sang from the palm fronds, and people milled about, most dressed casually and barefoot.

Pocky and I walked around, captivated by the village's rural simplicity. Everyone we passed smiled and bowed. I felt relaxed due to the welcoming attitude of the local people.

As we walked past a row of shacks, a couple of teenage girls joined us, one holding a crying baby. Always resourceful, Pocky reached in his pocket for something to soothe the wailing infant. He handed her a crisp dollar bill.

This seemed to do the trick. The baby grabbed the bill and stopped fussing, waving the money in a tight little fist. When the mother smiled at us, her eyes twinkled. We grinned back. No matter who we are in the world, or our means, religion, or propensity for suffering, we all love happy babies.

When the friend of the mother asked whether we were American, I was surprised at the clarity of her English. I said, "We're from Colorado."

The girl nodded. She had long straight hair and a pretty smile. She introduced us to Minh, her friend and the mother of the baby. Minh also had long hair, which she had tied back away from her narrow face. When she smiled at us, her warmth was genuine. I decided she was a good person to interview about happiness.

Diving right in, I asked Minh what made her happy.

Her friend translated. "A simple life." Minh's baby buried her pink face in her mother's breast. She still clasped the dollar in her small hand.

The air smelled sweet and the sky was cloudless. We continued to walk as Minh led us toward a palm tree and a spot of shade.

"What makes me happy are the flowers," she said, pointing to the orchids clinging to the palm trees that surrounded the village; tiny white orchids, bursts of canary-yellow orchids, fat red orchids that drooped from the trunks of the palms all around us. How had I not noticed these gorgeous flowers while strolling the village? They were everywhere. My heart felt full, relishing the surprising beauty of what had been previously unseen.

"Not so long ago, all we grew here were poppies. That is, flowers for opium," Minh told us while rocking her sleepy baby from side to side. "My father and grandparents are all drug addicts. Opium has devastated our lives."

Her friend and translator nodded, frowning. "This is true for all of us in the village."

Minh went on. "The government helped us remove the poppies and plant other flowers. This makes me happy because my baby can grow up and lead a good life without becoming addicted to opium like so many of our people."

My heart sank a bit. The flowers pleased her not because of their simple beauty, but because they represented a way to avoid addiction. Another diamond in the rough, this teenage mother had been able to find hope in her surroundings despite the desperate cycle of damage in her life caused by drug addiction. She could look at the orchids and see a beautiful future for her daughter.

"With the orchids, there are less drugs," Minh said. Her baby was sleeping now, quieted by her mother's attentiveness.

The serene tone she used to speak about such hardship impressed me, as did her equally tranquil friend.

I said in a quiet voice, "You are so good with your baby. Very patient. What is your advice about how to raise a happy child?"

Minh said, "In my country, adults love children. Including children who are not their own. My child is not just mine; this whole village is my child's parent."

She pointed to a group of very young children huddled together, chatting and laughing. There were no parents hovering nearby. Farther away, a group of boys, probably around ten years of age, played together, called out in rowdy voices. The boys looked industrious and engaged. Their heated discussion involved kicking rocks and brandishing sticks in a wild game.

Minh caught my eye. "Children must discover their own path; what is good, what is bad."

In the United States, parents orchestrate play dates. These usually involve the latest computer gadgets, or outings to legally mandated "safe" playgrounds with rubber crash mats. Back home, kids rarely experience the joys of simply playing in the dirt with rocks and sticks.

Minh's friend explained that it was time for Minh to feed her baby. She wished us well on our holiday in Thailand, and said they both hoped we would return to their village one day.

After we said goodbye, the image of the young mother and her baby stayed with me; a girl who had found strength in her small village, the people around her, and her simple life. She also found hope and beauty in choosing orchids instead of drugs for her family.

THE JOY OF STICKS AND ROCKS

On our walk back to the main road, Pocky and I paused to watch the young boys play. They ran and jumped and called out, rocketing with high energy and enthusiasm. These boys were poor, but rich in spirit, and a kind of eagerness for life sparkled in their dark eyes.

When I held up my camera and asked if I could take their picture, they offered up ear-to-ear smiles for the perfect Kodak moment. As I snapped the photo, it occurred to me how much play fires up and nourishes the brain, leading to creativity and innovation. Play is the business of childhood, but our bodies were designed to play throughout our lives. I wanted to join in the fun.

When I asked the kids to teach Pocky and me how to play, using my hands to help them understand our desire to join in, the boys became more excited. Several of them took Pocky by the hand while three or four crowded around me. They didn't speak English, so they showed us how to play the game by mimicking the moves of what seemed to be a form of street hockey. The skills involved a few kicks and hits with the stick.

The boys were all in. I was totally taken up by the glorious present of the uninhibited, full-on enthusiasm they displayed. Pocky got right into it, too. What a joy it was to see him running about and laughing so uninhibitedly. I have always loved Pocky's boyishness. He is a kid at heart.

The village boys illustrated for me one of the greatest sources of personal happiness: spontaneity. I didn't have to join in to learn from them. Simply watching the boys play infected me with their joie de vivre. What a gift. They welcomed us into their game, running barefoot through the dirt and laughing. They were completely in the moment.

If I could acquire these boys' openness to experiencing the joy of a simple moment, and allow that joy to spread to every cell in my body, I knew I could find peace and happiness in my life.

PAIN AND PLEASURE IN PHUKET

Our last stop in Thailand occurred on the shores of the Andaman Sea. Phuket's storied beaches offered incredible vistas, clear blue seas, delicious cuisine, and the gorgeous Phi Phi Islands. On our first day, we sailed out to visit the film location for the movie *The Beach*, starring Leonardo DiCaprio. Maya Bay was even more striking than in the movie, with pristine sand, azure skies, and thick forests of tropical trees.

Back at the hotel, we booked a couple's massage on the beach. There were only a few other people out on the sand, even though the temperature was perfect with a slight ocean breeze. The water was calm, and when we walked out on the pier, we could see fish swimming in the clear blue water.

We lay down for our massages within earshot of the waves. Relaxing and releasing all the stored tension in our bodies, we expected this would be the sensual icing on our vacation cake.

My masseuse appeared. A big woman with muscular arms, she kneaded my muscles one by one, wringing them until I yelped. I had been expecting smooth, soothing strokes, but Thai massage took pleasure and pain to a whole new level.

A few minutes into the wonderful agony, I looked over at Pocky. His masseuse had climbed on top of him. She had his foot in her hand and was bending his leg backward to an extent I did not think possible. Just as I was about to joke around with him, my therapist suddenly unblocked all the tension in my body; my thumbs, arms, legs, knees, elbows, and feet zinged with electric energy. I had no idea how blocked I'd been, and how painful the unblocking process could be. I screamed.

After the masseuses finished, I asked my therapist to explain how Thai massage works on the body.

She said, "Traditional Thai massage is an ancient healing system that blends relaxation techniques with assisted yoga stretches and applied pressure, similar to acupressure. We apply this pressure to certain areas of the body to release blockages in the energy flow."

I got that. I asked, "What exactly is the energy you unblock?"

She crossed her thick arms. "In releasing blocked energy, we seek to balance the elements of life—space, air, fire, earth, wind, and water.

When the elements are balanced, the body becomes healthy and in harmony. Pain, discomfort, illness, and disease are reduced, or pushed away altogether."

I nodded. Western medicine focused on the avoidance of pain, but Eastern medicine worked to embrace and free the pain—different approaches to the same problem of imbalance.

The masseuse tilted her head to one side. She had large dark eyes and a strong jaw. Her physicality and good health gave her a kind of glow. "When we are out of balance with the forces of the universe, we are out of harmony, and our health suffers. This causes sickness in the body, mind, and spirit. Our choices and lifestyle can create such imbalances. Choices about diet, exercise, profession, and relationships all have the potential to create physical, emotional, or spiritual imbalances. Thai massage seeks to release the imbalances trapped in our bodies through habitual patterns in thought and actions."

Unlike Western medicine, Eastern medicine accepts pain as part of life. Health practitioners teach people to choose to think about pain as something to be revered and released instead of denied, averted, or buried inside. Acceptance, rather than drugging, seems wise. Pain is a season, something to sit with, and not wish away. The way we choose to meet our pain could empower us to determine our own happiness.

Phuket has seen much pain and suffering. The 2004 tsunami has been memorialized in a huge bronze sculpture. At night, the memorial by the beach is bathed in blue light. It looks like a circular ocean wave, frozen in time to honor those killed and swept away by the tsunami. Buildings in the beachfront towns of Patong, Karon, Kamala, and Kata are relatively new, an eerie reminder that every building there was destroyed. Yet the people are warm, friendly, and always smiling.

The people of Phuket are living examples of how to find pleasure again after pain.

THOUGHTS ON THAILAND'S SIAMESE RUBIES

On our last night in Phuket, we celebrated my birthday on the beach-front patio of a lovely seaside restaurant. Basking in the warmth of the evening, I sipped a cold blue-cheese-stuffed-olive martini. As a dramatic sunset full of pinks, blues, and vivid tangerine settled over the Andaman Sea, I thought about how this moment in my life would never come again. Nor would the joy of taking it all in. The sunset was the best birthday gift ever! Pure happiness rose up inside of me, and I felt a deep appreciation for the indescribable beauty of nature, the love of the people I had met, and the richness of the beautiful colors and textures of Thailand.

I remembered how uncertain I had been at the beginning of the trip. I'd had no idea if I would be able to talk with the people I met. I'd wondered if they would even want to share their stories with me. Yet it had all been so easy, so simple. The people of Thailand had an ancient wisdom that I respected. I reflected on their steadfastness in the midst of despair, reviewing all the stories I had heard. I reveled in the connection I felt to the people through their tears and stories, through our laughter, and shared feelings about life.

In the glow of the fire-red sky, I took inventory of the many jewels Thailand had given me on this trip, the first of my adventures in happiness on the blue dot. As a psychotherapist, it's my job to analyze life. You might call it an occupational hazard. My travels in Thailand had allowed me to get out of my analytical head to directly experience the world and its greatest gift: the present moment.

As I looked out over the waves that had once caused complete destruction, I was witnessing the beauty of a calm sea. The tsunami had passed, as all our personal storms do. Calm seas return when we find artful, mindful ways to deal with our internal storms, like meditation, long walks, listening to music, and for me, honoring as many sunsets as I can.

Through the tranquility cultivated in stillness, happiness stays alive in the faith that today's pain will transform into tomorrow's pleasure.

I made a silent birthday vow. Like Minh, I would learn to appreciate the orchids around me and not get caught in the poppies of the past. I would define myself by my joy instead of my pain. I would open myself up more to the deliciousness of life.

Pocky appeared beside me and set two more blue-cheese-stuffed-olive martinis on the table. "How about another cold one, honey?" he said with an impish grin.

I returned his smile, and we joined hands. Then we watched the pinks and blues of the sunset's afterglow turn the sea before us to a misty violet.

Chapter 2

CAMBODIA AND VIETNAM: PINK SAPPHIRES

A kind of hesitant elation filled my spirit when our plane took off for Phnom Penh. As fascinating as Thailand had been, I expected Cambodia would be even more of an adventure. I was about to set foot in a war-torn country rich in culture and history, and I knew this land full of open beaches, lush landscapes, captivating cities, and magnificent temples would be one of contradictions.

While en route to our next destination, I read about the land and its people. A surprising statistic jumped off the page: 63 percent of the population was under the age of thirty. I knew this striking statistic reflected the brutal genocide of the Khmer Rouge during the 1970s. However, I wasn't prepared for the graphic details I would discover in learning about the horrors the Cambodians faced during this frightful period in their history.

We traveled by motor coach to Siem Reap, the gateway city to Angkor Archaeological Park. Our hotel was comfortable, and we went to bed early. Pocky woke me before dawn. We had signed up to take a sunrise trip to the magical lost world of Angkor Wat, which translates to "capital city," or "holy city." The temple, a UNESCO World Heritage site, is the largest religious monument in the world, and covers some four hundred acres.

Our small tour group chatted as the bus drove through the darkness. After a short bus ride, we disembarked, and everyone fell silent as we joined a throng of people amassed in a dark meadow. With only flashlights in hand to illuminate our way, we traversed the electric-moss-green land framed by ancient stone walls, and moved in unison with saffron-robed monks, tourists from all over the world, and Cambodian families. Children ran around in the darkness. We had all gathered together to watch the sunrise over the historic temple.

As the pre-dawn grayness lifted, the sky turned orange, red, and purple behind the dark outline of the expansive temple. The vibrant colors were made even more dramatic in the reflection of the moat at the foot of the holy city. As I watched the beautiful colors brighten and shift, I considered the sight a metaphor for Cambodia: beauty rising out of darkness.

Pocky and I stood close, watching the sky unfold like a new flower. It's difficult to convey the beauty of this remarkable setting. As international food writer Anthony Bourdain once stated, places like Angkor Wat defy description, and "seem to demand silence, like a love affair you can never talk about. For a while after, you fumble for words, trying vainly to assemble a private narrative, an explanation, a comfortable way to frame where you've been, and what's happened. In the end, you're just happy you were there—with your eyes open—and lived to see it."

I was indeed happy to be there observing the natural beauty spread out before us, even as the darkness lingered. The ancient stone was hugged by the gigantic roots of banyan trees that fell like waterfalls over the temple ruins. Energetic monkeys played in the crevices.

Light and dark, living together.

We followed a guide toward the building, a young man in a white shirt and slacks. As we stood by the entrance to the site, he said, "Angor Wat is the largest monument of its kind, and was built by the largest empire in the world at the time. It was constructed between 1113 and

1150, erected to honor the Hindu god Vishnu, and it is here that the religions of Hinduism and Buddhism meet. This is because one of Vishnu's incarnations was as the Buddha, the Enlightened One."

We walked along the tourist path, looking at the ruins. The detailed, dramatic bas-reliefs and stone inscriptions adorning the temple walls impressed us in their intricacy and number. These walls held many secrets.

The guide explained, "The bas-reliefs tell the story of palace life, and reveal information about the marketplace. They also describe epic naval battles, depict famous leaders and warriors, and share Hindu sagas." He pointed at specific images to illustrate his points. "Since there is no written history for the period when the temple was erected, the reliefs and inscriptions provide the only window into the events and culture of the time."

Pocky led me forward to look at the most breathtaking bas-relief. Chiseled in three parallel layers, it depicted thirty-seven heavens and thirty-two hells above and below the earth, all carved in stone. Pocky and I marveled at the intricacy of this beautiful and painstakingly carved artwork. Detailed images of luxurious mansions, depicting gorgeous women attending the fortunate, sat opposite the terrors of underworld tortures, including having one's bones smashed and tongue pulled out.

Our guide said, "The Khmer Rouge used some of the methods shown here as a blueprint for their torture."

His chilling yet casual reference to the fanatical genocide conducted by Marxist leader Pol Pot and the Khmer Rouge gave me goose bumps. I shivered and leaned closer to Pocky. I found it hard to believe such atrocities had happened as recently as 1979.

I did not know it at the time, but Angkor Wat's bewitching backdrop to monstrous brutality would become one of the themes I would explore in Cambodia. Such contradictions would have much to teach me about happiness.

THE KILLING FIELDS

On our second day in Cambodia, we booked a tour at one of the Killing Fields. It was in these fields that 1.7 million out of a population of 7 million people were brutally murdered in Cambodia. These people died from starvation, overwork, or outright massacre.

Pocky and I took a bus with other tourists from our hotel to the site, and stood waiting for our guide. Birds sang in the trees against a startling blue sky. The heat was thick and intense. It was hotter here than in Thailand, and I felt as if I could not get any relief from the relentless sun.

Our guide was a small middle-aged gentleman named Kimsan. He had a broad face, and stood barely five feet in height. His voice was almost robotic, striking polite and gracious tones while delivering information with a certain steeliness. I had the feeling he had an interesting personal story buried underneath the rote general history he so expertly shared.

Kimsan led us over to a massive glass case. "In order to build this memorial, the skulls of thousands of executed Cambodians were exhumed. They now sit behind this glass."

Carefully laid out next to the skulls were many of the killing tools—machetes, knives, and crude devices made of metal and wood.

We stood in silence, taking in the shocking sight of rows of human remains and the implements used to take the lives of millions of innocent people.

Expressionless, Kimsan said, "In the early 1990s, mass graves were uncovered throughout my country. Each grave held the remains of many dead. Some held hundreds."

I was having a hard time getting my mind around the horror of these facts. I had read Joel Brinkley's book, *Cambodia's Curse: The Modern History of a Troubled Land*. He recounted how the villagers had piled the remains of the dead in barns or other outbuildings. According to Brinkley, the villagers claimed the skulls still spoke to them.

I thought of this as I stared at row upon row of white skulls.

Kimsan offered us bottles of water and asked if we needed anything else. Aware of our emotional shock, he catered to us to make sure we were okay. When we said we were ready to continue the tour, he led us toward the field. Together, we wandered the killing field, the experience, a lesson in the history of the horror of genocide.

Kimsan said, "After the revolution, the Khmer Rouge declared themselves in power and began to execute their dream of an authentic Cambodia, free from Western influence. Their dream involved creating a perfect communist state, one they defined as a place where no citizen would ever be considered better than another. This was communism at its most dangerous, and led to the killing of nearly a quarter of our people."

Despite the jungle heat, chills ran up and down my spine. I shivered and crossed my arms over my chest, hugging myself under the sear of the sun. Pocky gave me a look, then patted my back gently. I knew he was equally disturbed by the vibe in the fields. Man's inhumanity knew no bounds.

Kimsan told us how in the eyes of the Khmer Rouge, equality meant no one was supposed to be higher in social status than a farmer. So they closed all the schools in Phnom Penh, then forced the evacuation of the cities. People were relocated to slave labor farms. "The Khmer Rouge demanded the workers triple the rice production. That task impossible, their lives became full of pain and suffering," he said.

We walked past small bamboo shelters with waist-high fences that blocked foot traffic. Kimsan told us these were the sites of mass graves. Pocky reached for my hand as we walked around a dozen massive earth mounds.

Kimsan waited for us to catch up, then said, "The Khmer Rouge had no use for the educated. So they were killed and their bodies dispatched here. Anyone accused of having ties to the Western world was also murdered here. The Khmer Rouge had no use for anyone who couldn't work in the rice fields, so those too young to work died here too."

Pocky and I looked at each other. Children had been mass murdered. Tears welled up in my eyes. I felt sick. I wished to forget everything he had told us, I wanted to unlearn all of the history Kimsan had so stoically relayed.

As we moved on, Kimsan made a comment about his size, saying he had been malnourished as a child. I suddenly realized he'd spent his childhood under the Khmer Rouge and must have some very dark stories to tell. My mind whirled.

Kimsan said, "My people died to the sound of music from loudspeakers, music played to drown out their screams. The Khmer Rouge didn't want to spend money on guns, so they dug huge pits. The victims were told to kneel down, then they were struck on the head, their throats cut with machetes."

Pocky squeezed my hand. The chills and the intense heat were taking a toll on me. I wasn't sure how much more I could take.

Kimsan led us over to a tall tree that had tiny bracelets hanging from its branches. The scene looked like something in a Tim Burton film, cartoonish and strange. Pocky and I looked into each other's eyes, fearful of what we would hear next.

"This is where they crushed the babies," Kimsan said.

I didn't hear the rest, it was just too much—all those skulls, the nightmare stories of torture, the murdered children. I held onto Pocky's hand and tuned out. As Kimsan continued to speak, I put on my sunglasses and stared into the distance, sending my thoughts across the sun dappled field. I became completely disconnected.

KIMSAN'S STORY

What I experienced in the killing field is an example of what often happens to people in trauma. They dissociate from the horror and try to explain away or run from the pain. A coping mechanism, it has its place, but can also cause lasting damage.

I reeled from the reality of the Killing Fields. But as I looked down at Kimsan, I found myself wondering what he had done in order to survive his traumatic childhood. I felt shaky and sort of out of it, so I wasn't sure I could get it together enough to ask him about his life. But I experienced a strong urge to try, so I jumped in.

I invited him to have something cold to drink with me. He agreed, and we walked to a little tourist café on the edge of the field. Pocky excused himself and wandered off. After Kimsan and I sat down together at a small table in the shade, I asked him if he would tell me his own story.

"Certainly," he said. But his demeanor belied his response. He immediately became nervous and hesitant. He picked at the label on his bottled water and repeatedly cleared his throat. The shade of the sidewalk umbrella felt good after hours in the sun and I drank my water quickly.

When I asked him how old he was, he said he didn't know his birthday or his age. He said most Cambodians don't celebrate their birthdays. This surprised me, and I wondered even more about his childhood. I knew he'd been around for the horror, so I waited patiently for him to share his story.

Finally, Kimsan began to speak in a dreamlike voice. He did not look at me, but spoke carefully while staring at his water bottle. "I was born in Phnom Penh. I was a small child when Pol Pot and his communist party came into power. My father was an educator. The Khmer Rouge took particular aim at intellectuals, so our family fled Phnom Penh for the countryside."

He took a sip of his drink, then continued. "A few years later, when I was probably about seven years old, a truck filled with Khmer Rouge came through the small village where we lived. The men gathered up all the children. They kidnapped me. They put me in a truck with the other children, and we were taken far away to a brainwashing school near the Vietnamese border."

I thought about the young Cambodian children I had seen running around at Angkor Wat, how happy and carefree they'd seemed. This made the unfolding story seem even more gruesome.

Kimsan said, "I spent two years there. None of us dared to try to escape because they warned us that the field outside the camp was filled with mines. They said there were wild tigers and escaping would mean certain death."

He spoke without any emotion, as if in a trance. As a psychotherapist, I could see that he had found a way to temporarily disconnect from his story and the frightening emotions he had felt at the time.

"I was brainwashed to forget about my family and join the Khmer Rouge. They said we were training to become excellent people, and they changed my name to Kim."

He paused to sip some water. Still not looking at me, he said, "When I was probably about nine, I was taken to work in a security camp, where enemies of Pol Pot's regime were tortured until they confessed that they were educated. Then they were murdered. The soldiers were training me to be a torturer. They made me watch them pull out fingernails, place electrically-charged clips on nipples, hang people upside down and dip them in buckets of urine, and rape women using electric prods. They planned to train me to take over some of the torturing by the time I reached the age of twelve."

I shuddered. I couldn't believe the small gentleman in front of me would ever be capable of such evil, such brutality and cruelty. I wondered why he had made revisiting the pain he had suffered his life's work. Each day he exposed himself again to the source of his own trauma.

I waited patiently for him to continue. This was not an easy story to tell, and I felt honored he was sharing it with me. So many Cambodians his age must have had similar stories. Their suffering was unimaginable.

It's part of my job as a therapist to listen to stories of tragedy, loss, violence, and abuse. Providing people with an opportunity to process the details of their painful experiences can work like a healing balm. It's an important step in enabling them to mend and move forward in their lives. Some stories are very difficult to hear, and I've had to learn to compartmentalize so that I can be present with my clients while they share with me. But I'd never heard a story quite like Kimsan's. The intensity of the horror he had been through felt surreal.

He told me, "I contracted malaria before I was old enough to begin to do the torturing. Because I was of no use anymore, I was turned out into the jungle. My captors didn't want to bother with a sick kid. I didn't know where I was because of the fever. Somehow I met an older woman in the jungle and she knew that a certain flower can cure malaria. She helped me recover. After that, I spent most of my teen years in an orphanage." He paused, reflecting. "You know, I never had shoes as a boy."

I sat forward in my seat, listening intently. Around me, people laughed and spoke in a variety of languages. Elsewhere in the country, people Kimsan's age were still suffering from the trauma of their youth.

"After the genocide had ended, when I was probably fourteen or fifteen, I was washing my clothes in the river one day when a girl around my age motioned to me. I went over to the pile of rocks where she stood. She looked friendly and nice. I climbed up to her, and she pulled an old photograph out of her shorts pocket. It was a picture of me with many people I didn't recognize. She told me they were my family, and pointed to herself in the picture. She looked the same, small and pretty. She said it was easy for her to recognize me because I hadn't changed much. Malnutrition had stunted our growth."

When I'd been a teenager during the time of the Killing Fields, all I'd had to worry about was homework and having a bad Farrah Fawcett hair day—a crushing contrast between my own teen years and Kimsan's.

"The girl said my name wasn't Kim. My name was Kimsan. I will never forget that moment. It was as if a great light had suddenly shone on my darkness. The name 'Kimsan' seemed strange, yet familiar, too. It took some getting used to."

He pushed back from the table and crossed his short legs at the knee. "The girl told me she was my cousin. We traveled together to the area where I had last seen my family. We visited my old home, but there was nobody around. I went back every day, and every day no one was home. After five years, I gave up. I imagined my family had all fallen victim to the Killing Fields."

He crossed his arms, his eyes distant. "I have no solid memory of my mother or father. I have no idea what day I was born." He looked at me. "I still have nightmares. Mostly about the torture camps."

"I'm sure you do," I said.

He looked away. "I have found happiness with my new family. My wife and I were married in 2002, and we have two children."

He had told me so much, I was worried I had pushed him too hard. So I decided to change the subject, encouraging him to talk about more normal aspects of life. "So what do you think is the key to a good marriage?" I asked.

He flashed a brilliant smile. This was the first time I'd seen him smile, and it changed his face. He was, I realized, a handsome man. "A good marriage is one where the wife is frugal with money, and a good mother to the children. Cambodians typically don't celebrate birthdays, but I enjoy romance, and I like to lavish my wife with special gifts on hers. I always take her extended family out for a nice dinner on that day, too."

I returned his smile. "That's beautiful. You'll have let my husband in on your tradition of lavishing the wife with special gifts."

His smile widened and he let out a small laugh.

Pocky was waiting for me at another table. I would have to tell him about this. Lavishing sounded good to me—especially since I would now be bathing him in frangipani.

Even with all Kimsan had been through, he had not lost the art of finding joy. Or love. He must have erected protective walls inside his mind during the brutality he had suffered. But his emotional self-protection had not turned into an emotional prison. It warmed my heart to know he had found love and healing with his new family.

I asked him, "And what do you believe is the key to being a good parent?"

His expression changed and he leaned forward. "Good parenting means teaching your kids to do their homework. Nowadays, education is highly valued in Cambodia, as are teachers."

I nodded in agreement. His generation had lost out, but they would make sure their children and grandchildren did not fall behind the rest of the world.

I ached to ask him the most obvious questions: *How do you give tours, day after day, of the places where you and your people were so traumatized? Doesn't this rip open the wounds all over again?* But I approached these difficult questions carefully.

"I'm surprised you don't seem to harbor any anger. You're so calm when you talk about your past," I said, watching to see if I'd offended him.

He shrugged. "I don't look at it that way. Instead of feeling like a victim, I believe my past is part of my karma. I probably did bad things in a past life to deserve what happened to me in this one. Accepting this helps me focus on doing good karma so the future will be better."

I sat back in my seat. Wow. His acceptance blew me away. Talk about a belief system that worked! I thought about how limiting it is for us to hold onto the wrongs of the past and fuss over the little things in life. Kimsan's story gave new perspective to the concept "Don't sweat the small stuff." This man had persevered in spite of overwhelming odds, and had found peace in his mind.

I wanted to know more about how he had transcended his pain. I said, "It seems like surviving the pain of the past would be hard enough. Isn't it terribly difficult for you to conduct tours through the Killing Fields? Don't you long to get away from the pain of all that happened to you and your family?" I felt my breath catch in my throat. I worried I'd been too direct. The last thing I wanted to do was add to this man's pain.

He shrugged again. "I've spent so much time in the Killing Fields that I'm used to the pain. I carry a lot of sadness inside me regardless. But because I accept what's happened in the past as part of my fate, I don't feel angry. When I was around eighteen or nineteen, I became a Buddhist monk. I learned to calm my mind. My teachers helped me focus on leaving the past behind to live in the only time we really have, that is, the present. Every minute spent agonizing over the past is a minute stolen from what really matters. I learned about good karma and doing good things in order to have a better next life."

"What kinds of good things have you been focused on?"

He thought for a few seconds. "Well, I try to be a good husband and father. And I learned English so that I could be a good provider. I learned to speak English at New Life Church while reading the Bible. After that, I was able to get a job as a waiter in a tourist hotel, and now I work as a guide."

I nodded, impressed by his industriousness. "Is there any advice you have for people who are looking for more happiness in life?"

He thought, staring off into the distance, then said, "I find happiness when I think about how much my country has overcome. All of us didn't die. The people who lived have a duty to make a good and noble life, to honor those who had their lives taken away. My life is very humble compared to yours in the USA, but I have much gratitude for the life I live in my country today."

I thanked him for his time. He had been so open with me about his most traumatic life experiences, I could hardly believe it.

Trauma has a tendency to get locked in the brain and the body. If not addressed, such pain can wreak havoc with emotions and behavior. There exists a variety of psychological and physiological treatments for trauma. Kimsan's method involved accepting the trauma of his past by spinning the story of his life through the eyes of karma. He also healed himself by repeatedly exposing himself to the Killing Fields to desensitize the impact the trauma had on him.

Resiliency is strengthened by belief systems that enable us to look at the circumstances in our lives in ways that move us forward. Kimsan's story inspired me. The astonishing resiliency of the Cambodian people inspired me as well. Meeting such strong people reinforced in my mind how we can all find happiness and lead a good life despite our past circumstances.

VIETNAM

I learned about Vietnam on TV as a young child. Graphic images accompanied terrible stories from reporters in the field covering the long and drawn out Vietnam War. To vacation in a place I had only seen as war-torn seemed counterintuitive. But as I was discovering, the counterintuitive plays a big part in uncovering the gems of happiness.

As we traveled from Cambodia to Vietnam, I read up on the country's history, intrigued by how it had been sequestered from the outside world until the 1990s. I looked forward to seeing the iconic vistas of rice paddies, white-sand beaches, and peaceful waterways dotted with pagodas. I also hoped to catch glimpses of the rainforest and the people of the most rural villages.

We would be staying in Hanoi, a city with an interesting blend of Chinese, French, and Southeast Asian cultural influences. The capital city after North and South Vietnam reunified in 1975, Hanoi was of interest to a circle of our friends and relatives. Our friends Jim and Jenny, and Pocky's sister Lisa and her husband Ed, accompanied us on this adventure. As a Vietnam War veteran, Ed hoped the visit would open the door to healing for him.

I hoped Vietnam could teach me more about how people are able to face hardships and move ahead to lives of satisfaction and happiness. Vietnam seemed like a good place to research this further.

PUT ON A HAPPY FACE

We stayed in a beautifully preserved one-hundred-year-old hotel located in the middle of the bustling streets of Hanoi. After recovering from jetlag, we roamed the city by foot. Hanoi was famous for its colonial architecture, motorbike traffic, tranquil parks and lakes, and ancient temples. We walked through the infamous Hanoi Hilton, where American prisoners of war were held, and visited the Ho Chi Minh Mausoleum, where the amazingly well-preserved body of the former president of the Communist Party of Vietnam is on display behind glass.

Then we took a rickshaw to the lively Old Quarter, which was filled with locals peddling baked goods, herbs, jewelry, and silk. Our day ended with a water puppet show in which the puppets danced on water, a Vietnamese tradition that dates back to the eleventh century.

The following morning, we got up early and boarded a motor coach for a picturesque countryside ride to the water. We would be setting sail on a junk to travel through H Long Bay—the "bay of the descending dragon."

We sat together in the exotic wooden boat, oohing and ahhing as we slid through beautiful emerald waters filled with towering limestone islands. The islands are nearly 250 million years old, and there are a thousand of them, many covered with the thick jungle of rainforests.

The day had been sunny and hot, but as we approached the first of the islands, a thick fog descended and totally engulfed the shoreline. We disembarked in the eerie mist, and followed a dirt path to the edge of the island, where we then followed a steep path lined with trees. Then we entered a dark cave. My heart pounded with excitement, and I held tight to Pocky's hand.

Sung Sot Cave (or, the Cave of Surprises) had smooth walls, and seemed quite small. But as we walked deeper in, the vastness revealed itself. The colorfully lit grotto featured thousands of glittering stalactites and stalagmites. I was reminded of chandeliers.

As we wandered through the huge dark cavern, I felt like I'd entered another world, a world of ice and darkness, cool air, and rich earth.

The next day we headed to the water again, this time for a week-long cruise down the legendary Mekong River, often referred to as "the rice bowl of Asia" due to the endless emerald rice fields along the banks. The twelfth longest river in the world, the Mekong flows for 2,700 miles through China, Laos, Cambodia, Thailand, Myanmar, and Vietnam.

Pocky stared out the window of our motor coach, fascinated by passing trucks filled with cages. After at least a dozen trucks had passed, Pocky pointed to the cages and said, "Those are rats!"

Our guide explained the rats were a delicacy. He told us we would be stopping at a market soon, where we could enjoy barbecued rat on a stick, or we could opt for some "KFC"—Kentucky Fried Crickets.

Everyone laughed.

When we stopped at the market, we wandered around and examined the wares. A vendor placed the most beautiful gray, velvet-like critter on my chest. It was a tarantula—and it was alive!

After the shock wore off and the fear left my body, the pretty spider and I bonded. But when my new friend started crawling toward my face, then it was time to say goodbye.

As we continued walking through the market, I saw that anything with the ability to swim, crawl, or walk provided protein for the people of Vietnam. I tasted a "special wine." The yellow liquid came from a huge jar with a three-foot snake curled up at the bottom. The snake, fortunately, was in an eternal slumber. It tasted bitter, more like medicine than wine. The elder who poured the wine promised me good health.

In fact, after that, I was not ill again for two years.

We left the market and joined the travelers gathered in the lounge on the deck of the riverboat. We were served a much-better-tasting, welcome-aboard coconut drink. I began a conversation with the woman hired to interpret for some of the passengers on board the ship. Her name was Rose.

Rose and I continued our conversation as the ship sailed, and almost from the start, she seemed like an old friend. Educated and articulate, her easygoing, fun-loving nature won me over right away. The special warmth she radiated made her a fine conversationalist. But occasionally she hinted at a deep sadness, which told me Rose had a story to tell.

At the end of our last day on the water, Rose and I lingered on the main deck. We sat side by side, as we had on our first day, staring at the green water. Everyone else had gone to their rooms to pack or rest.

Rose's dark eyes sparkled when I revealed I was writing a book about happiness.

"I'd love to find out your thoughts," I told her.

She looked surprised. "I'm not used to talking about my thoughts. I don't know what I could tell you about happiness." She leaned in close and whispered, "But, well, why not?"

We laughed.

Rose made me promise not to use her real name. "Please call me Rose in your book," she said in a soft voice.

"Sure, that's no problem," I promised her.

We went downstairs to the dining room. It was a little too early for dinner, so we had the place to ourselves. The gentle rocking of the ship soothed as we sat close to each other at an empty table.

Rose said, "I want to help you understand what it is like for a woman in my country. So I will tell you a story about my family."

I nodded. I wanted to learn about her family so that I could know more about her.

Her dark eyes were full of light. "I have two sisters, and our mother is still alive. When I was young my parents tried to have a third child. They were hoping for a son, of course, even though the communist government at the time limited families to two children."

I nodded again. I had read about that, and about how women had abortions as they tried to make sure their second child was a boy.

She frowned. "Here it is like gold to have a son because sons are the ones who take care of their parents. Sons will take in parents when they get old, you see. But instead of getting a son, my parents had a third daughter. This was not good. They hid my youngest sister, but this did not last. When it was time for her to enter school, my family was strictly penalized, and the government cut off some of our financial support."

Her face held a solemn expression, and I touched her hand to express my understanding. I asked her, "Have things changed since you were a child?"

Pocky and our friends took their seats in a far corner of the expansive dining room. I was pleased Pocky had left us alone so that I could speak privately to Rose. His intuition seemed to kick in at important moments.

Rose said, "There is another thing I want you to understand, but probably you cannot fully comprehend this as a woman from the West. Women here are supposed to live in little boxes of happy and less-than. By that, I mean we are always supposed to be less than we are, and happier than we really are. If we do not do this, then there are problems."

"What kind of problems?"

She frowned. "Besides putting on a happy face when we are not happy, we women are encouraged not to come across as cleverer than our spouses. We have to play dumb all the time. This is true also at work, and we must play dumb for the men we work with. If we are perceived to be smarter in any way, we are severely dealt with." She sighed deeply. "As a child, I had no idea how bad life could be for an adult woman."

I felt sick. Poor Rose. She was in such a dramatic position of inequality. I felt suffocated just listening to her. What a waste of female energy, intelligence, and productivity.

"Do you have a daughter?" I asked her.

"No, in that, I have been lucky. I have a nine-year-old son. It will benefit my country, and the young women of my country, to make certain my son learns to respect women. The main problem in raising my son is—" Her voice hushed, and I leaned closer so that she could whisper. "Well, my husband. You see, I am in a difficult marriage. My husband is having an affair."

Tears streamed from her beautiful eyes. Overcome with emotion, she let the tears fall, then sobbed.

I felt awful for her, and wanted to help in some way. I knew I couldn't take her pain away, but at least I could continue to let her to reveal her real self, something her culture did not encourage.

She wiped her eyes and said, "He goes out late whenever, wherever, and with whomever he wants. Women here are taught to swallow their feelings, put on a happy face, and not complain. The men are free to do whatever they wish."

Her face contorted, and for a moment, this beautiful, composed, highly intelligent woman looked like a frightened animal. Her composure had changed as well. She was hunched over, keeping watch from the corners of her eyes to make sure no one stood within earshot. She placed a hand on her chest and took a deep breath, composing herself so that she could retake control of her emotions.

I poured water from a pitcher on the table into a glass and set it in front of her. "Why don't you leave him?"

Her eyes went wide. She took a long drink of water and stared at me in silence. This was the longest moment of silence in our time together.

"I can't," she confessed. She replaced the glass on the wood table a little too hard. "My family would lose face. Do you know what this expression really means? What it means to 'lose face'?"

"I think so. I'm not sure," I said.

She leaned in. "Look at the homes around Hanoi. *Really* look at them. Sometimes you can see how only the front is painted and looks good, the face of the house. The rest of the house is a mess. Do you see? This is how we are."

It struck me as wasteful that half of the country's talent and wisdom was repressed. This represented a massive loss of human potential, and incurred serious personal and economic costs. The silencing of women was bad for the country and all its citizens. Having to wear a happy face in the world was creepy and unnatural. I couldn't imagine having to suppress all my feelings, hide my intelligence, and not share my opinions—for a lifetime.

As I listened to Rose speak, I could tell her ability to feel happiness was also suppressed. I wondered what this did to her health. Studies show that suppressed emotions can cause depression, sleep disturbances, and exhaustion. Living in such a repressed manner would never lead to happiness.

After she dried her eyes with a napkin, I said, "Rose, how do you make it through your days? Do you do anything just for fun?"

She looked at me, her eyes glistening. "I don't know. It's difficult. Because my husband is the oldest son in his family and obligated to care for them, I have to live with my mother-in-law. She never liked me. She went to a fortune-teller after we got engaged, she wanted to find out whether I would be a good daughter-in-law. My husband and I bribed the fortune-teller, so she said all the right things."

We laughed a little. She said many Vietnamese go to fortune-tellers for advice on life. This is what they do instead of seeking counseling from a therapist.

She shook her head. "My mother-in-law is awful, actually. Me and my other sisters-in-law pay for her to go to a Laughing Tai Chi class."

"Now that's a good idea!" I said.

We both laughed. As she began to talk about her mother-in-law's awful nature, I had a small-world moment. So many people around the world all say the same thing, but of course we aren't all expected to live with our mothers-in-law.

"Does the class help?" I asked.

"With her? Not much," Rose said with a grin.

We laughed louder. Pocky glanced over at us and smiled. He raised his glass at us in appreciation.

Rose said, "You know what makes me happy? Cooking with my girlfriends and sisters-in-law—*that* makes me happy. We laugh like you and I are now, and we gossip. Oh, how we gossip! We feel safe with each other, you know? Enough to complain about our husbands, but within limits. Honestly, it feels so good to speak the truth with them. To be who I really am. They know. They understand."

I smiled and nodded, glad that she had people to share her true self with. Admitting what she felt to her girlfriends in private would help her avoid the unhealthy side effects of repressing her real self in public. What would any of us women do without our close girlfriends?

Rose leaned toward me. "I also love my work. In your book, you can't describe the real work I do, please. Make up some other job for me, okay? I am afraid someone might read what I've said to you today and retaliate somehow on my family."

I nodded. "Yes, of course. What job would you like me to give you?"

She laughed. "How about you make me an interpreter? You can say I'm a housewife, too, because that part is true."

"Perfect!"

She smiled with relief, then grew serious when she said, "My work gives me a temporary feeling of independence. It helps me discover new ideas so I can grow—at least it gives me this illusion. But I am tired of acting less intelligent than my male colleagues. It is so hard to constantly play a role, you know?"

No, I didn't know. I wasn't sure what to say.

"Sometimes, some days, I don't know who I really am. The happy face person, or Rose."

How hard it must be for a woman to grow in this stifling society; how impossible the prospect seems, and how beautiful that Rose still tried. The fear and suppression she lived with every day bothered me. I tried to put on a happy face for Rose, but I couldn't. Her name would forever remind me of a beautiful flower that had not been allowed to fully bloom.

"One more thing for your happiness list," she said with a big smile. Now she wanted to cheer *me* up. "Music is happiness. Music makes me merry, so my girlfriends and I sing karaoke. I wish you could come with us. I bet you're good at it!"

"Me?" I burst out laughing. "Me and karaoke?" I instantly thought of Pocky, and what a riot it would be to sing karaoke together. Something for the bucket list.

Rose laughed, too. "It's very popular here. We have karaoke places on every block—like Starbucks!"

We laughed harder.

Rose had the best laugh, rolling like hills, and youthful. I would have missed out on that laugh if she hadn't chosen to be vulnerable and share her story with me. So many parts of ourselves are not revealed to others as our guarded natures hinder us from fully sharing who we are. In this way, we deny ourselves the chance to be a blessing to others. I will always cherish my memory of Rose's laugh.

"Thank you for bringing me happiness," she whispered as we hugged each other goodbye.

MEMORIES ON THE MEKONG

We continued to sail down the Mekong River, heading south to Ho Chi Minh City, once called Saigon. The striking natural beauty of the environment included the lush green trees and paddy fields, mists that came and went, and the changing colors of the river. The water would go from rust to muddy brown to olive green. We traveled slowly downriver to the sound of the boat cutting through the water as sunlight bounced off the waves. Here and there, we glimpsed life onshore. Most of the time it felt like we were alone in the natural world.

The breeze felt nice on my skin, but floating by so much poverty disturbed me. I observed the tiny villages along the riverbanks where people lived in the smallest of shacks. Villages full of barefoot kids with raggedy clothes and scraggly hair. Stick-thin men in small boats catching fish. The banks of the river seemed a dumping ground for rubbish. Birds swooped down to capture enticing garbage. Sometimes the people waved to us as we passed. I wondered if they thought we were from another world.

I had time to process what I'd seen and heard in North Vietnam. I thought about Rose and her singing. And I reflected on the power of music to uplift. The most popular religion in Vietnam is Buddhism. Most Buddhist practices involve chanting in some form. *Puja*, a word from the ancient Tamil culture meaning "to do with flowers," is a musical offering involving chants and drums. It is a way to honor and show reverence to the Buddha. Chanting and music help followers memorize the holy texts. How lovely that Rose and her friends honored each other with their own kind of puja—karaoke.

Sitting on the deck, floating down the slow river, I found myself in a twilight between the Vietnam of today and the Vietnam I recalled from my youth. I remembered the numerous newspaper headlines about fighting along the Mekong. The TV reports on all the war casualties, and the steadily increasing number of dead soldiers. I thought about all the pain inflicted by the draft, and the many families I knew who would forever have an empty seat at their dinner table.

Thinking about the war made me want to talk to Ed, Pocky's sister's husband, who had been a first lieutenant in the US Army, and stationed in Vietnam. I asked him to tell me about his time in Vietnam, and his impressions from our trip.

Ed is a formidable guy, with a sturdy build, thick white hair, and a goatee—think, Colonel Sanders meets college professor. He is one of the nicest people I've ever known. Firmly planted in his deck chair, he stroked his beard as he spoke to me.

"I remember Saigon as a big city with a lot of rundown buildings. I'm curious, and just a little uneasy, about traveling there again. My last memory of Saigon is bad; the place was a mess. The people seemed nice, but booze and drugs were all over the place, so it was a pretty screwed-up time. I worked in a giant warehouse just outside the city, doing military intelligence." In a hushed voice, he added, "The worst day of my stay here was on New Year's Eve, 1971. At night, one of us always kept watch over the warehouse, and that night it was my turn. I heard an explosion in the back of the building, and ran back there. A South Vietnamese soldier who had been hired to burn our intelligence had accidentally set off some kind of explosion. While I stood there staring at the guy, his skin fell off. He screamed in pain. It was terrible. There was nothing I could do. I couldn't believe my eyes. The skin was shedding, you know, like a snake!"

Ed took a moment to collect himself. When he continued to speak, his voice was unsteady. "I rushed him to the nearest hospital, but because it was an American hospital, they didn't want to admit him. I convinced them to at least bandage him up, and they did. Then they sent us off with a couple of Vietnamese soldiers who said they knew the way to a Vietnamese hospital. It was pitch black, and I had no idea where we were. The soldiers drove and drove, past miles and miles of rice paddies. These soldiers didn't speak a bit of English. The poor burned guy continued to scream in pain. It was a nightmare. Finally, we reached the Vietnamese hospital. They admitted the man, fortunately. I later heard he had miraculously survived."

Ed shifted gears to another painful memory. "When the army returned to America, the people in our own country hated us. They hated us because we lost the war. Or they hated us because we participated in an unpopular war. I was flipped off and cussed at. I was afraid to let people know I had ever been in Vietnam."

I remembered how much antagonism there had been at the time, all the protests against the war, the violence in our own country between protesters and those in support of the soldiers. "So I guess Vietnam was not your first choice for a family vacation," I said with a small smile.

Ed smiled back. "I have to admit, I hesitated before agreeing to this trip. I wasn't sure what to expect. Maybe the bad memories will still be there to haunt me. We'll see how it goes. So far, so good. I've been interested to experience parts of Vietnam I didn't get to appreciate when I was here before."

The boat had arrived at a wide expanse of water where many riverboats congregated. I leaned on the rail, staring down at the water. I was feeling so very far away from wartime Vietnam. I breathed in the rich, moist air, appreciating the natural beauty and unique character of the river, the thick patches of tropical trees and grasses, and the silhouettes of fishermen casting their nets. I loved the way the trip down the Mekong had slowed us down, making me feel less civilized, more primal.

JOY AT LES ENFANTS DE KBAL KOH

A few miles farther south, we stopped in a little village on the water. We disembarked so that we could purchase locally made trinkets and visit the local school. At the small building housing Les Enfants de Kbal Koh, the boys and girls wore crisply pressed school uniforms. We had purchased supplies for the children; basics, like pencils, paper, and books in English. In return, the children would sing for us. The first song they chose was, of all things, "Old MacDonald Had a Farm."

They encouraged us to sing along, so we did. We sang quite a few rounds, covering many animal impressions, mooing and clucking and making funny faces. We all laughed, catching eyes and giggling.

I spoke to two girls who looked like best friends. They sat together, their dark hair flowing down their thin backs. I asked what made them happy. One of the girls spoke up right away.

"We're happiest when we sing! We know how to count to ten in English, too!"

I was impressed with her impeccable English. "Really?"

The girls looked at each other, and in unison, began to chant, "One, two, three, four, five, six, seven, eight, nine, ten!"

Both girls had huge smiles on their pretty little faces. Such pride and confidence. I hoped they would not be forced to hide their intelligence as they grew up.

The girls continued to talk, taking turns to tell me their thoughts. They said they were both ten years old, and agreed that the two boys who sat behind them in class made them happy. When I asked why, they giggled and said the boys made them laugh because they were always getting into trouble and acting silly. Their joy was infectious. Boys act silly and make girls laugh everywhere in the world, a sort of international language of happiness.

I looked around the room as the group began to sing another round. Everyone looked so happy. If adults could find joy in the simple things like kids do—if we were intentional about it—we would open up our awareness to these moments. If we incorporated joy intentionally, and made it into a daily practice, moments of pure happiness would become more common for us, even automatic.

The way we process joy has a lot to do with how we create long-lasting happiness in our lives. It isn't enough to just notice the special moments. We should take those moments and breathe in the feeling of joy, allowing it to fill our bodies. This is a healthy, healing practice.

Our biology is designed for happiness. The body processes joy with a particular signature, as it does with every emotion. Essentially, the body memorizes ways to emote. So the less joy we feel, the less able we are to feel it. The more joy we acknowledge and allow ourselves to appreciate, the more joy we will feel.

"With a 'moo, moo' here, and a 'moo, moo' there, here a 'moo,' there a 'moo,' everywhere a 'moo, moo' . . . " Pocky playfully sang the lyrics as we walked back to the boat, and I couldn't stop laughing.

We are so like this; he, the little boy being silly, and me, the little girl laughing at him.

HAI ON LIFE

We finally left the river behind. It felt strange to be back on land again. We found seats in a crowded bus headed for Ho Chi Minh City. I sat next to a middle-aged Vietnamese man who looked like a businessman on his way home from work.

The modern city teemed with rush hour traffic. Skyscrapers lit up the night sky, cars and bicycles and pedestrians hustled along busy streets.

So much of the city was new, it looked nothing like the rundown communist cities of North Vietnam.

Ed sat across the aisle from me. He leaned over to say, "The city is better than I expected. It seems like this place has a new energy to it. It's good to see Saigon has returned to normal."

Ho Chi Minh City had a special significance to me as well. I clearly recalled the fall of Saigon at the end of the war, and the nationwide relief and grief when the last American soldiers left Vietnam. This was two years after the war officially ended in 1975. It took the United States a long time to recover from that war. For many people, there will be no return to normal.

I stared out the bus window. Ho Chi Minh City had a cool, urban feel. With a population of eight million, it is the largest in Vietnam. People dressed in expensive suits and skirts, the neon lights above advertising stores and restaurants, cafés and tea houses, clubs and bars. The wide streets lined with trees reminded me of Paris. I spotted upscale dress shops, some filled with gorgeous silks. I made a note to stop at one of them, as I wanted to take home a custom-made dress. I could feel the excitement of a city brimming with money, art, culture, and life.

The man sitting next to me had noted my increasing excitement as I watched the city from our window. I introduced myself and told him I was an American on my first trip to Vietnam. With a twinkle in his eye, he said his name was Hai. He lived in the city, and was on his way home to his wife.

"I make the money, and she spends it," he said with a small smile.

I laughed and told him that is exactly what I might hear from a man on his way home from work in America. He nodded, smiling broadly.

I asked Hai what people in Vietnam thought about Americans. Since Ed was within earshot, I hoped the answer would be positive.

Slightly smaller than me, Hai looked up at me when he spoke. In a matter-of-fact way, he said, "My father was in the American War."

In Vietnam, what we call the Vietnam War is referred to as the American War.

Hai continued. "Most people in Ho Chi Minh City have moved on from those times. Most of us look at the war as something in the past." He glanced out the window and then looked back at me. "We are feeling happy these days. The Americans bring us tourism, and we welcome that. Tourism is a strong part of our economy, and with strong tourism, we have less hunger."

I was happy to hear we were welcome in South Vietnam. "Life here has a cosmopolitan feel," I said.

"I like living in the South. Our country is developing now, and communism is less influential. There is more open-mindedness here."

I took that opportunity to ask about happiness. "What do you think was the key to cultivating happiness after the war?"

He continued to stare out the window for a while, then he looked at me and said, "If we focus less on the past destruction and problems involving our countries, and more on the good we can do together now and in the future, good karma will happen. I trust in that."

Karma again.

Apparently, the concept of karma had enabled Hai and the people of Vietnam to forgive the past and move on. This enabled them to enjoy a happier present that would lead to a happier future. As Martin Luther King Jr. said, "Darkness cannot drive out darkness; only light can do that. Hate cannot drive out hate; only love can do that." This is the heart of forgiveness.

In our brief conversation, Hai had given me a window into what it means to forgive. Forgiveness doesn't always mean reconciliation. But Hai had made the choice to welcome American tourists to his city. He chose to focus on how everyone could move forward together with good works that might heal the destruction of the past.

People like Hai and Ed will never forget the effects the war had on their lives. But their elegant, bittersweet steps made me happy. Both men had been able to make peace with the horrors of the past in order to create space for more joy and good works in their lives.

As the bus pulled to a stop and I said goodbye to Hai, I thought about contrasts. Dark and light, happiness and sadness, war and peace. My visit to Cambodia and Vietnam had been full of such contradictions—pain and pleasure, extreme beauty, and unspeakable horror. But such is life. How would we know happiness without experiencing sadness?

As the Buddha said, "Pain is inevitable; suffering is optional." Like my diamonds in the rough back home, Kimsan, Rose, and Hai had overcome their pain, and they served as shining examples of resilience. These people sparkled in my mind like pink sapphires, beautiful examples of overcoming intense suffering. They warmed my heart.

HIGH IN THE CITY

On our last night in Ho Chi Minh City, the girls and I hit a laid-back bar on a crowded street corner while the guys roamed around town. Jenny, Lisa, and I were giddy with sensory overload. Over foamy drafts of beer, called *bia hois*, we chatted about our experiences. We laughed about the tarantula, and the snake juice. Everything was so weird and exotic, colorful and exciting, in Vietnam.

Our table overlooked a busy intersection. As I finished my first beer, I realized I was high on the vibe of this vibrant city. Rickety scooters dodged cars and people, horns honked, and pedestrians scattered. The air smelled of grilled meat. I watched people practicing Tai Chi in white pajama-like outfits. Women walked by carrying baskets on their heads, and boys on bicycles passed us, their baskets overflowing with fragrant flowers. Lines formed in front of the many vendors who peddled their wares at the crowded market across the street. The rich tapestry of colors and sights, smells and sounds, was exhilarating.

A tuk-tuk driver caught my eye. Throngs of cars and people stood between us, but we acknowledged each other through the crowd. His smile was beautiful. He looked weary, but proud and happy.

The evening heat made it particularly easy to drink beer. So did all the spicy food the waitress brought to our table—dried beef, meat cooked over open fire, pho and pho ga, chicken noodle soup and sticky rice with deep-fried hard-boiled eggs. For dessert, we had a rich crème caramel.

Pocky and Jim joined us at the table while we were finishing our sweet custard.

"Where's Ed?" Pocky's sister Lisa asked.

"Right here!" Ed sat down beside his wife.

"Where'd you go?" Pocky asked him.

Ed took a deep breath. "I decided to take a cab and visit some of my old haunts. I actually found the hospital door I entered that New Year's Eve carrying the wounded Vietnamese soldier," he said.

"No way!" Jim said.

"Wow," I gushed, as Lisa put her hand on her husband's broad back.

Ed's eyes brightened. "It's just an empty building now, but I remember that door. When I saw it, everything came flooding back—the explosion, walking in and finding the guy in such agony." He shook his head, the images too much even now, so many decades later. "But I had a great conversation with a Vietnamese man who was here in Saigon when I was. I met him as I walked through the market. It was good swapping stories with him. He was really friendly."

Nobody interrupted. Lisa massaged her husband's tense muscles as he talked.

"I'm relieved the Vietnamese people have been able to forgive the past. Like that guy on the bus you were talking to, Lisa. These people have moved ahead to better lives." He looked at me. "I'm really glad we came to Vietnam."

Pocky broke the silence that followed. "Come on, buddy, let me buy you a beer," he said, standing up to head for the bar. When I raised my empty glass, Pocky winked at me. "Okay, okay. You too, honey."

I was high that night, but not on beer. Ed had been revitalized on the trip, and so had I. There were times when I felt heartbroken by the devastation and destruction experienced by the people of Cambodia and Vietnam, and my spirits dampened—the exact opposite of what I had intended on this adventure in happiness. But then I thought of my discussion with the monk in Thailand, about how he'd pointed out the inevitability of suffering in life. How our ability to maintain happiness is found in the way we meet our suffering, instead of being defined by it.

Rose and Kimsan knew suffering, and I will forever be humbled by their stories and their openness in sharing them with me. Something magical happens when people from different places take the time to connect. We have a lot to learn from one another. The people of Vietnam and Cambodia presented me with lessons in resiliency, the keys to lasting happiness.

As I sat back and observed my laughing friends amidst the thriving, buzzing streets of the once war-torn city of Hanoi, I was surrounded by proof that good can rise out of devastation. This filled me with hope.

Part II

EUROPE: INNER SUMMER, FAIRYTALES, AND BLUE LIGHTS

Chapter 3

NORWAY: THE HAPPIEST PLACE ON EARTH

As the plane flew us from Denver to Oslo, I couldn't fall asleep. Restless, I looked with envy at my snoozing husband. The long flight was taking a toll on me. I'd already watched a couple of movies and I was still wide awake. Bored and wired, I flipped open my window shade.

Instead of the darkness I expected, the night sky was splashed with color. I watched a brilliant and ethereal light show in delight. Neon greens flashed on and off, like curtains opening and closing in the atmosphere—rapidly materializing, then disappearing in a fizzling white glow. The spectacle seemed like a beautiful dream.

Each time the lights faded, I clasped my hands in a kind of prayer to the light gods, willing them to bring back the show. Each time, the fantastic sky lights appeared again, playing a celestial game of hide-and-seek. I wanted to wake all the sleepers on the plane, yelling out to them, "Hey! You're missing the show! Wake up and check out the view!"

Instead, I nudged my husband. "Pocky, wake up. You gotta see this!"

Pocky opened his eyes and gave me a blank look. Then he peered out the window. His eyes widened when he caught a glimpse of the fantastic glimmering lights in the darkness. He leaned over me like he wanted to give me a hug, and said, "Incredible. That's . . . amaze . . . hon . . . "

He fell asleep again, leaning hard against my shoulder. I shifted him carefully to his own seat, and rearranged his blanket.

Elated by what I'd seen, I waved to a flight attendant walking up the aisle and asked her in a hushed voice, "Have you seen this?"

She stared out my window. On cue, another colorful curtain of lights opened and closed.

This wasn't her first heavenly light show. "Ah, yes. These are the Northern Lights, the Aurora Borealis. Unusual to see at this time of year, and at this elevation. You are very lucky!"

She smiled, then continued on her way down the aisle.

Sitting there in the eerie silence of the dark cabin, I felt oddly alone. Unable to share the Aurora Borealis with everyone around me reawakened a familiar, if unexpected, loneliness; the same deep-seated loneliness that had overwhelmed me when I'd first joined the ranks of the real walking dead, a confusing kind of emptiness experienced by a woman who seemingly had it all.

Sometimes surprising emotions rise up in us and we're not sure why. I allowed the subtle waves of sadness to wash over me, and tried to understand why this unwanted feeling had revisited me at such an awe-inspiring moment.

My work as a psychotherapist has given me the privilege of listening to thousands of stories of pain and loss. Occasionally, the sadness of my clients' stories add to my feelings of melancholy, despite my efforts to detach from them. But this sadness, I attributed to the remnants of feelings I'd had during an earlier time, a time in my life when I'd lost three people I loved in a three-year period while I attended college. A close friend, who was like a sister to me, died, then my father, then my mother. A divorce when I was in my thirties had been another time of intense sadness.

As the plane flew through the cold night air, I reflected on those times, and how much my father, a lover of travel, science, and nature, would have enjoyed the magnificence of the Northern Lights.

We are not designed to hold on to an emotion for a long period of time, and as I observed my own emotions on that silent night, they transformed into a feeling of peacefulness, and I finally fell asleep.

From everything I had read, Norway had much to teach me about happiness, even though it wasn't at the top of my bucket list. I preferred traveling to places offering warmer weather, but had a feeling the region would radiate warmth in other ways.

In a land of fjords and legends, the Nordics are known for their practicality. But scratch the surface, and you will find something else entirely. Their Viking heritage has provided them with fantastic folklore, rich in tales of the savage seas, epic conquests, and the kind of magical thinking that once led sailors to believe in sea monsters.

A blend of practicality and imagination can provide a balance that helps foster a happy life. I wanted to meet people who would tell me more about this so that I might uncover the secrets of what research has shown—that Norway is the happiest place in the world.

KOSELIG AND THE INNER SUMMER

On our first day in Oslo, I felt groggy and sleep deprived. In desperate need of fresh air, Pocky and I left our hotel for a walk on the Oslo Harbor Promenade.

The minute we arrived on the bustling walkway, my jet lag began to fade. Everyone around us was dressed in bright colors, their smiling faces rosy from the cold. Young men rode unicycles. Girls in leggings blew gigantic bubbles. Long-legged parents pushed their little ones in mod strollers. The place had a fashionable, carnival atmosphere that made me feel alive.

Pocky and I gazed at the people as we walked along the marina, and we admired the stunning view of ships moored in the harbor. We noted the wild, grassy dirt trails that led from the main drag, paths winding around jagged rocks framed by world-famous fjords. We could see in the distance the long, narrow, and very deep inlets formed by the sea in between steep slopes of the mountainous coast. Colorful glass, wood, and concrete buildings lined the promenade, creating a cheerful atmosphere. Sidewalk cafés featured cooking demonstrations, and the aroma of grilling meat filled the air.

I realized I was hungry, so I walked over to a food cart to order what looked like barbecued beef on a skewer. Pocky caught up and stood beside me. He put his hand on mine, indicating I should wait to order.

"What?" I said to him.

"Uh, that's reindeer," he said, smiling.

"Yes, fish is over on this side," the vendor said with a huge smile.

"Oops." I laughed.

"Well done!" she said to me. "I see your inner summer shining through, and that makes you well on your way to becoming a Norwegian. Det var bra! This is what we say when things are very good."

"I like the idea of my inner summer shining through," I replied.

She nodded. "This is what we must do in life, learn how to find our inner summer. What Norwegians cultivate to survive the long nights of winter. We all do that here. It's called the endless need for koselig."

"If that's a kind of beer, I'm all in," Pocky said. "Det var bra!"

The vendor offered me a fish skewer, then handed one to Pocky. A young man dressed in striped pants and a bold yellow shirt passed us on a unicycle. I laughed in between bites.

"You wanna ride one of those, honey?" Pocky said, his eyes daring me to say yes.

"Sure," I said, joking.

The vendor's smile widened. "Yes, do ride! It is a matter of koselig."

I smiled at her, puzzled, as I couldn't figure out what *koselig* meant.

An older man stood in line behind us. Clothed traditionally, he wore a handmade black-and-white sweater trimmed with red and yellow embroidery and gold buttons. He said to us, "You wish to know the meaning of koselig?"

I nodded, surprised at his willing participation in the conversation. This kind of openness turned out to be a hallmark of the attitude of the people I met in Norway.

The man said, "My dear, 'koselig' is the feeling of being cozy."

The food vendor added, "It means 'intimacy,' 'warmth,' 'happiness.' 'To be content.'"

You could have knocked me over with a fish skewer. What were the chances that the first word I would learn in Norwegian would be a word for happiness?

"So how do you achieve koselig?" I asked.

The vendor said, "To achieve koselig, you will need koselig objects. In winter months, they can be found in the blankets the cafés place on their outdoor chairs, and in the quaint shops with candlelit entrances."

The old man said, "At home, koselig is wholesome food, waffles made from scratch. In the mountains, it's passing the flask of cognac around."

Comfort food, I thought. *A universal.*

"You want to know how to make me koselig?" Pocky said, taking my hand in his.

I laughed. We then said our goodbyes and continued our walk along the waterfront, passing ultra-modern restaurants, museums, and art galleries.

After a mile or so, I said, "We need to find our koselig object."

Pocky grinned. "I know just the thing."

He led me over to a restaurant overlooking the water, and nodded to a waiter. After we took our seats, Pocky ordered us microbrews. When the frosty glasses arrived, we toasted to our successful quest for koselig.

The beer tasted terrific, fresh and malty. We ordered up a big plate of mussels, which were the best I'd ever tasted. We had a delightful gelato for dessert. During the remainder of our stay, we sampled traditional Norwegian fare, like lamb and cabbage soup, big fat meatballs, and thick fish stew. I always passed on the reindeer, however. I couldn't get myself to eat Rudolph.

The restaurant had a friendly, relaxing brand of hospitality that encouraged conversation. I noticed a wide variety of accents, both patrons and servers speaking myriad languages. Everyone seemed joyous, excited, amped up. People around us were enjoying the beautiful autumn day.

After our meal, Pocky and I walked arm in arm under the star-filled sky. As the cold evening arrived and we reached the well-lit lobby of our warm hotel, I felt the ultimate feeling of koselig.

Now I understood. I could see it all around me—a bright happiness. Forget Disneyland; Norway was the happiest place on earth.

The World Happiness Report, published by the United Nations, measures subjective well-being. In the 2017 report, Norway was rated the highest in this category, with other countries in Scandinavia rounding out the top five slots. The top countries rank highest for those factors known to create happiness: caring, freedom, generosity, honesty, health, adequate income, and good governance. In contrast, the US ranked fourteenth in the report—down from third place, just a decade ago.

A DOCTORATE IN PRACTICALITY

The next day over hot coffee, we decided to learn some Viking history. Enthused by the prospect of seeing the iconic Vikingskipshuset Museum, we jumped out of our cab and hurried to join a tour group. The entrance was like a church, with high ceilings and a roof that came to a pointy peak. Pocky leaned in and whispered in an alarming yet charming Viking accent, "Call me Thor!"

I laughed.

"Over here, please!" our tour leader called. She was tall and lovely, with glossy brown hair that fell all the way down her back. She had a gorgeous white smile and beautiful blue eyes. "Welcome to the Vikingskipshuset Museum. My name is Kari."

Everyone gathered around her.

"Here is where we house three Viking longships. You may view these ships as some obscure relics from long ago, however their discovery began a fantastic dialogue with the present, illuminating twelve thousand years of history sweeping and ambitious in scope. Together, we will explore the many secrets of the Viking ships."

Kari had earned a PhD in history, and she described for the group her specialization in Viking burial rituals. Her beauty and intelligence piqued my interest. She exuded a degree of self-confidence refreshing to see in a young woman.

She shepherded the group into a cavernous room housing the spectacularly preserved Oseberg longship. Pocky and I walked around it, examining the construction as Kari told us the history.

"This, ladies and gentlemen, is what legends are made of. A ship around a thousand years older than the USA. Radioactive carbon dating sets construction at 834 AD. Can you imagine digging this up in your backyard? Well, that's exactly what happened to the Norwegian farmer who discovered this beautifully preserved ship on his land back in 1904."

Silence fell over our group. I tried to imagine finding an ancient relic buried in our yard.

Kari said, "And when they dug it up, the once great ship had turned into a cemetery. It held the remains of many nobles, as well as the remains of thirteen horses, four dogs, and two oxen. Ancient beliefs called for burial rituals conducted so that the valkyries—the beautiful maidens who attended Odin, the god of death—would appear. They were said to escort the dead to a shining Valhalla, a great hall where Odin received the honored warrior dead. This was a kind of paradise, where warriors battled all day, then found all their wounds healed by night."

Kari pointed out the flat bottom, wide middle, and tall bow and stern. "The special design allowed for perfect transport over oceans and fjords. Look closely at the bow. See the slithering snake carved in the wood? The snake leads the way on the journey, scaring away all enemies."

I examined the snake carefully, admiring the artistry.

"Discoveries also included the remains of women dressed in expensive fabrics. These were possibly priestesses to the Nordic Goddess Freyja. The Vikings believed the priestesses could talk to the Nordic gods. They spoke to the gods through the water to keep the Vikings safe at sea."

Pocky and I exchanged glances. We both loved a good myth.

Kari told us, "Vikings were the lords of the oceans. Leif Eriksson landed on the American coast in a longship around the year 1000, long before Columbus arrived."

What an amazing culture. The people were strong enough to live through cold winters and summers blazing with the Midnight Sun, and brave enough to cross the ocean, yet they were full of fantasies about protective princesses and wooden serpents to keep them safe in the long dark nights. They believed in both the practical and the fantastical.

Our guide said, "The importance of learning about and understanding our ancestors and their beliefs cannot be understated. One of the ways we learn about them involves a concept called 'scaffolding.' Our modern minds have a mosaic quality inherited from our ancestors. There is an evolution of thought, one that cannot be understood unless our ancestors are understood as well."

The idea of a mosaic mind intrigued me. Bits and pieces of our ancestors that become our identity as well, forming the way we look at the world. How fascinating.

I thought Kari would be a great candidate for an interview, so I took her aside and asked if she would be interested in speaking to me about her ideas on happiness.

She replied, "Absolutely. I am happy in every area of my life. Except taxes. The taxes in Norway are overwhelming!"

I nodded empathetically. Another reminder that we live in a small world.

After the tour ended, Pocky and I followed Kari to a picnic table in a courtyard between stately buildings. Surrounded by manicured lawns, birch and spruce trees, the courtyard was full of young families, the air sweetened by the sound of children playing. A cloudless sky overhead and perfect weather punctuated the idyllic scene.

I noticed Kari wore little makeup; a natural beauty. When I shared with her the details of our happiness adventure on the blue dot, her eyes lit up. She asked how long Pocky and I had been married.

We looked at each other and shrugged, doing the math in our heads. Everyone laughed. Pocky then excused himself to grab something for us to eat at a nearby café.

"Are you married?" I asked Kari.

She shook her head. "No, I share my life with a partner. He and I are monogamous, but that is not always the case with partnerships. However, most of my friends do choose fidelity."

Kari had regaled me with tales of magical priestesses and serpents, yet she obviously had a pragmatic side. I thought about the balance between practical thinking and pursuing our wildest dreams. While being practical may lead to less disappointment, chasing our dreams can create a more passionate existence. I wondered how she felt about that.

"So when you were a little girl, did you dream of walking down the aisle? Did you want a fantasy wedding?"

She shrugged. "All little girls have dreams. Brave knights on white horses coming to the rescue. Looking beautiful, wearing ball gowns and white dresses. But as grown women, we understand the difference between fantasy and reality. I believe this lies at the heart of happiness. That is, living in the truth."

Kari's straightforwardness, her confidence, and comfort in her own skin, turned out to be common among the Norwegians I would meet. Their ability to share their unfiltered opinions gave me the freedom to share mine without concern for saving face or bruising someone else's ego.

I asked Kari, "How does your partnership make you happy?"

She smiled. "My partner and I find happiness in the freedom to choose who we want to be with, and when. In the beauty of honoring who we are today, and not putting limits on who we will become tomorrow. This allows us to let each other be who we really are; that is, authentically ourselves. It provides us room to grow and change. In Norway, we don't believe in committing to a relationship and staying in it if it becomes unhappy. Because of this, there are fewer marriages in Norway these days."

The Norwegian trend away from marriage minimized the emotional pain of divorce. But I wondered if the practical side of this kind of partnership eliminated some of the romantic aspects of a loving relationship.

Kari said, "The benefits we receive from the government are the same for marrieds and singles. We have financial contracts for property and assets. If the partnership doesn't work, these contracts are simply dissolved. There is no need for divorce attorneys. My own partnership is extremely happy, but if it were not, I would just end the contract and move on—without the pain and expense of a divorce."

Wow. If only American breakups could be that simple. I had nursed so many clients through heartbreaking divorces. Marriages had lasted back when people had shorter life spans. Now, when people married young, they often outlived their marriages. Perhaps a dissolvable partnership would be an idea worth considering.

I thought about my conversation with Rose in Vietnam, and how her emotional floodgates had opened as she recounted her years of suppression and the marital betrayal she had to endure. Kari did not have that kind of relationship. Two women from two different cultures; modern women with very different opportunities in life.

We continued to chat. The lack of drama around hot-button issues gave the conversation a certain openness and clarity, free of the dictates of political correctness. How refreshing it would be if we lived in a world where *all* our opinions found acceptance. Why couldn't we speak freely about what we believed even if we didn't agree? If we were more accepting of our differences, our conversations would be less dramatic and more dynamic, not muddled up by pretense or watered down by fear.

Pocky sat down next to me and doled out bottled water and thick cheese sandwiches.

"So, what about naming the children? How does that work in a partnership?" I asked between bites.

Kari sipped her water. "They can be given either one of their parents' names. Often both last names are combined."

Pocky said, "My name's a real tongue-twister. Our kids would have some interesting names, wouldn't they, honey?"

I smiled and nodded.

Kari folded her napkin, placing it on top of her paper plate. "I think it is easier to be happy in Norway because of all the benefits we receive from the government. Since education is free all the way through college, we can become as highly educated as we like without incurring any debt."

I had to agree. If you can't afford decent schooling, it is more difficult to become successful in America.

"How did you like your sandwich?" Kari asked Pocky. Then she scooped up his trash and placed it in a small paper bag.

"Hit the spot!" he said.

"A nice, sensible picnic. My favorite," she said with a twinkle in her eye.

I was still thinking about free education. "How wonderful that you took full advantage of the system by earning your PhD," I said.

She nodded enthusiastically. "It makes me very happy to work with the tourists at the museum. I enjoy helping them get a unique view of my homeland. What fun it is to discuss our different perspectives and broaden our world views together."

An older man had taken a seat at the opposite end of our picnic table. "I lead a happy life myself," he chimed in.

We all turned to look at him.

"Where are you from?" he asked Pocky and me.

"Colorado," I answered.

"I hear you are outdoor people there. I am, too. I walk everywhere, and this makes me young," he said with pride in his steely blue eyes.

"Good for you, my friend," Pocky said with a smile. He reached over and shook the man's hand. "Pocky's my name."

The man did not smile in return. "My name is Steinar."

"So how did you come upon your happy life?" Pocky asked, nudging me under the table. It was the first time Pocky had participated in an interview, and he seemed to be enjoying himself.

Steinar said, "I used to run a travel consultancy business. I am retired now. I worked very hard in my life, and have enough saved up for a good retirement. I like the freedom of winding down, having the time to enjoy life more. I also like to drive people around in my car. That way I can earn a little extra money. And it gives me a chance to practice my English. But mostly it helps keep me out of my wife's way."

I laughed. Steinar remained serious.

"How long have you been married?" Pocky asked.

Steinar searched the beautiful blue sky. "A long, long time." He did not look happy. Then he said, "The reason I got married was because my wife and my mother-in-law pressured me. But, it all turned out okay."

He did not laugh. Was he serious?

"Is it easy to retire in Norway?" Pocky asked to change the subject.

Steinar leaned in. "The taxes are high. Mine can be as high as 50 percent, and there's a 25 percent value-added tax."

Pocky whistled. "So how were you able to afford to retire?"

"Well, we have something you in the USA do not have," Steinar said.

"I'm all ears," Pocky told him.

Steinar raised his thick gray eyebrows. "Land! We live in a large area, with a relatively small number of people. We are surrounded by bodies of water teeming with fish. We are blessed with many resources. Norway is particularly rich in oil."

Pocky nodded. "So, with funds generated from high taxes and oil reserves, everyone's education and other basic needs are paid for."

"Basic needs—and luxurious ones, too! We have the luxury of providing for our future generations. So *this* is how we can retire." Steinar smiled at last. "Retirement is a big change. But you know something? I actually love what I do now. Driving tourists is good work."

"So you want to keep at it, keep working?" Pocky asked.

Steinar nodded. "I think it's good to keep working for as long as possible, even if you can retire comfortably. Working keeps a person thinking and learning. It keeps you sharp and gives life purpose," he said with a twinkle in his eyes.

"I agree," Pocky said, his eyes trained on me. We often discussed the idea of retirement, and what we might do to replace the work lives we both enjoyed.

Steinar said, "Because we are encouraged to choose careers based on our personal interests, Norwegians tend to be happy with our careers. And we don't have to spend our time worrying that all our resources will go to taking care of ourselves and our loved ones if we get sick, or when we are too old to work."

I let out a deep sigh. What a relief it would be to know our basic needs would always be met. Maslow's Hierarchy of Needs states that when the fundamental need for food, water, rest, safety, and security are met, we can focus on the deeper human need for relationships, accomplishments, and self-actualization. When this is the case, we can be rooted in the present because we don't have to worry about the future.

Steinar flipped the top off a microbrew. He handed one to Pocky, and both men took long swallows.

Wiping the froth from his lips, Steinar smiled again. "How old do you think I am?" he asked us.

"I would guess sixty," Kari said.

"I am seventy-two. I'm getting on now, so I want to do all the enjoying I can!"

"Here's to that," Pocky said, raising his beer.

"Skål!"

Channeling his inner Viking, Pocky pointed to the beer and said, "I think I found my koselig object."

I turned to Kari. "What's your koselig object?"

Her eyes widened. "My goodness, where did you learn about that?"

Pocky and I laughed. "A cute old man told us," I said.

"Well, my koselig object is my wonderful Wüsthof knives. They bring me so much happiness, because I love to cook," Kari said. "They were given to me by a dear friend, a journalist, in fact. Actually, she might be a good person for you to talk to for your book. You may enjoy her insights. Do you want me to try to arrange a meeting?"

"That would be wonderful," I said.

"She lives with her husband and young children very near your hotel," Kari said, checking her watch. She took out a small notebook and a pen. She handed them to me. "Thank you for the marvelous lunch. My next tour is in a few minutes."

I wrote down my contact information, and Kari stood up to go. "Delightful to have met you! I will be in touch soon."

In the hotel room that night, I couldn't sleep. I lay on my back, imagining a world with free education and enough money for retirement for everyone. Then my thoughts shifted, and my mind filled with images of Vikings, Leif Erikson, valkyries, and priestesses talking to Nordic Gods through the cold deep water.

BUCKET LIST MARRIAGE

I awoke early to a message from Kari on my phone. Her friend was available, and expecting us. Pocky and I scrambled to get ready, then enjoyed the short walk to Svein and Anne's apartment.

"I can't believe how lucky we are," I said.

"Couldn't be more convenient," Pocky agreed.

"Hey, are we lost?" I said, pointing to an unfamiliar street sign.

He laughed. "Must have made a wrong turn."

We retraced our steps and arrived at Svein and Anne's building on time. We hiked up the stairs to their apartment and met them at the door. I shook hands with Svein, a handsome blond with an athletic build, while Pocky greeted Anne, a natural beauty with shoulder-length blonde hair. Both looked to be in their mid-forties.

After we settled in the living area of their apartment, Anne said, "Kari told me about your exciting book project. How fun to be a part of it."

Two young children with white-blond hair entered the room and closed in on their parents. Svein scooped up the little boy. His older sister, looking pretty in a white eyelet dress, sat on the couch beside her mother, and smiled at me. The living area oozed comfort, with a lived-in vibe and the stuff of life scattered around; a toy here, a coffee cup there, books and piles of clean laundry. There was none of the nervous energy you find in homes where people feel they must tidy up for visitors.

Anne and Svein's relaxed way of entertaining felt refreshing to me. There is a difference between entertaining and hospitality. Entertaining has an air of Martha Stewart perfection. Hospitality evokes a less formal generosity of spirit that feels more familial. This much less stressful approach to entertaining impressed me, and I decided I'd keep it in mind.

I said, "We are so touched you opened your home to us. Kari tells me you're a journalist."

Anne nodded. "I was. I mean, I still am, but I decided to focus on a particular cause that would make a big difference. So I work with an alcohol and drug organization."

Their home had a small patio with a view of downtown Oslo. Pocky and Svein went to look at the city from the balcony. When they returned, Svein sat beside his wife on the leather couch.

He said, "Your book about happiness sounds intriguing." He turned to his wife. "What makes you happy?" he said, placing a hand on her thigh.

"Doing good for others. And you?" Anne asked him, smiling into his eyes.

"All of this," he said, waving his arms to indicate his home, his wife, and kids.

The boy was stretched out on the carpet playing with colorful Brio cars and a train set. His sister remained seated by their mother, listening and quietly watching the adults.

Svein continued. "We've been married since 2003, but it seems like yesterday. Where did all these kids come from?" He laughed.

"How old are you, young lady?" Pocky asked the girl.

"I'm nine," she said proudly. "Would you like a piece of fruit?"

"Well, yes, I would, thank you very much," Pocky said.

The girl stood up and began to wait on us, offering us sliced fruit and pastry from the serving trays set out on the coffee table. Her brother bounced up off the floor and scooped a piece of watermelon. He gobbled it down in a matter of seconds.

His sister laughed. "I think watermelon makes my brother happy."

Anne's family treated one another with respect, the parents including the children rather than tucking them away while the adults talked. I admired this approach to childrearing.

Anne told me, "You've come to the right place to write about your subject. They say we are one of the happiest places in the world."

Svein added, "I think an important factor in achieving happiness is for women to be treated equally. Anne and I are on equal footing, and that makes our life balanced and pleasant."

His wife smiled. "You know what I think? I believe a good marriage is essential for happiness," she said, nodding her head.

I asked her, "And what do you think makes a good marriage?"

"Common interests. For instance, children!" She laughed. "Being a good parent is important. But so is small talk, touching base."

She reached down and patted her son's head. He continued to play with the toy cars, oblivious and content.

Anne continued. "Also, it's important to try to put yourself in the other person's shoes. Say you're sorry when you're wrong. Be respectful when speaking with each other. Take turns nurturing the kids."

"That's a great list," I said.

"We nurture the kids equally but our styles are very different," Svein added, jumping up to grab his son from a precarious climb up the back of the sofa.

Anne smiled at her husband. "I suppose when the children get older, I'll have to be a bit stricter. But right now, I just enjoy seeing them find their own limits."

I told her, "You and Svein have a real flow; you work well together. You seem to have a happy marriage."

She leaned in. "You want to know a little secret? I got married because it was on my bucket list." She laughed. "I find crossing things off my bucket list makes me happy, too."

Svein stood over us. "I married Anne because I wanted to be in a relationship that had a strong commitment. I wanted to value that instead of my personal freedom."

Anne looked up at her husband. Her eyes softened. I could see the appreciation and deep love in her face. Their respect for each other was obvious, because they took turns speaking and listening, tending to the children and interacting with their guests. And they showed respect for each other's opinions and life choices. I loved how they tuned in to each other so attentively.

"So what do you think about partnerships?" I asked.

Anne shrugged. "The benefits are the same whether a couple marries or not. I don't see much difference with regard to the well-being of the children. In divorce, the custody rights are the same."

Svein added, "I think it's really important to spend time with the children, no matter what your situation. My father was a leader in politics here, and I didn't spend much time with him while growing up. This is not the case for me with my children." He glanced at the two kids. "At this stage in our lives, I'm happy our career choices allow flexibility so we can spend time together as a family."

"So how is the political system structured here?" Pocky asked.

Svein sat down on the couch again. "There are eight political parties in our legislature. None of them can gain power alone. They build coalitions with enough support to form a government, so there is a lot of cooperation between the parties."

Cooperation in politics sounded about as fanciful as talking to gods through the water. Pocky and I exchanged glances. If only we had a little more of *that* in America.

Svein said, "Even though he was a politician, my father lived a relatively modest, low-profile existence."

That would be a nice change at home, too, I thought.

Pocky asked about the monarchy.

"King Harald V and Queen Sonja are now in their eighties. Their son is Crown Prince Haakon, and their daughter is Princess Martha Louise," Svein said.

Anne said, "It's a great pastime amongst the Norwegian people to share gossip about the royal family. Prince Haakon married an uneducated woman he met at a rock concert. Before that, they had a child out of wedlock."

Svein raised his eyebrows. "And Princess Martha Louise talks to angels. She even plans to use her psychic powers at an alternative therapy center to help heal people."

The little boy, tired of his trucks, crawled into his dad's lap. The daughter brought the fruit trays into the kitchen, then sat beside her mother again. At one point the children played catch, and the ball missed Pocky's head by a centimeter. Everyone laughed. Anne and Svein's interaction with their children had an ease about it. They didn't worry if the kids dropped crumbs on the floor or climbed on the furniture. Parenting seemed second nature to them, and they appeared to understand the importance of free play.

I asked Svein, "What religion are you, if you don't mind my asking?"

"We belong to the Protestant church, but actually, we don't attend. I mean, we do on holidays, and, well, after the shooting . . . "

"The what?" Pocky asked.

Svein spoke in a low voice. "A terrible thing happened here several years ago. There were two attacks; a car bomb in the city, then a vicious attack at the summer camp on the island of Utøya. "

Anne explained, "The camp was organized by the AUF, the youth division of the ruling Norwegian party. There were many children of officials attending the camp. Many of them died, seventy-seven in all."

I remembered the horrific incident from the news reports. Such a terrible tragedy.

"Anne and others went to the church to gather and grieve," Svein said. "It was the biggest loss of life in Norway since World War II."

Anne said, "I felt such a sense of spirituality at that time. I also attended church after my grandfather passed. When I sat there during the service, I strongly sensed my grandfather's presence. I felt his spirit all around me. During such events, the church has brought me great comfort."

Svein hugged his wife. Then he said, "I would like to believe there is life after death, but I don't. Not really. In fact, I really wish I did, because I think it is too depressing to think this is it, that our life just stops."

Anne nodded in agreement. "I believe the same as Svein. Although, if I had a major challenge in my life I had to sort out, I think I would become more spiritual. Maybe it's because of the comfort I received from the church in times of great sadness."

The children were playing together quietly when we said our goodbyes. I thanked Svein and Anne for their hospitality, and wished them continued happiness. They had everything they needed to remain happy: a committed bond, a wonderful relationship with their children, a nice home, careers they loved that provided them with adequate income and family time. Anne also had a spiritual connection she could rely on in troubled times.

As we walked back to the hotel, Pocky and I discussed what we had observed. I told him I wanted to become a more relaxed hostess. And we agreed it would bring us more happiness if I let go of my perfectionism.

FANTASTICAL FJORDS

After a light lunch, we walked down to the harbor and boarded a ship for a three-hour tour. We sailed along peaceful bays and beautiful beaches, then we headed out to sea, passing gorgeous lighthouses, powerful symbols of safety in a storm. I looked forward to seeing the fjords, including the Geirangerfjord and the Nærøyfjord, which are UNESCO World

Heritage sites. The Sognafjord is the longest one, and the Hardangerfjord is famous for its cherry and apple trees.

We sailed by tiny islands glimmering in the sunshine. Summer homes adorned with flower gardens looked especially charming with the majestic cliffs in the background.

I watched everything we passed with a feeling of incredulity. The journey had an epic, slow-motion feel to it, and the extreme natural beauty inspired joy and awe.

Studies indicate that feeling awestruck can be healing. When we feel awe, we are inspired. We may even change our basic ways of thinking. The power of awe helps us forget our problems, or at least feel that our issues are less significant. Understanding how small we really are in this incredible, vast, beautiful world can make us feel happier. It can make us feel deep gratitude that we are here, playing our unique, small part on the world stage.

As we sailed past the fjords, I remembered the awesome sunset I had observed in Thailand on my birthday. But it doesn't take a trip to the fjords or a Thai beach to feel that kind of awe. Plenty of natural beauty existed back home. All I had to do was tune in to it.

"Aye, matey!" Pocky said in his best pirate. "What are you thinking about, honey?"

I grinned at him. "Just thinking about how much happier I am now, and how much I enjoy being here with you," I said.

"I always knew you had a thing for pirates," Pocky said, putting his arm around me. "Look at the cliffs over there."

A voice came over the loudspeaker. Our guide announced, "These inlets have enormous cliffs, hundreds of meters high, which are impossible to traverse by land. The impenetrable coast made sailors out of the Norwegians, forcing us to take to the sea to travel and trade. In days past, Norway ruled the Northern Way."

"Shiver me timbers," Pocky said.

I laughed.

"Our many fjords were created by ice, stone, and rock during a series of ice ages. However, the fjords are virtually ice-free today. That's because the warm air from the currents in the Gulf Stream, aided by the Coriolis effect, have raised area temperatures. Now the temperature along Norway's fjords is about forty degrees warmer than in similar latitudes in other places."

I wondered what this meant for the future of the fjords. Still, the air was cold, and I sat close to Pocky.

When our tour came to an end, we decided to take a last stroll on the promenade. We mingled with the brightly dressed crowd, then found a restaurant, where we ordered big bowls of mussels and pints of beer. We had learned so much about the Norwegian people. The moment was bittersweet, and we were quiet, knowing we had to leave this city so wonderfully grounded in the practical, and lit up by the magical.

Chapter 4

DENMARK AND SWEDEN:
HIPPIES AND FAIRYTALES

When our plane touched down in Copenhagen, I looked forward to seeing the countryside. The old Danish myth of the Viking Prince Amled of Jutland had inspired one of my favorite works of Shakespeare's, *Hamlet*. The famous Dane Hans Christian Anderson wrote many of my favorite fairytales, including "The Emperor's New Clothes," "The Little Mermaid," and "The Ugly Duckling." While in Denmark, I expected to be inspired in my own writing about happiness.

Our hotel was in a great location, close to many important sites around Copenhagen. As a result, we could walk almost everywhere.

We weren't alone in avoiding car travel. Bike lanes lined every street, and the many bike parking lots were filled with yards of crowded bike racks.

We enjoyed walking in the crisp air along the crystal-clear waterways and crossing cobblestone streets through the picturesque city. Eventually we made our way to the charming neighborhood of Christanshavn, which was filled with gorgeous green parks.

We passed a group of men seated at an outdoor café, all dressed in blue and wearing the same blue hat. I couldn't help laughing. When I stopped to ask them what their matching outfits were all about, they told me: Fun. That's it; it was just for fun. One of the men told me how they all got together every year and went wandering.

Wandering.

Yes! This was what we had been doing as well. I'd been especially aware of this ever since we'd arrived in Scandinavia, mainly because we walked so much, allowing ourselves to go wherever our feet took us. Goal-less, unscheduled wandering was so different from my way of life back home, where packed daily schedules never allowed room for a casual midday stroll. The aimless walking was good for me, allowing me to see more of the places we visited, while lifting my mood and spirit.

We continued our drift through the neighborhood, which reminded me of a European Disneyland for adults. Charming canals filled with boats, old and new, cut through the middle of the hamlet. The streets were lined with sidewalk cafés, quaint shops, and colorful nineteenth-century houses.

On our way to the Tivoli Gardens, the world's second oldest operating amusement park, we took a wrong turn and ended up at Freetown Christiana. A one-time military base, the eighty-four acres had been occupied by squatters and artists in 1971 as a social experiment. The area was still full of hippies, and many more like-minded folks had flocked to the neighborhood in order to live a non-traditional lifestyle. There were whimsical homes with giant potted plants, beer gardens with colorful banners, and murals everywhere. The area looked like a charming Danish village, but with an artistic bent. Some of the buildings sported intricate paintings of dragons and Hindu gods, and others were decorated with rainbows and strange fantastical creatures. Freetown Christiana even had its own flag; a red field with three yellow circles to represent the three *o*'s in "love, love, love," from the lyric in the Beatles song "All You Need Is Love."

"I feel like we're on our way to Burning Man," Pocky said.

I laughed. I had been taking stock of the charm of the place. The people were as colorful as the surroundings. They had chosen not to be defined by others' ideas of normal. The place had a fun-house vibe to it, a bit confusing yet mesmerizing.

One shop we entered sold hash and marijuana alongside homemade jewelry. Grass is legal in Colorado, so we had the same shops, but here they sold some forty different kinds of hash!

At some point the atmosphere changed, and I no longer felt comfortable. Signs declared No Photos Allowed, with the hash booths manned by masked men wearing robber-style bandanas and dark sunglasses.

Pocky held my arm tightly. "I think we better get out of here," he said.

"Yeah, I think you're right," I said.

"Let's retrace our steps back to the entrance," he advised, walking faster.

But when we turned the corner, the atmosphere changed again, the brightly colored houses and shops, inviting. We noticed a home constructed completely from glass windows; a glass house. Even the trash cans were painted in psychedelic colors. We strolled beside a canal where people lived on houseboats. They looked serene and happy.

We decided to stop at a café for lunch. They served us delicious vegan sandwiches and coffee.

We walked out of the hippy village under a sign that said EU This Way. Pocky grinned, and led the way to the Tivoli Gardens.

The magical entrance had Russian-style architecture and dome roofs. As we entered, thousands of little white lights instantly lit up, and all around us, the gardens sparkled. We walked past old-fashioned buildings, flowers in every shade, and vast green lawns that led to a gorgeous outdoor terrace with a beautiful reflecting pool. Packed with people, Tivoli had a festival vibe that apparently appealed to all ages.

"Looks like half the park is kiddie rides, and half is white-knucklers," Pocky said.

"Let's just wander," I suggested.

"Absolutely," Pocky agreed.

We kept walking through the delightful gardens. We passed all kinds of rides, street entertainers, and musicians.

"I read that Walt Disney visited Tivoli a bunch of times and became inspired," Pocky said.

I could believe it. The park had been built in 1843, so it had a long history, and had probably served as a model for other amusement parks.

We stopped to watch the carousel. Horses, giraffes, and a colorful sleigh went around and around. I got lost in the old-fashioned organ music infusing the evening's fairytale atmosphere. It felt like anything could happen, even the fairytale ending—*and they lived happily ever after.*

Pocky was looking at a map for the gardens. He interrupted my fantasy. "Hey, they say here that by some miracle, Tivoli only sustained minor damage during World War II."

How far away a war seemed as we walked past the sparkling glass pavilions, crowded carnival games, and throngs of giddy kids waiting to ride the bumper cars. My sister, Kristi, and I spent hours on bumper cars, never tiring of them.

We stopped at a charming beer garden. Pocky bought us a couple of drafts, and we sat down on small white metal bar stools.

"Skål!"

Overhead, a ride called the Star Flyer lifted riders high into the sky and spun them around and around. We drank to squeals of frightened happiness and shouts of joy.

Research has shown that it is real-life experiences—not material things—that lead to happiness. Cornell psychology professor Thomas Gilovich co-authored a study with colleagues published in *Psychological Science* that looked at anticipation as an indicator of happiness. In the study, they discovered that looking forward to something provides benefits, and experiences provide more enduring levels of happiness.

After the beer, we walked to an outdoor theatre where a concert had just begun. We relaxed in the last available seats and listened to the enchanting music under the stars as a terrific fireworks display lit up the night sky. I was thrilled to be applauding minstrels in the gardens that had inspired Hans Christian Andersen's "Nattergalen." "The Nightingale" is a story about the power of music. In the story, a nightingale's song is so enchanting that Death spares the life of the dying Chinese emperor.

THE HUNGRY AND THE DEAD

"Okay, Julia Child, you got the directions to the cooking school?" Pocky asked with a grin.

We were getting ready to leave the hotel, but we had stopped in the lobby while I searched my purse.

"I have no idea what I did with it," I admitted.

Pocky sat down.

I'm very organized, but when I have moments where I'm lost and confused about something, he knows to leave me alone.

"Found 'em!" I raised the directions above my head in victory.

Pocky stood up again.

"I'm starving! I hope we cook some good food," I said.

I had booked a cooking class at a local chef's house. Her name was Katrine. I'd signed us up because I thought it would be a good way to meet a local with whom I might have discussions about happiness. But I had no idea what kind of food we might cook.

We hurried out to the waiting taxi. Katrine's place was outside the city. After all the city walking we'd been doing, it felt strange to be riding in a car in the countryside.

As we drove through quiet neighborhoods, I wondered about walking and happiness. The University of Cambridge in England developed an app for a study conducted to find the link between happiness and movement. During the seventeen-month study, they found people were happier when they physically moved more. This made sense to me. If we walked more in the United States, we might be a happier country, as well as a slimmer, healthier one.

When we pulled into Katrine's driveway, she stepped outside her ultra-modern home. A petite woman in her thirties, she wore large round glasses that accented her round face.

"Velkommen, welcome. Come in!" she said, giving the driver a small wave.

She ushered us inside. Her home was light and airy, with many windows. We followed her from the great room into a huge modern kitchen. The open floor plan had a crisp, clean feel, and the room was filled with the delicious aroma of herbs, apples, and freshly baked bread. A cookbook sat in a bookstand next to her range. The book cover had her name on it. Katrine was an author as well as a cooking teacher.

As she toured us though the kitchen, she pointed out all the solar energy features. Then she handed me an apron and an apple to peel, slice, and core. But before I could begin slicing, Katrine pointed out a special apple-chopping gadget sitting on the kitchen island. I placed the apple in the machine and cranked the handle.

The menu for our lunch included apple rye bread, beetroot salad with horseradish, pig's cheeks, and salmon fillets with pickled fennel. I got pretty queasy when I heard about the pig's cheeks, but Katrine said not to worry; she'd prepared those herself.

As we cooked, we talked about life. She got right into it without missing a beat.

"You are writing a book on happiness? Well, I'd buy a copy!"

"I'd like a copy of yours, too," I said.

"This cookbook was a labor of love, I can tell you," Katrine said. "And that's what it's all about, isn't it? Love *is* happiness. So, for me, cooking is happiness."

I removed the diced apple from the chopper.

"We have many sayings in Denmark," Katrine said. "Many of these sayings are about food." She began slicing a fat cucumber. "To 'go cucumber' means to 'go nuts,' or like what you would say, 'go bananas.'"

Pocky said with a laugh, "I don't believe I'll go bananas for pig's cheeks."

"Ah, you might be surprised," Katrine said. "Never say never."

Katrine showed us how to knead the dough, and I folded in the diced apples. After setting the loaf on a pie tin, she slid it in the oven and removed a delicious-looking loaf that was already done.

"Magic!" She laughed. "Now, on to the fennel salmon."

Pocky got busy chopping fennel. He loves to cook, especially his special spaghetti sauce. Friends and family ask for it every time they visit us, which makes my job simple. I make the tossed salad.

When I pointed to a large landscape portrait on the wall, Katrine said, "My partner loves photography. That is his latest piece."

"It's beautiful."

"It's how we met. Doing what we love. We met on the beach; him, with his camera, and me, taking in the sun. I love nothing more than stretching out in the sun naked. It is my release, my ultimate freedom."

"So you're a nudist?" I asked.

She shook her head. "No, there are no labels here. In our country we take communal showers. Even in the public pool we have supervised naked scrub-downs before being allowed to swim. And we have family nude swim nights. It is so much more natural to be without clothes. Clothes are a mask."

Katrine turned her attention to the beets, showing me how to prepare them for the salad. She said, "My partner, he loves photography, and I love my cooking business."

She reached over and put a hand on Pocky's forearm, as if to say, "That's enough chopped fennel." He smiled and stopped his furious chopping.

She said, "My work makes me happy every day."

I wondered how many Americans would be able to say that. So many don't like their jobs, but people have expensive lifestyles and debt, including college loans that must be paid. Many people have little choice about what they do to pay the bills.

Katrine said, "It is important to us that we get educated in what we love to do. We get paid to go to university."

Pocky handed her the pile of chopped fennel. "How do you mean? Does the government cover the cost of everything?"

She nodded. "Our tuition and some living expenses are covered, so we can get as many degrees as we want. But not everyone takes advantage of free university."

"I can't believe people don't take advantage of that," I said, thinking about all the people I knew with delayed careers due to a fear of overwhelming tuition costs.

"Because it is free, people don't always see college education as a privilege, so some don't take advantage of it," she explained. "Still, our crime rates are low, so the uneducated are not resorting to crime. The only homeless are those people who choose to live that lifestyle."

"Why do you have such a low crime rate?" Pocky asked her.

"I suppose it is because everyone is taken care of so there is no real need to steal," she replied. "I feel safe and secure living here."

She explained how to poach the salmon, then instructed us on how to put the finishing touches on the beetroot salad. Then she told us our lunch was ready.

She had set the table by the window with white plates and fresh flowers, which had the feel of a modern farm table.

"Here you go," she said, pointing to our seats. She handed us each a bottle of a microbrew. "My village's pride and joy."

As she brought the food to the table, she told us the name of each dish in Danish. When I shrugged my shoulders, finding it difficult to pronounce the words, she repeated them, making sounds we don't use in English. I raised my beer in a white flag gesture, remaining silent instead of butchering her language.

"Eat all the pig's cheeks you want, Mr. Pocky," Katrine said with a grin. "I know they're your favorite."

Despite our misgivings, both Pocky and I tried the strange meat. The rich flavor was a pleasant surprise.

Katrine said, "It is important to try new things. Probably, for you, it's not every day you can say you ate pig's cheeks, right?" She laughed. "People here love it, especially my partner."

Her eyes sparkled when she spoke of him.

"Are you and your partner married?" I asked.

She shook her head. "No. I believe monogamy is important, but I don't see the need for marriage. Our rights are equal either way. We get the same protections from the government; there is no tax advantage. Here, there isn't the burden of waiting for marriage to have sex or live together. If it doesn't work out, then we are free to leave and find our happiness elsewhere."

Pocky interrupted. "I love the fennel. It really brings out the flavor of the fish."

She smiled at him. "That's exactly right. At first it seems a bit counterintuitive to use such a strong flavor with such a subtle fish. But as you can see, their opposite properties work well together. Kind of like people."

Kind of like the Scandinavians, with their practical approach to life and their fanciful myths.

"Let's be sure to get this recipe, honey," Pocky said to me, his mouth full.

"Oh, I have all the recipes here for you, no worries," Katrine said. "Fennel is near and dear to my heart. My mother used it when I got very sick. She swears the fennel cured me."

"From what?" I asked.

Katrine looked out the window at her manicured backyard. The sunlight splashed across the pretty garden of brightly colored flowers. "When I was a little girl, I lived in isolation for two years. I was diagnosed with cancer when I was just a few years old. My father was very busy working to provide for us, so most of my care fell to my mother, who was a homemaker. I had to undergo months of chemotherapy. But my mother didn't trust the doctors' treatments. She trusted the fennel. I suppose that's how I got so interested in herbs and cooking."

I nodded my head. Of course. Her childhood challenges had led her to embrace a life she loved.

"Yes, I am very fortunate. That experience gave me a certain joy for life. A feeling that every day I have now is a gift. Because of the sickness, I embrace life differently—from different ways of thinking to different ways of cooking," she said with a laugh. "Maybe that's why I love pig's cheeks so much."

Pocky laughed.

I asked her, "Do you have children?"

"Not yet. The trend in Denmark is to wait until we are older. I might think about it in a few more years. But not too long, because of all the infertility issues that come with age."

"What other trends can you tell us about?" I asked.

"In Denmark, there is a trend toward rainbow families. This is when a woman has a child with a homosexual man. Both people may have partners, and, if so, they all raise the child together. So many ways to love, yeah?"

"There certainly are," I answered. "So what are your beliefs on religion? Do you attend church?"

Katrine frowned. "No, because I don't understand this intellectually. I mean, I want to believe in God and an afterlife. I do. But my common sense, and my knowledge of modern science, tells me that God is just a beautiful fiction."

"So you weren't raised with a faith?" I asked her.

"I had religion classes in school, but I had too many questions. My teachers didn't like me asking questions. Among my friends, some believe in God, and some are atheists. I suppose if there is a religion here, it is the religion of not thinking of ourselves as special or better than anyone else. I guess it is the church of sameness, and honestly, some of us are questioning that, too."

I felt her frustration. "Back home, it's almost a religion to stand out," I said.

Katrine threw her hands up and said "C'est la vie!"

We laughed.

She said, "I do love Christmas, though, with all the beautiful lights and festivals. I love giving gifts and having fun. Although I don't love the winter and the long, long nights. I really don't enjoy that part. There is a bit of a seasonal depression I feel in the wintertime."

"A Dane talking about depression?" Pocky said, "No! I don't believe it!"

She gave him a little smile. "Yes, I'm afraid depression happens to even the happiest of us," she admitted.

When we finished our delicious meal, we helped Katrine with the dishes, and she gave us the salmon recipe. The taxi arrived and we hugged her goodbye.

After the long drive back to Copenhagen, I wanted to get out and walk, so Pocky and I went wandering.

We found ourselves at the gates of the Assistens Cemetery. Established in 1760, for many years the cemetery stood behind a poor church. Now the green oasis felt more like a park than a memorial for the dead. The grounds were filled with the scent of roses and other aromatic flowers.

We walked through the lush grounds to a botanical garden, where we discovered plant species from all over the world. We admired the Manchurian cherry trees and lively cinnamon bushes. The hanging trees seemed to weep for the lost.

Throughout the park, people sat on blankets reading books and having picnics while kids ran around in the sunshine. The cemetery was full of life, with women rocking babies in strollers, and old men and women sitting in lawn chairs. The park was alive, and very unlike American cemeteries. I loved the scene, because the vibe supported my belief that our deceased loved ones should be celebrated instead of lamented, and the place had the added benefit of being a fabulous use of green space.

I said to Pocky, "What if all our cemeteries were turned into public parks? How would that change our perspective on death?"

He took my arm. "How would it change how we see life?"

We found Hans Christian Anderson's grave, an ethereal sight in the bright afternoon sun. I thought about one of my favorite quotes from the great author: "Life itself is the most wonderful fairytale."

We left the cemetery to head for the Langelinie Pier to see the Little Mermaid statue. Known as Den Lille Havfrue, the bronze statue was erected in 1913, and is an icon of Copenhagen. Originally written as a ballet in 1836, the story of the Little Mermaid has had hundreds of adaptations and interpretations.

I stared at the silent statue, a life-size figure of a small girl sitting on a large rock overlooking the vast sea. The sculpture made the story come alive in my heart, and her humble beauty struck me in ways it wouldn't have, had the statue been large and grand.

DINING WITH DANES

After a morning spent visiting some of Copenhagen's wonderful museums and art galleries, Pocky and I made our way down Strøget, the main shopping street in the downtown area. The boutiques and galleries had urban-chic interiors that felt fresh and modern.

We wandered into the Nyhayn neighborhood and walked along a canal with beautiful ships, some historical. On the other side of the street were seventeenth- and eighteenth-century townhomes painted gold, red, and blue, intermingled with cafés and shops. I felt like we had time-traveled from the sleek urban present into the quaint past.

It turned out to be a lovely way to spend our last day in the city, absorbing its unique flavor, scents, and culture. Before we knew it, it was time to get to our next adventure: Dining with Danes.

The program is an international one, a cultural eating exchange that allows participants to meet people from around the world. We had trouble finding the hosts' address, so we were a little late. Apparently we were great at wandering, but not so great at reading Danish maps.

The couple welcomed us inside their comfortable contemporary home. I gave Emma the bottle of wine we'd purchased for them, then we all stood out on the balcony to enjoy the charming view of their courtyard. The space below us resembled a small city park with trees and benches scattered about.

Emma had a healthy, natural look, her blonde hair swept up in a casual bun. She excused herself and headed for the kitchen. In a few minutes, she returned with a plate of fragrant meat and a wood tray holding fresh apples topped with whipped cream.

Simon, who was tall, with an athletic build and outdoorsy good looks, said, "We're going down to the courtyard to dine. It's such a lovely time of year." He motioned us to follow them through the kitchen.

Simon and Pocky picked up the dinner plates, decanters, and glasses. I grabbed a couple of wine bottles off the kitchen countertop. Emma added a quiche to her tray of food. Their daughter opened the front door for us, and closed it behind us without locking it. As she followed us down the stairs, Emma told us she was their youngest. Their three daughters ranged in age from eleven to twenty-two.

"We're lucky to have a young one still," Emma said. "We barely see our other girls, they are so busy with their own lives."

"They grow up so fast," I said, thinking about when my daughter was eleven. Now she was an adult, but it seemed like yesterday she'd been a child.

The park-like courtyard was occupied by people from the surrounding apartments. Kids of all ages ran around as we set up our picnic table. Four families enjoyed their dinners nearby. Emma waved to the neighbors while her daughter ran to join the other children. I noticed they played simple games like tag and rock collecting.

Literary greats have told us through the years that the key to happiness lies in sharing. Charlotte Brontë wrote in one of her letters, "Happiness quite unshared can scarcely be called happiness; it has no taste." Virginia Woolf said in *The Common Reader*, "Pleasure has no relish unless we share it."

There is scientific data to back up such statements. A study by Nathaniel Lambert and his colleagues at Brigham Young University found that the act of sharing happiness boosts well-being. The researchers also discovered that the more people share their happiness with others during the day, the happier and more positive they are at day's end. When we have happy news, what's the first thing we want to do? Find someone to share it with.

After Emma poured the wine, we all took our seats and toasted one another. "Skål!"

"So what have you discovered about our city so far?" Simon asked as he set the food on dinner plates and served us.

"We feel like we step in and out of time here," I said. "From the past to the present, and back to the past."

He laughed. "Indeed, well said."

I continued. "It's amazing how we can be walking in Tivoli and feel the old-fashioned charm there, then turn the corner and walk past sophisticated minimalist architecture of the present day. Danish people seem to have two sides to them—the romance of the old world, and the sleek practicality of today. It's intriguing."

"I suppose we do have these sides to us," Emma said.

"Speaking of time, I feel it marching on. I just turned fifty a few days ago," Simon said, running a hand through his gray hair.

"And I'm just a few years behind him," Emma said, rolling her eyes.

I nodded. "That's one of the reasons we're here. I didn't want to wait until we retired to travel."

It surprised me to be speaking candidly about such things. Back home, people didn't usually mention age while socializing.

"Bravo!" Simon said. "So many people put things off instead of truly living."

Simon had made up a plate for their daughter. When he called her, she ran up and joined us for the meal.

Pocky said, "The way the government supports education here is interesting. The idea that you can become whatever you want, and not have to choose your profession based on how much you can earn, is something else."

Simon nodded. "I enjoy accounting, so that is my profession."

Emma said, "We all work. I don't know any stay-at-home moms. The government provides wonderful childcare so both parents can work full time."

My clients struggle with work-life balance. If they work, they feel like they miss out on raising the children. If they don't work, there are financial issues, and they often have a hard time reentering the workforce. Parents have a difficult time finding affordable daycare. In Denmark, they seemed to have a much better balance.

"Anything else about our city interest you?" Simon asked.

"We can't believe all the bikes," Pocky said with a laugh.

Emma said, "They say there are two bikes for every Dane. We have eight!"

Simon finished his wine and poured more all around. "We have many bikes of our own, yes, but we also share many things. Like cars, for instance. We can't possibly all have a car, so when we need one, we borrow it. Everyone does this. We have associations we can join that allow us to share almost everything."

"Where do you live in America?" their daughter asked.

"We live in Colorado, which is in the western part of the United States," Pocky told her.

"And what is the capital?" she asked him.

"Denver, and that's where we live," Pocky said. "What do you want to be when you grow up?"

"I want to be a flute player," she said with a huge smile.

"Speaking of sharing, how about sharing dessert?" Emma said.

Simon scooped the whipped-cream concoction onto some plates and passed them around. The fresh apples and whipped cream tasted light and only slightly sweet. Perfection!

Simon told us, "We belong to an association so we can share this courtyard."

His daughter kissed him on the cheek, then she excused herself and ran back to her friends.

Emma leaned over to me. "Simon and I want all our girls to figure out what they love to do, then do that."

Simon added, "Yes, especially since Emma and I feel very blessed to have found careers we both enjoy. I believe it makes our marriage even stronger to be so happy professionally."

Emma nodded. "When we get home from our workday, we share everything—the chores, cooking, laundry, marketing, all the fun!" she said with a laugh.

"There is so much to do during each day. I often feel I won't have enough time to do all that I want to do in this lifetime," Simon said.

I asked, "So, what do you think happens when we die? Do you believe in an afterlife?"

"There's a question!" Emma said, staring into her husband's eyes.

Simon said, "I believe in the here and now. I guess you could call that my religion."

He poured us each a small glass of a fruit cordial.

Emma said, "I believe in the grief and pain I suffer when I lose those I love. That is very real to me. I don't really fear death, though. It's just part of life. It's hardest on those left behind."

After dinner, we said our goodbyes. As Pocky and I walked back to our hotel, we talked about how much we liked their lifestyle, the shared courtyard, and the idea of sharing cars. We discussed all the ways we could apply the sharing concept at home—bike sharing, car sharing, party decoration sharing, lawn mower sharing, cross-county skis sharing. Just look in the average American basement or garage, packed with unused or rarely used items! Sharing what we have with others would lead to saving resources, as well as expenses.

Marriage is the ultimate form of sharing—love, duties, children, experiences, travel, work, home. The people we'd met in Copenhagen seemed to have that mastered. It was impressive, and filled me with hope for my clients, for all of us.

I held Pocky's hand as we found our way through the city we'd come to love.

A SIDE TRIP TO SWEDEN

In the morning, we took a train from Copenhagen to Malmö, Sweden. We wanted to spend a day exploring the city. I looked forward to more wandering.

A true blend of the old and new, the city's commercial center was full of busy traffic and tall glass buildings that gave way to Old Town's cobblestone streets and brick buildings, some with colorful façades. In Old Town, we stumbled into some sort of festival with musical acts, tons of street food, and artists selling their work.

After spending time at the festival, we took a stroll along the sleek city streets dotted with chic bars, modern coffee shops, and urban markets. This led us to the waterfront, which was lined with green parks and stunning views of the Oresund Bridge. We decided to duck into a café, grab a patio seat, and get a quick bite.

A friendly waitress seated us. "Can I get you anything to drink?" she asked.

"Absolutely. What's your favorite beer?" Pocky asked her.

"Me? I like Lervig," she said. "But everyone is different." She caught the eye of a friend on the street and waved at him. Her demeanor was upbeat and energetic.

"We'll have two, and bring us the best of whatever you have in the kitchen," Pocky told her.

She laughed at that. "Where are you from?" Her eyes went wide when Pocky told her. "I want to live in America one day," she said, placing a hand over her heart.

Pocky and I smiled. "Why?" I asked her.

"Because here, it's so . . . stuffy," she said. "One minute, I'll be right back with your beers."

I kept my eye on her as she darted around the busy restaurant. The young woman exuded happiness. I watched the way she filled coffee cups with a smile and flirted with the waiters. In her early twenties, with a tall and sturdy build, she had a striking presence.

"Here you go," she said, setting two beer bottles on the table. Her name tag said Louise. "You know, I want to move to America to sing country-western music. I just love it!"

I was surprised. "Really?"

"Yes. I sang Merle Haggard and Johnny Cash before I learned to write my own songs." She beamed. "I'm not what you call normal for around here." She nodded toward the crowded dining room.

"Besides writing country-western music, what else makes you different?" I asked her.

"Well, I'm a big girl, for one thing," Louise said, placing her hands on her hips and standing a little taller. "And most people I know aren't working to buy a plane ticket to Nashville."

"Good for you!" Pocky said, raising his bottle.

"Got big dreams, huh?" I said, smiling at her.

Louise nodded. "I do. And Nashville is where they happen every day."

"I wish I could hear your music," I said.

"My musical skills came from my father. He was a musician. Hang on, I have to go get your order."

"I hope she makes it," Pocky said, sipping his beer. "What's your dream, honey?"

"I'm living it now," I told him. I wasn't kidding.

I enjoyed the quiet that settled between us in that moment. It felt so right. As we sat and watched the world go by, I thought about an article in the *Journal of Happiness* that said imagining a future happiness like a dream coming true helps us to perceive our life as being meaningful. This helps make us happy and adds to our well-being.

I said to Pocky, "All the beer has tasted so great on this trip."

He laughed. "It's true."

Louise delivered two fat juicy burgers. "This is our signature dish," she said. She placed a generous basket of fries on our table. "I can't wait to go to America. I think I would fit in better there."

"How so?" I asked.

"Here, I'm kind of out of place. Everything about me is big. I'm big, I have a big personality, big dreams. But everyone here is the same. I feel like it's not really encouraged to be special or talented. I kind of feel dimmed. Like it's hard to let my artistic side flow because of the pressure to conform."

She hurried off.

I thought about what she had said as I chowed down on what turned out to be a memorable burger. I could see the benefits of promoting fairness and equality, but not at the expense of limiting individual dreams. As philosopher Henry David Thoreau said, "Dreams are the touchstones of our characters."

I wished young and spirited Louise the best in pursuing the life she imagined for herself.

Chapter 5

THE NETHERLANDS: WINDMILLS AND BLUE LIGHTS

We flew to the Netherlands and landed at Schiphol International Airport on a runway dramatically below sea level. I found it thrilling to visit a place that relied on windmills and dykes to keep an entire ocean at bay. With more than half its surface area below sea level, the "Low Country" is also home to one of the tallest populations in the world. There would be many highs and lows here—one of the hallmarks of our adventures in happiness on the blue dot.

The Netherlands has two capitals: Amsterdam in the north, the constitutional capital; and The Hague in the south, the seat of government. I thought this was another example of the duality of the Low Country, a place known for legal soft drugs, like cannabis and magic mushrooms, that can be purchased in bars, and where prostitution, same-sex marriages, and euthanasia are legal—all this, despite the country's conservative history. The Netherlands once sent disillusioned Protestant worshipers across the Atlantic in search of religious freedom. Now the people are free in so many other ways.

Pocky and I traveled by bus into the heart of Amsterdam. I immediately pointed out all the odd-looking buildings. "Look, they're leaning," I said.

Pocky explained how the city had been built on a system of canals and constructed on wooden piles driven into the earth. "Over the centuries, the earth has given way, leaving the city leaning to the left."

I laughed. Time and gravity had given the place a left-of-center vibe, creating a visually stunning metaphor for its culture and politics.

We walked around the quiet city in the cool, crisp air, enjoying the sunny morning perfect for aimless wandering. The streets did not feel crowded. There was a lightness to the paths along the Amstel that was infused by all the movement; people were biking, jogging, walking, sailing. Colorful tulips were in bloom everywhere. The city reminded me of a painting by Rembrandt or Vermeer, two of the most famous Dutch artists.

Pocky suggested we take a sail down the canals. I readily agreed. With 165 canals, it was simple for us to sign up for a guided tour.

The boat had a single deck with a cabin made of glass windows. There were other passengers, too, perhaps a dozen people onboard. "We're wandering by boat now," I told Pocky as we took our seats in the stern.

He laughed. We had become the happy wanderers made famous in the old song.

BLUE LIGHT IN THE RED LIGHT DISTRICT

We floated past museums, the Anne Frank House, and lots of houseboats, including one called the *Poezenboot*, or "cat boat." "This is where the stray cats of the city live," our guide announced over the loudspeaker.

Pocky and I looked at each other. What a creative idea.

We disembarked as evening fell and the city was lighting up. The streetlights and colorful neon signs were reflected in the water of the canals, making the city look like an abstract oil painting.

We wandered by the Oude Kerk ("old church"), one of the oldest buildings in Amsterdam. We passed contemporary coffee shops, busy restaurants, and art galleries, not realizing we were entering the heart of the city's Red Light District.

I had read about the storefronts where women put themselves on display in big glass windows. In fact, Amsterdam had one of the most famous Red Light Districts in the world, with some five-hundred-such windows and thousands of working prostitutes. As we sauntered the streets, we noticed erotic graffiti on the exterior walls of churches and day care centers, integrating sex and prostitution into the neighborhood.

We stopped at a former brothel from the seventeenth century that had been turned into a museum, and learned about the history of the Red Light District. The rules of conduct for the district included the following: When the window curtains are closed, this means the women are busy. When the light is on, the woman in the window is available. If she smiles at you, this means she is interested. At that point, you may open the door to negotiate price and activities. There are many sexual fantasies to choose from, each with its own fee.

I asked Pocky if he thought we might hire a woman and interview her for my book. He stopped walking to stare at me as if I had gone out of my mind.

"I want to know if they're happy, if they make the men happy," I explained.

He laughed. "That's such a great idea," he said, shaking his head. I knew he was not on board, but would go along with my idea.

We looked in each of the storefronts we passed, checking out the women in the windows. The scene made my skin crawl. The women looked bored, some dejected. They did not look happy, and the vibe was seedy and sad.

We stopped at a window with several prostitutes sitting on stools. One of the women was intelligent looking and attractive, with long dark hair. She might have been forty; not young. I thought she was probably experienced, with a story to tell. I pointed her out to Pocky, and we watched her. She was wearing a low-cut red dress with stiletto heels.

She smiled at Pocky. Bingo!

She opened the door and came outside, and we stood together in the alley.

"I wonder if you would see us for twenty minutes," I said.

She looked at me, then at Pocky. Her face was impassive. She had seen it all, and my request was nothing new.

"No, it's not like that," I said. "I'm writing a book about happiness, and I'd like to hear what you have to say. Could we pay you to talk to you?"

"Talk?" She raised her dark eyebrows skeptically.

I nodded. "Yes."

She said, "I'll do it for fifty Euro, but he stays outside."

I would have preferred to have Pocky around for moral support, but I understood her decision. I turned to look at Pocky and he motioned me to go ahead with a wave of his hand. He looked uncomfortable as I left him in the alley by himself.

I followed the woman into a dimly lit room. A queen-size bed with a black plastic cover took up most of the very limited space. The walls were blank, painted black and red. A few shelves over the bed displayed various sex toys. The hot and stuffy room smelled like sex and Lysol.

The woman sat on a stool by the bed. Feeling exceedingly awkward, I perched on the foot of the bed across from her.

"Where are you from, lady?" she asked with an accent that wasn't Dutch.

"I live in Colorado."

"What are you doing here?"

"I'm a therapist, and I'm interested in learning what makes people happy. I've been traveling the world talking to people about happiness.

I saw you and, well, I thought you'd be a great voice to add to the conversation."

I could feel my face grow hot. I didn't want her to think I was taking advantage of her as a person with a "less-than" job. I added, "You must see a lot of people who are not very happy. Right?"

"Right. Hold on, love. I'll be right back."

She flashed me a beautiful smile, then she disappeared out the door.

What are you doing here? The woman's voice echoed in my mind. What the hell *was* I doing there? Maybe I had gone too far this time.

I sat frozen on the bed. I had no idea where she had gone or when she would be back. I imagined all the naked bodies that had been in this room, lying on the black plastic cover beneath me. I tried not to freak out.

The woman walked back in. A wide-eyed Pocky followed behind.

"You have ten minutes," she said.

Pocky and I looked at each other. He leaned against the wall, looking as awkward as I felt.

"I suppose I should tell you a few things before you continue. See that blue light?" She pointed to the light above the door. I nodded. "That blue light means I'm transsexual." She paused. "You still want the interview?"

I couldn't believe it. I hadn't even suspected it. My heart sped up. I smiled and said, "Absolutely." Whatever she had to tell me about happiness would be even more interesting, I thought.

She sat down on the stool again. "My name is Daniela. I was born in Ecuador, where homosexuality is illegal. I went to jail for being a homosexual. Twice."

Her tone was oddly matter-of-fact.

"I saved my money, and I left Ecuador and came to Amsterdam. Being instantly accepted here has helped me live in the truth of who I am."

I nodded. No matter who we are, we want to live in that truth.

"I knew I was homosexual from when I was a boy. I couldn't hide the truth. So here I am."

I nodded again. I was impressed with her courage. Daniela had risked everything to be herself and live her truth, leaving her country to be in a place where she could find acceptance.

"Do you identify as a woman or a man?" I asked her.

"Well, lady, what I identify with isn't really in *any* category. But I guess if I had to describe it in simple terms, I'd have to say I am a woman."

"You're very attractive," I said.

"Thank you," she said with a small smile. "The joys and pains of breast augmentation, and the help of a fabulous plastic surgeon, got me here. I'm especially proud of these." She grabbed her hips. "Something about a woman's hips I find incredibly sexy and powerful."

I glanced over at Pocky. He looked like he was going to faint.

Daniela riffled through her purse. "Here," she said, handing me a small plastic card.

It was her Ecuadorian driver's license. The photo was of a dark-haired man, the gender listed as male. She handed me a second card. Her Amsterdam driver's license had a flattering photo of her with the gender listed as female.

"Stunning," I said. I handed the cards back to her. Choosing my words carefully, I said, "So you found happiness in being able to have the freedom to explore your sexuality, find your identity?"

She nodded. "That, and the ability to make three hundred dollars a day with health insurance benefits and a nice retirement plan. That makes me happy, too," she said with a smile. "I earn enough to send money back to my family in Ecuador."

I asked her, "How did your family react to your gender change?"

She shrugged. "They helped me through it as much as they could. They don't know I'm a prostitute, though. I told them I'm working as a maid," she said with a small laugh. "I was raised Catholic. I attend the Catholic church here every Sunday."

"So do you work with men or women, or both?"

Daniela tilted her head to the side. "I only see men. I have strict rules about what I will and won't do. I don't kiss, and my clients need to be sober. If things get out of hand, I have a button on the wall right here." She brushed a long manicured finger across a plastic buzzer by the head of the bed. "If I feel unsafe, I press this button and the police come to take care of the problem. They come right away."

"So you feel safe here," I said.

She nodded. "Very. I am my own boss, a business woman who is free to be herself in a society that doesn't judge me."

"Tell me about your life outside of work," I said.

She smiled at me. "I share an apartment with my fabulously hot young boyfriend. We enjoy traveling the world—like you do. He likes warm, fantasy island destinations, and I like fine art and culture. It's our diversity that makes us such a great couple."

I smiled at her. "You sound like you found your happiness." I glanced at my watch. " I've taken up much more of your time than we agreed on," I said apologetically.

Pocky stepped forward and handed her some cash.

"Don't worry about the extra time. It's on the house," she said, smiling.

Pocky headed for the door. He'd had enough.

I said goodbye, and followed Pocky down the stairs.

"She works really hard, and is financially responsible," I said, and Pocky nodded in agreement.

We stepped out into the late afternoon sunshine. The subtle breeze was refreshing. Pocky suggested we find a café and order up a couple of Heinekens. I seconded the motion, and we left the Red Light District.

We found a café overlooking a sun-dappled canal. The men at the table next to ours were eating raw herrings and onions with their fingers.

"You want what they're having?" I asked Pocky.

"I think I'm about adventured out for the night. Let's save that one for tomorrow," he said with a smile.

As I sipped the cold beer and stared out at the calm waters of the canal, I thought about how much I had enjoyed the conversation with a prostitute who, in an effort to be true to herself, had found her happiness.

WINDMILLS

We spent the night in a comfortable hotel, and in the morning, hired a driver to take us to see the windmills. Franco greeted us in the hotel lobby dressed in a suit and tie. He was in his sixties, with a gray mustache, glasses, and thinning hair.

He guided us outside to his beautifully detailed compact car. We drove out of the city and into the countryside.

Franco was the perfect guide, full of information and happy to share it with us. "We have an incredible highway system in Holland. Look over there. Cameras are strategically placed all around to catch speeders. So driving here is very safe, unlike in my homeland."

"Where are you from?" I asked him.

"Chile. I do miss it. Not the Chile I left behind, but the Chile of my youth."

Most of us miss the land of our youth, even if we never leave it.

"What brought you to Amsterdam?" I asked.

"I fought in the army in 1973 during the Chilean coup d'état, but I was able to escape afterward. I arrived here and almost immediately met my beautiful wife. She's from a high family."

I wasn't sure what that meant. "High, as in noble?"

He shook his head. "No, 'high' means 'well-heeled.'"

He pointed out the Kinderdijk mills in the distance. We were almost there.

When I stepped out of the car, I felt dizzy. I was standing in a vast field, looking up at the massive ancient machines spinning in the wind. These windmills had been used for everything from pumping water to grinding grain and sawing logs. Where I stood had once been the ocean floor. Using the wind to prevent flooding of land below sea level was all in a day's work for these majestic structures. They were true marvels of landscape engineering that had successfully pumped an entire nation into existence.

I took Pocky's hand. "I feel like I'm walking back in time again," I said, admiring the white of the sails against the gray of the overcast sky.

He nodded.

Franco told us, "At the end of the sixteenth century, a man by the name of van Uitgeest invented the first sawmill powered by the wind. This eliminated hand sawing, and revolutionized the ship-building industry. The Dutch were able to build ships much faster than anyone in the world. Some of these mills date back to the thirteenth century."

"But if this was a swamp back then, where did all the wood come from?" I asked.

"The forests in Poland. The land there was cleared in the seventeenth century to support Dutch ship building," he explained.

Everything about the scene felt epic. My mind whirled at the technological achievements that had allowed the Dutch to control the exotic spice trade routes and have a dry homeland.

Pocky said, "So these machines once helped the Dutch rule the world's oceans?"

Franco nodded.

I'd thought of windmills as charming curiosities, objects for the masters to paint and include on Delft Blue pottery. I had no idea how essential they had been to the Dutch.

"I never tire of looking at them, at their ethereal beauty," Franco said.

He seemed like a person I could ask about happiness. I stood beside him, looking upward. "Franco, what makes you happy?" I asked.

"For me? My beautiful wife, of course, and . . . " He stared out over the field of tall grass fluttering in the wind patterns created by the windmills. "Great art. I love the art scene in Amsterdam. I love the masters' paintings of the windmills. I also enjoy the wonderful sensibilities of the young modern painters. Being happy, it's really a lifestyle."

I said, "We had an interesting conversation with a woman in the Red Light District about how her lifestyle made her happy, mostly because she is free to be herself in Amsterdam without the persecution and prosecution she experienced in Ecuador."

He nodded. "As a child in Chile, I wasn't raised to be accepting of prostitution, homosexuality, or transgender people. But after living here and getting to know so many people from so many different lifestyles, I appreciate the accepting nature and openmindedness of the city. And now that the refugees are here in greater and greater numbers, I pray that respect for all kinds continues."

Pocky said, "Which refugees are here in great numbers?"

Franco said, "Iraqi Christians and Syrian Muslims."

As we returned to the city, I thought about how Franco had been raised in a different culture. Yet, like Daniela, he had found ways to enjoy a new culture through living in Amsterdam. I hoped the refugees would be able to have a similar experience.

We don't always see eye to eye with those whose belief systems are very different from our own. But we can look for the good in people. Looking for the good in people creates happiness.

When we got back to the hotel, Pocky said he had just the place for us to chill out before we had to pack. He held my hand and led the way.

"Last chance," I said to Pocky, pointing to a group of people slinging down herrings with their fingers.

He shook his head. "I'd rather wear wooden clogs," he joked.

He gripped my hand a little tighter and led me inside a barroom. It was freezing cold.

"Brrrrrr. What *is* this place?" I said, clutching myself tightly.

"It's called the Ice Bar!" Pocky replied with a big smile.

The frozen room cast a purple glow, and the décor consisted of ice. The walls were made of ice. The glasses were carved from ice. Ice, ice, and more ice. It was like being inside an igloo.

Pocky hugged me close to warm me up. We sat at the bar and he ordered us two shots of gin.

"What are you doing?" I said. "You know I never drink gin. It gives me a headache."

He handed me the tasting menu. It listed gin, gin, and more gin. "Think of it as research," Pocky advised.

The bartender intervened. "Not many people know the Dutch invented gin."

"Of course you did!" I said, laughing. The Dutch had been more resourceful that I'd ever imagined.

"We call it jenever," our bartender explained. "It was originally invented for medicinal purposes in the sixteenth century. It has to be served at just the right temperature, of course. So it's minus ten degrees Celsius in here."

"Bottoms up!" Pocky said, taking a sip. "Wow. Powerful stuff!"

Shivering, I shook my head. "I think I'll pass."

Pocky picked up the shot glass and handed it to me. "You need to be more open to new experiences," he said with a grin.

He was right. I lifted the glass to my lips and took the teeniest of sips. It was delicious, instantly warming me from my lips to my belly and out to my fingers and toes.

I took another tiny sip. The gin burned its way down my throat. In the rush that it gave me, I remembered the dance of the Northern Lights that had begun this adventure. I grinned at Pocky and shot the damn drink down.

"Come on, honey, your lips are turning blue," Pocky said when he finished his drink.

We stepped out of the Ice Bar and walked past the canals for the last time. So many pretty houseboats caught my eye. I began to imagine what it would be like to live on one. What would that life be like?

"Where are we going next, honey?" Pocky asked me, his arm around my shoulders.

"Somewhere warm," I said, laughing in spite of my chattering teeth.

Part III

LATIN AMERICA: HARDSHIP
AND HAPPINESS

Chapter 6

MEXICO: LAND OF ENCHANTMENT

It was freezing cold when we left the ground in Denver, so landing in Cabo in the warm, humid afternoon air gave me a thrill. As we exited the terminal on our way to ground transportation, the palm trees swayed in the breeze and smiling young men offered us bottles of Corona beer, the perfect welcoming drink for this lush tropical setting.

I was with my three best girlfriends on our annual winter getaway. The vacation had begun perfectly.

"Why, yes, thank you," Pam said, handing one of the handsome entrepreneurs a wad of pesos.

She took four tall bottles out of his ice bucket, holding his gaze an extra second or two before passing out the beer chain-gang style. Blonde and fit, Pam's a Type A, turned desert rat. She moved to Tucson from Colorado, and developed a love of snakes, lizards, and other sand critters. Our MacGyver, we know Pam will get the job done if something needs fixing.

"Salúd!" the four of us said in unison, clinking bottles.

"Gotta love Mexico," Sam said. The only brunette in our group, she's funny and a lot of fun.

"Can't wait to get out of these winter clothes and head for the pool," Diane agreed. Always enthusiastic, she energizes the rest of us.

Sam leaned in. "Girls, it's time to enter the zone. You know what that means, right?"

"No work," I said.

"No worry," Pam said.

"Just girl time," Diane said, and we clinked bottles again.

A van waited for us on the curb, ready to drive us to the beachside resort where we'd be staying for a few days of relaxation. I was looking forward to talking to my friends, hanging out in the warm sun, reading, and doing some exploring. I was interested in finding out about the Mexican culture, the fiestas and the mariachis, and especially El Día de los Muertos, the Day of the Dead.

On the plane, I had buried myself in a book about the history of Mexico. I became fascinated by the country's ancient roots in Aztec sacrifice. The Olmecs believed the universe would come to an end and the sun would cease its path around the earth unless there were human sacrifices. The Aztec sun god Huitzilopochtli was often depicted with his tongue sticking out, a sacred gesture to suggest his thirst for human blood.

As our van crawled through the traffic, I took note of all the Mexican flags on the shops and car antennas. The Mexican flag depicts an Aztec legend that states wandering people discovered an eagle eating a snake on top of a prickly pear cactus on a rock in the middle of Lake Texoco. This was, legend has it, the sign the travelers needed to make camp and establish Mexico-Tenochitlán. This occurred in the 1300s, and the city would evolve into Mexico City. The nation would become a powerful empire—Mesoamerica—a land reaching from central Mexico through Belize, Guatemala, El Salvador, Honduras, Nicaragua, and northern Costa Rica.

I had read that we would be vacationing in the Ring of Fire, one of the earth's most violent earthquake and volcano zones. Mexico is a land rich with fire—and with gold. As I looked out the van window at the busy streets, the colorfully dressed people, the crowded markets, and sidewalk cafés, I could feel the raw intensity of the place we were visiting. It excited me, and I couldn't wait to mingle with the people and find out their secrets.

Sam was making Pam and Diane laugh, which brought my attention back inside the van. My friends' faces shone with good humor. I thought about what a treasure our friendship had been over the years, and what it meant to discover and encounter treasure in the world. How sometimes our real treasure sits right in front of us every day, in our relationships with friends and family, yet we miss it somehow, bewitched by striving for more in life.

Staring out the window of the van again, I remembered all the fun we'd had over the decades we've known one another. When we were in junior high, our Spanish class went to Mexico on a school trip. Sam took me shopping for the perfect bikini. I didn't know it at the time, but she'd made the same shopping trip with another girl in our class. On our first day at the beach, I was mortified to discover Sam had talked both of us into buying the same dark-blue-and-hot-pink bikini. Her pranks had only improved over the years.

I was smiling as I thought about this, about us. I loved these three women. Just being in their presence brought me back to myself. They felt the same way. It's as if the world we lived in apart from each other blew us a little off course. The grounding we felt in each other's presence returned us to ourselves. Our annual getaway helped me to get back in touch with my dreams, reminding me every time we got together to focus on what I care about.

The van pulled up the long driveway of a beautiful resort nestled on the Sea of Cortez. The place looked luxurious, with tall palm trees shading grassy lawns lined with colorful flowers, sapphire-blue pools, and beachy bars and restaurants—everything we would need to enjoy our stay.

The bellhop brought us to our room, which turned out to be a lovely suite overlooking the rocky shoreline and turquoise water.

LIKE YOUR LOVE

By late afternoon, we were stretched out on hammocks by the infinity pool. I would lift my head slightly whenever I wanted to look out at the sun-dappled Pacific. We all jumped in the pool for a water aerobics class, then somebody announced a game of blackout Bingo.

Uh oh.

Pam turned to me. "You have to play," she said. "You know you have supernatural blackout Bingo powers."

This was true. I don't play drinking games very often, but when I do, I often win.

"First prize is an all-day spa package," Pam said, eyebrows raised.

Sam and Diane took off for the room and a short siesta. Pam and I picked up two Bingo cards, and settled in a couple of lounge chairs. The ocean glistened in the distance. In no time at all, I'd won the spa day. And I didn't even feel tipsy.

Later that evening, showered and primped, we headed out on the town to a must-try restaurant we'd heard about from the hotel concierge.

The wild ride to the city was fast and furious. It seemed our driver had once been a race car driver. I held on to the door handle the entire way, feeling the afternoon Bingo beers crawling up my throat. When he let us out at the entrance to the restaurant, my stomach settled down again.

The restaurant had a beautiful courtyard lit up by many lanterns of various sizes hanging from the tall, old trees. The lights cast a gentle glow on tables draped with crisp white linen. We all breathed a collective sigh of awesome as we wound our way to our table.

A waiter greeted us with, "Buenas noches!" He pulled out our chairs, bowing slightly.

The romance of the language and the pretty lights, and the fact that we had switched our bathing suits and flip-flops for colorful sundresses, made me believe anything could happen that night.

"So nice to see so many señoritas with such beautiful smiles," our waiter said.

Carlos introduced himself. He had been hustling, the patio buzzing with celebrations, loud tables of friends and families, and intimate couples enthralled with one another.

"What can I offer you beautiful women this evening? Sangria? Margaritas?" Carlos had a full head of black hair and a huge magnetic smile. He was there to make us happy.

"We'll have four of your best margaritas," Pam said with a twinkle in her eye.

"Our best? Of course. Made especially for you. Here is the tequila menu." He handed a slim menu to Pam.

"I'd like to look this over for a minute," she said, studying it carefully.

"I like a woman who knows her tequila!" Carlos smiled, lingering.

"Cazadores," Pam pronounced, setting the menu on the table.

Carlos nodded his approval. "Excellent! I'll return with your drinks. And some chips and salsa."

I smiled at Pam, who grinned in return.

Carlos returned with a tray holding four giant glasses. Wow, these were big margaritas. It was cooler now that the sun had set, but we all sighed with pleasure, lifting the icy glasses to our lips.

"Is it top notch, do you think?" Diane asked Pam about the drink.

"Close, very close," Pam said.

"Still, it's not in the same league as yours," Diane said.

We all agreed. Pam made the best margaritas in the Western Hemisphere. Maybe the world.

"The quest for the best margarita continues," Sam said, laughing.

Carlos returned with our chips and salsa. "How are my favorite women this evening?" he asked with a bright white smile.

"Carlos, you beam happiness!" Diane told him.

He nodded. "I am a happy man. A *very* happy man!"

"What's your secret?" I asked.

He leaned on the table, smiling. "Well, I tell you. I am married to a woman who sincerely likes me. This is everything. Love only goes so far. Like is better, I think. To have a woman who likes me is heaven on earth."

I sat back in my seat. How unusual—and profound.

"I love that idea," Diane said with a half smile.

"How long have you been married?" Pam asked him.

"Twenty years," he said.

Carlos gave us a nod and excused himself to tend to his other tables.

We were silent as we pored over the dinner menu. I began to think about Pocky. On occasion, we were too short with each other. We're supposed to love our spouses the most, but sometimes we treat them the worst. Keeping friendship alive in love is a simple yet profound way to honor those who are most important to us.

I put down the menu. I had work to do when my vacation was over.

When Carlos returned, we ordered mahi mahi, shrimp scampi, lobster enchiladas, tostada salad, and more margaritas with plenty of fresh lime. And when we were done sharing all the food, we ordered more.

Sam rubbed her arm. "I have a whole new skin. It's soft instead of dry."

I agreed. "I know, it's amazing. My mile-high skin loves the tropics! My body finally feels completely hydrated."

"After all the drinks we had today, we should be hydrated," joked Sam. "Seriously, though, you're glowing."

I laughed. "Maybe that's because you're looking at the blackout Bingo first prize winner!"

My friends cheered and Pam said, "I told her she's still got it."

Carlos arrived at the table with a plate of ceviche. "Yes, please," Pam said, downing the last of her margarita.

"This is on the house," Carlos said.

"Carlos, you are too good to us," I said.

He nodded, serious for a minute. "That's the secret to happiness. Being too good to others. Well, that, and going to mass every Sunday," he said with a wink.

I sat forward in my chair. "What other keys to happiness do you have for me, Carlos? I'm actually writing a book about happiness."

He looked pleased. "I know a lot of people who need to read that book. Let me think, now."

Carlos looked out at the twinkling lights of the patio. I admired the way he took his time, even with so many customers to attend to. His attitude was common in Mexico. Except for the racecar taxi driver, the people didn't seem to rush. The whole country took its time in a way I never did at home. Everything from the proper tequila to the proper answer given its due. Such a great way to live.

Finally, Carlos said, "I enjoy spending time with my family, and devote much of my time to my Catholic faith. Whether I am in church worshipping the Lord, or out in the community doing good works, I like helping those in need in my city." He smiled at me. "And I get great happiness from jogging to stay healthy, too."

I nodded. Family, faith, purpose, and exercise. I asked, "What is your favorite religious tradition?"

"That is easy. When we honor our ancestors during El Día de los Muertos." His face fell for a moment. "My grandfather went home to the Lord last month. I look forward to visiting with him this year. I have so much I'd like to tell him."

This really piqued my interest. Talking to the dead as a way of staying happy in life?

"When is the Day of the Dead?" I asked.

He said, "We believe the dead have spirits. On the day you call Halloween, the veil between the world of the dead and our world is at its thinnest. Spirits can communicate with our world. So on the following day, All Saints' Day, we celebrate El Día de los Muertos."

Diane leaned over to ask, "How do you celebrate the dead?"

Carlos crossed his arms. "Oh, we do different things. The celebration begins on the night of Halloween, when the gates of heaven open. Some people paint their faces and carry candles. The next day, we bring gifts to the graves of our loved ones. People make altars there with flowers and the special foods our ancestors used to enjoy. These are a kind of offering in their memory. We sit for hours at the graves, talking and telling stories. The graveyard is like a park; it is filled with people having picnics and laughing. It is very beautiful."

I said, "That sounds so lovely."

"What a special way to keep the memory of your loved ones alive," Diane said.

Carlos nodded at us. "It is sacred. I'm not sure if I believe the spirits come to us on such days, but I do believe in spirits. I believe they visit us here on earth and are benevolent. That they have messages for us, wisdom."

Interesting. "So are you afraid of death?" I asked him.

He shook his head, his thick hair shifting, shining in the scattered lights. "No, I am not. When I die, I will return home to be with my Lord. It will be joyous and all my suffering will be over. My family talks about death; everyone I know laughs about it. We celebrate death, so death is a part of our life."

When another waiter signaled him, Carlos excused himself. "They are waiting for me. A pleasure to speak with you this evening," he said, heading for a large party that had just been seated.

A mariachi group entered the courtyard. They serenaded us with the classic song "Guantanamera," the band weaving around our table like strolling minstrels. The evening had a dream-like quality to it, and I didn't want it to end.

When we arrived back at our resort, Diane talked us into going to the bar to listen to a band. She urged us onto the dance floor, then moved from table to table, gathering dancers. She was like the pied piper of salsa. Her enthusiasm was so infectious, it wasn't long before the whole place was up on the dance floor.

I hadn't laughed that hard in a long time.

As we walked through the resort's tropical gardens to our suite, I stared up at the heavens. And then, boom! A magnificent shooting star crossed the night sky. The darkness brought on by the new moon made the brilliant trajectory even more vibrant and memorable. I wouldn't forget this night, or this wonderful place.

IT'S ALL IN THE *DETALLES*

On our last day in Cabo, we decided to leave the cozy confines of our resort and walk the beaches. I loved the feeling of the sun on my face, the sand between my toes, and aimless wandering. We were letting the day take us where it wanted.

By now, we all had a bronze glow. In addition to the sun's rays, I'd absorbed the Mexican spirit: I was slowing down, socializing more readily, making good conversation a priority. Most of the time at home, I'm so busy I don't take the time to do this. Our culture has lost the art of pausing, stopping to appreciate the beautiful moments. Mexico was helping me remember to pause and appreciate.

We left the beach for a marketplace not far from the water. People sold local goods from small huts, and most greeted us with big smiles. We walked past stalls filled with trinkets, foodstuffs, handmade clothing, pottery, and other items.

Pam is not an avid shopper, so she remained down by the water's edge.

"Hey, Pam, come check this out!" I called to her, holding up a magenta bowl.

She held her hands at her hips, keeping a beat only she heard, fanning out her fingers like she sensed something in the air along the empty stretch of beach. I had no idea what she was doing.

I moved to a booth selling little terra cotta sculptures. The hand-painted statuettes were of mermaids and whales, fish and suns, and Aztec symbols. When I turned around, Sam had disappeared.

Diane caught up to me. "Where'd they go?"

We walked back to the sand and found Sam. "Pam, get back here! No girl left behind, right?" Diane yelled, and I laughed.

We found Sam standing outside a beachside bar. A weighted-down chalkboard sat low in the sand. The sign said Ocean Massages next to an elaborate chalk drawing of a treasure chest with a swarthy pirate in the background.

Pam beckoned us over. "Look! Massage, ocean waves, *and* margaritas!" She led the way inside the beach bar.

We collapsed in the bar's oversized bamboo chairs that made gigantic circles around our heads. Sitting there made me feel like a glamorous actress in an old Humphrey Bogart film.

Beautiful young men in bright floral shirts brought us drinks. Wow.

"This is the salt life," Pam said with a grin.

We sipped cool margaritas with a twist of lime, then ordered ceviche and fish tacos. The food was cheap, fresh, and delicious. Sam ran reconnaissance and discovered a massage only cost thirty-four dollars for a full hour. A bargain!

I laid down on a massage table on an open-air platform tucked behind white curtains fluttering in the sea breeze. As I settled under a clean white sheet, I could hear the soothing sound of ocean waves in the distance. The masseuse was named Perla, and she worked her magic on muscles I never knew needed to be pressed and tugged and awakened. The heat and humidity nourished every pore of my skin.

After my massage, I seemed to float across the sand as Perla escorted me to an oceanfront table. One by one, my friends joined me there, all of us dreamy-eyed and relaxed.

Our masseuses were friends, too. Perla, Luz, and America were dressed in aqua scrubs, and they all had smiles that could brighten the darkest night. After Perla handed us each a glass of exotic juice, I asked if they might join us.

We tried to chat, but their English was as bad as our Spanish, so all of us struggled with the language barrier. After a few false starts, Perla called a friend who was nearby, as he had a business selling timeshares on the beach. Sergio spoke excellent English, and could serve as our translator.

He walked up, beaming. Sergio was handsome, dark and rugged looking. "Buenas tardes, guapas!" he said.

America smiled at him. Her dark eyes twinkled. Particularly animated, she seemed to be the natural leader of the group. Luz, her older sister, was quieter. Perla was intelligent and thoughtful.

"What did he say?" Diane asked us.

"'Good afternoon, beautiful,'" Sergio explained, sitting down at our table. "You need some help?"

I told him, "We're trying to find out what makes your friends happy."

He smiled. "Bueno." He turned to Luz. "Como puede encontrar la felicidad?"

This is one of the reasons I love the Spanish language. The translation of this question is "How do you encounter happiness?" Encountering happiness. Finding happiness. As if happiness has to be searched for and uncovered. Has to be dug up and excavated. Has to be held onto and fought for. From my seat overlooking the Pacific, I thought about how beautiful it is when happiness washes over us like a frothy wave.

Luz said she found happiness in thinking about her children. Sergio translated, "She feels the best part of being a woman is being a mother. She has two young children."

Perla said her work and her family made her happy. "She appreciates honesty, and is sentimental. She feels beauty fully, like seeing the rising moon, wild animals, or pretty flowers," Sergio said.

I smiled at Perla.

He translated America next. "She says that family and friends make her happy. She loves to cook, then eat and drink with them. She was close to her grandmother, who passed recently. In her dreams, her grandmother visits and tells her how to help the other family members. Her spirit is still around and present."

Interesting. I smiled at the women and said, "Thank you, Sergio. So, can you ask them what frightens them?"

The women all said they were afraid of the violence and drugs that plagued Mexico. They were all hoping the violence would soon stop. They cared deeply about the environment and wanted to keep their homes safe and beautiful.

Luz confided she was worried about divorce. Her friends consoled her with looks of compassion.

I asked Sergio to ask the women about their dreams.

He nodded and turned to them. Each masseuse spoke in turn, then he told us, "They say that as businesswomen they wish to have better, more profitable careers, but for now they enjoy the work they do." One woman wanted to become a chef; another, a doctor; the third, a travel agent. Everyone wanted to travel. Luz wanted to go to Las Vegas to see the lights; America dreamed of Peru and Machu Picchu; and Pearla wanted to visit New York City. Sergio said, "But they are in no rush to travel. If it happens one day, that will be fine, but in the meantime they are satisfied with their lives."

Impressive, how they could be happy with their lives, secure in knowing they were where they needed to be. How rare to find this kind of personal serenity in the United States, where people rarely live peacefully in the present because we are so caught up in the allure of the future.

When I asked about the role of women in Mexico, the women snorted, all talking at once.

Sergio translated. "They say the men in their lives are still macho. Their husbands believe their role is to make the money and head up the family. These women agree they allow their men to think they are in charge, but in reality, the women do everything—they work and run the household." Sergio laughed. "This is very good information for me. I better make sure I am really in charge at home."

I laughed, then turned serious. "Sergio, can you ask them what makes them most happy?"

His question caused the women to talk heatedly among themselves. I sat forward in my chair, anxious to hear their answers.

Eventually, Sergio told me what they had discussed. "They talked about the importance of giving *detalles*—thoughtful little gifts—to the people they love. This act makes them very happy. They admire women who are hard workers, good mothers who also dress sexy. They agreed that happiness depends on their children receiving a good education. They all hope to be able to save money for this. Happiness comes from praying for their own children, and for all of God's children. They pray for the children in Africa who are hungry, and for the elderly every-where who suffer abuse."

I nodded. Individual happiness is dependent on the happiness of others, your own loved ones and the people of the world.

Sergio told us the women honor the elderly by taking care of them. They work to keep their relationships strong, which they agree is best accomplished by living geographically close. They stay near their families, and remain close to their friends.

Sergio added, "They also talked about the magical healing powers of siestas. Siestas make them happy." He grinned.

My friends were drinking their margaritas and chatting quietly. The masseuses giggled together. This made me think about female friendships. In ancient times, women had to be more interdependent in order to care for their families, feed everyone, and remain safe. History is full of incredible sisterhood moments. Modern living is different. Many families are scattered around the globe, and so often women feel isolated.

This is why female friendships are so important. Our friendships help us reduce stress by encouraging us to open up and do what we enjoy. Happiness can be laughing together, dancing to mariachi music, or getting massages on the Sea of Cortez.

At Michigan State University, two studies were conducted on the influence of relationships on health. The participants were from nearly a hundred countries. These studies indicated that close relationships with both family and friends are linked to greater happiness, with friendships increasing in influence as the participants aged. Our friends can help us feel less stressed and more optimistic, and this may keep us healthier and help us live longer. Social people are happier people.

When Sergio stood up to go, I thanked him for his help. Then the women rose from the table, and we all hugged goodbye. It was our last day in Cabo, and we made sure to snap lots of photos.

We ate dinner at the resort at a table overlooking the frothy surf. The sun was setting in golden hues as light began to come on along the shoreline. Taking in the stunning view of the Pacific at land's end with my close girlfriends made me happy. We clinked wine glasses and vowed to meet again the following year.

Since we had run out of time, I donated my spa certificate. I hoped this would make some other woman happy.

HARDSHIP IN TIJUANA

Back at home, I longed to return to Mexico. I hadn't seen much of the country outside the beautiful resort.

Then Pocky and I had the opportunity to do an outreach project with our friends Jim, Colleen, Tad, and Betsi. We would be helping to build a home for a family in need as part of the Homes for Hope program. The small house would be built in Tijuana.

We flew to San Diego, where a bus picked us up to take us across the border to Mexico. We traveled the crowded, dirty streets of Tijuana, past the graffiti-covered walls of gritty buildings. The Tijuana River looked dry. We drove up into the less populated hills, the dust rising in our wake.

When we got off the bus, we were in a guarded, fenced-in camp. We were to stay in little apartments within the secured area. That night, we gathered with the other volunteers for Homes for Hope. Outside under the bright stars, we shared a wonderful Mexican buffet.

We rose early the next morning, dressed in our Homes for Hope T-shirts, and enjoyed a hearty breakfast. As the sun rose, the heat intensified until we were all sweating. A dozen volunteers climbed aboard the bus. Our ages ranged from fifteen to seventy.

The bus drove us across bumpy dirt roads to where a family waited for us to build them a new home.

The Sanchez family lived on a small plot of weedy land in a deserted, arid spot. They had a tiny shack with dirt floors and a blue plastic tarp for a front door. When they greeted us, they seemed thrilled to be the recipients of a new place to live.

Betsi, Colleen, and I were painters, the job given to those without any construction skills. Tad and Jim received handyman belts and hammers, but Pocky was handed a paintbrush. Tad and Jim strapped on their manly belts and strutted around the construction site.

"You sure you guys know which one's the dangerous end?" Pocky said. Jim and Tad chuckled.

The process took two full days, and we worked from sunup to sundown. The walls were constructed, each painted inside and out. We slept soundly at night, exhausted from the sun, the heat, and the physical labor.

On the afternoon of the second day, I took a break from my painting duties to visit with the Sanchez family. Arturo and Letitia had two children, ages eight and four.

I asked if I might enter the shack where they lived. The tarp served as an awning and provided protection from the rain. Their small one-room home was made from unpainted wood and had holes in the ceiling. Seating consisted of a red plastic chair and a white cooler. They all slept together on a double bed. Two pictures of Jesus hung above the family bed.

A man from the construction crew helped me with translations. The two of us used paint buckets as chairs. As we spoke, Leticia cooked mole in a huge pot that dwarfed their tiny stove. Her quiet strength filled the room.

Arturo sat in the red chair with the family cat. He had soft, expressive eyes and a mustache. He told me he met his wife when they were in their early thirties on a bus ride that lasted three days. "It was the best bus ride of my life," he said, his eyes locking with his wife's.

She laughed. "Yes, we talked and talked. It was the longest date I ever had."

Azul skipped to her mother's side. She wore a *High School Musical* T-shirt. Quiet and confident like her mother, she had helped us with the painting. Little Diego was all boy, full of energy and giggles, so adorable you just wanted to hug him.

Arturo told me, "I knew I wanted to marry her. In Leticia's family, it is the tradition to ask the father for permission to marry his daughter. In order for him to even consider it, I had to present what I had to offer the family. I would have to pay for her family, neighbors, and friends to come to a three-day wedding celebration. I would also have to buy a cow so there is plenty to eat. This costs $2,500, which takes so long to save here in Mexico. Weddings are a hard tradition, but one we respect."

He had little education, he explained, because his father had been an alcoholic, and he had worked to help out his mother. He now had a job at a taco restaurant and earned fifty-five dollars a week, but he said he'd keep saving forever in order to be a good husband to Leticia. She had a high school education and made some money cleaning houses.

Letitia spoke from her position at the stove. "It used to be the mother took care of the home and children, and the father went to work. My parents were like that. Now that is changing because most women can't afford to stay home. In many families now, the wife works *and* takes all the responsibility for caring for the children because the men don't think it's their job. But Arturo is really good at helping at home." She stopped stirring the mole to smile at him. She handed the spoon to Azul, allowing the girl to help. "And I like that women can have jobs, because Azul will be able to have more opportunities in her future."

I asked them, "What do you believe makes a happy life?"

Arturo said, "Keeping our family together. We don't need a lot of money and things. We just like being together."

Letitia agreed. She added, "We have lots of fiestas here in Mexico. Sometimes we go to church, and sometimes to the park, which is about an hour away. Now people will be able to come to our home, too. Happiness is seeing friends. We're happy when our kids are healthy and their basic needs are met. We want them to have it better than we did; we want them to flourish. That will make us very happy."

Diego ran to his mother, laughing. He grabbed his mother's hand, trying to drag her to where the rest of us were sitting. She said no; she had to watch the sauce to make sure it didn't burn.

I asked Azul what she wanted to do when she grew up.

She grinned. "I want to be a doctor, a teacher, or a veterinarian."

Diego said, "A policeman!"

Arturo said, "Both children are smart, so we want them to have a good education. Diego taught us how to use a cell phone!"

Everyone laughed.

I asked Arturo, "What kinds of things do you dream about?"

He set the cat down. "My dream is to be with Leticia forever."

Leticia stared at Arturo. "My dream is to get out of debt and have enough money for Azul and Diego to go to school, so they can get good jobs. I really don't need more than that."

Azul piped up, "My dream is to have my own room in our new house!"

Diego chimed in, "I want to play in our new house."

I thanked them for their time and followed my translator out, ducking under the sagging tarp. The sun was hard and bright, and I squinted until my eyes adjusted. I liked warm weather, but the desert was hard living.

When the house was nearly completed, Colleen and Betsi took the Sanchez family grocery shopping. While they were gone, we filled their new home with furniture—bunk beds for the kids, a new bed for Arturo and Leticia, a small kitchen table with four chairs—plus toys and clothing, everything donated by the volunteers.

When the family returned, the volunteers were waiting. We stood in a circle outside the new house. The Sanchez family joined us, and we each took a turn to speak about what we appreciated most about the last two days.

In private, we had admitted to one another how depressing it was to see such abject poverty. But we felt good that we had been able to help this wonderful family improve their living conditions. We'd helped turn hardship into a home.

Arturo began to weep. Leticia rubbed his back as he spoke while staring at the dirt. "I have had a difficult year. I was very close to my mother, and this year she got sick, then she died. It was very expensive to have her body prepared and transported to where she is buried. Then the rain started. Azul fell and broke her arm." He collected himself, adding, "We worried it would not heal right and that would cost more money.

I was so sad. All I did was worry I wouldn't be able to take care of my family. I almost gave up. On my birthday, I found out you were coming to build us this house. A hopeful sign that things were going to turn around for us." He smiled at us, his dark eyes glistening. "I feel like our family is blessed now, and things will continue to get better."

Letitia said, "Arturo was in a bad place, and we needed something to pull him out of it. We were in trouble. Now we have a real home. The house means stability for our family. It will protect us from the wind and rain. When it rains, our old roof leaks and the floor gets wet, and we get cold and sick. We will all be healthier now."

Azul said thank you, her pretty face bright with happiness. Diego squealed with delight as we all passed him around the circle. Everyone looked so happy. The connection we felt with one another in that moment brought us each pure joy.

And this joy was a lasting joy. All I need to do now is close my eyes and I'm right there again, in the dusty dry desert with the rest of the volunteers and the Sanchez family. Coming together to help people in need is one of the precious jewels of happiness.

We handed the keys to Leticia, and she opened the door to their new home. The Sanchez family went inside while we waited outside. We heard their shouts of joy. They had not expected to see the furnishings, the clothing, and toys.

They came to the front door to invite us all inside. I felt a chill, knowing I had played a small part in making their dreams come true, helping to turn their life of hardship into happiness.

THANK GOD TODAY, TRUST HIM TOMORROW

On the bus ride back to the US border, I chatted with Andrea, who was seven months pregnant and expecting her first child with her pro-athlete husband. Andrea's family had founded Homes for Hope, and I wanted to speak with her about how the experience not only changed the lives of the Sanchez family, but deeply impacted the volunteers as well.

We sat together at the front of the bus. She rubbed her round belly as she told me about her first experience building a home. "On our first trip to Mexico to build a home for an impoverished family, I saw another family living in a dilapidated bus. I was a little girl at the time, and I asked my dad if he was going to build a house for the bus people, too. He was so moved by my question that he made a decision. Soon after that, he moved us to Tijuana and launched Homes of Hope."

Wow, what an amazing man.

I asked her, "So how do you find happiness?"

She thought for a moment before saying, "It is difficult to watch people living in poverty and struggling with hard situations. But I thank God for today and trust him for tomorrow. Happiness for me is bringing out the best in other people. It is being clear about my purpose, which is to see the value in everyone and make things better for them. My family and I will stay in Tijuana trying to do this. We will keep on doing this indefinitely."

Her smile was happy, her face serene, peaceful.

On both of my trips to Mexico, I enjoyed living in ways that were in the moment, slow and rich, instead of distracted, too busy, always rushing. I appreciated the way the Mexican people would take the time to talk, and I admired how they awarded the highest priority to spending time with friends and family. I learned from the people I met about the importance of making the most of the life we've been given, and to be appreciative of the people we're fortunate to have with us on the journey—which is my definition of pure joy and lasting happiness.

Chapter 7

ARGENTINA: SIMPLICITY
AND SEDUCTION

In many ways, the next destination was a no-brainer. My daughter had been working in Buenos Aires for a year, and we were due for a visit.

Latin America, in general, intrigued me. The people there appeared to have some secrets to happiness. According to a Gallup Global Emotions study, positive emotions have remained relatively constant over the past ten years, but negative emotions have been increasing worldwide. Yet Latin America is home to many of the world's happiest nations because of a cultural tendency to focus on life's positives.

I hoped to find some answers to my questions about happiness in a land full of positive people.

OTRO MUNDO IN THE CITY OF THE DEAD

Delayed in Denver by a massive snowstorm, we had already lost a day when we arrived in Buenos Aires. My daughter Kaylee is an adventurous person, and has traveled the world while working in the hospitality industry. Pocky and I and my step-son Nick headed for our hotel, anxious to begin exploring Kaylee's newest hometown.

Kaylee greeted us in the hotel lobby with hugs all around, and we had a tearful and joyful reunion. Then, with Kaylee leading the way, we headed out. We walked to Recoleta, a nearby neighborhood named after the monks of the Order of the Recoletos, which means "recollections." The monks had taken vows of poverty, devoting their lives to prayer, spiritual meditation, and penitence.

We wandered the manicured streets made from quaint cobblestones, admiring the beautiful French architecture of a bygone era. The wide porches, bay windows, and tall glass doors of the pretty houses piqued our curiosity about how the residents lived. We wandered past charming plazas and cafés, smiling at the people we passed. All around us, the people seemed to be hugging and kissing one another, turning the ability to linger with one another into an art form. Affection spilled onto the streets, and it made me smile to see such displays of human warmth.

We would see this kind of public affection everywhere in Argentina. And why not? A romantic at heart, I identified with how the people unleashed their passions, from stopping to engage in conversation to dancing the tango to wrapping each other in heartfelt embraces that didn't leave anything to the imagination. The people displayed a no-holds-barred kind of joie de vivre. The country itself had an incredible power of seduction, and from the start, I gave into the seduction.

Kaylee had been busy traveling, and she had climbed Kilimanjaro, gone swimming with sharks, and tried all kinds of strange food. In a way, she was as full of life as Buenos Aires—open and engaging, a treasure of passion and surprises. That she'd spent a year living in this part of the world now made perfect sense to me.

Kaylee and Nick were raised as brother and sister, so they're as close as biological siblings. Nick looks like a young Pocky, with green eyes and curly brown hair. Free-spirited, uninhibited, and down to earth, he sees people and experiences through the lens of an artist. While we wandered

Recoleta, I told Kaylee how sorry we were that my sweet step-daughter Cara was missing out on the trip due to her busy work schedule.

Kaylee led us through tall black gates into a massive cemetery. We followed a wide path, a boulevard through the maze of mausoleums, each one more intriguing than the next. The place was thick with cobwebs, the mausoleums punctuated by chains with heavy locks. I felt like we had stumbled into a miniature city of death, with a skyline of ornate angels and crosses, saints, and winged cherubs.

Kaylee told us, "The cemetery bearing the name of the Order of the Recoletos wasn't established until after the monks were expelled from the country in 1822."

I looked around. Dusty coffins abounded. The statues of young women in poses that depicted them in the prime of life communicated life's fleeting youth and beauty.

We followed Kaylee down a winding path. "After the monks were expelled, Recoleta became home to the city's elite, and the cemetery served as the resting place for the country's powerful." She pointed out Evita's crypt.

Don't cry for me, Argentina.

As we wound our way through the maze of the dead, I could feel the ethereal energy of the 6,400 opulent tombs. Some resembled enchanted grottoes, others were like Gothic chapels. There were miniature temples and elegant little houses. The classic lines and charming individuality spoke to the fantastic.

"Where's Nick?" Pocky asked.

We searched the narrow corridors around the marble monuments until we found him. He was lying on his back on a crumbling pathway, his camera aimed upward, the marble angel in his viewfinder poised to take flight.

After Nick took the shot, I crouched down next to him. The sculptor had designed the angel so that she looked as if she were about to take off for the heavens.

"I'm getting some amazing shots," Nick said, giving his dad a thumbs up. A graphic designer, he had a gift for taking spectacular photos.

I stared up at the angel on top of the crypt. Such elaborate monuments made death seem magnificent and honorable. In this regard, there was less fear around death, and more glorification of the inevitable. I liked how death was being celebrated with mausoleums as different as the personalities of the departed being memorialized. My travels had been reshaping the way I looked at death, influenced by the way people in other countries integrated death into their lives.

Kaylee announced, "Okay, familia, now it's time for an Otro Mundo!"

I asked, "What is that?"

"Beer," Kaylee told me, laughing. She hooked her arm in mine, dragging me away from the monuments.

We walked to a nearby café, where Pocky found us a table on the patio overlooking an enormous tree. Kaylee told us the tree was several hundred years old. Its mammoth branches extended in all directions.

Our waitress brought over four tall glasses of a golden beer. The name of the beer, *Otro Mundo*, translates to "another world," which felt appropriate.

"To other worlds," Kaylee said, holding up her glass. "Welcome to my city."

The late afternoon sun glistened in her blonde hair. I felt transported to another world, Kaylee's world. I clinked glasses with her, a bit choked up. My daughter, an independent adult, living in her new home so far away from ours. Then I thought about what an adventure in happiness it was for me to go from being the mother of a baby to becoming the mother of young adults like Kaylee, Nick, and Cara. All three of them so full of life, engaged in their own individual ways with the world around them.

We split a delicious meat and cheese plate while watching the people who wandered past our table. Elegantly dressed residents sauntered by, passing one chic café after another. The Argentines wore high, elaborately decorated platform shoes. Balancing on the tricky cobblestones seemed second nature to them as they walked along in their flashy fashion statements. I loved their bold, confident spirit.

We spent the evening exploring the art galleries and famous landmarks.

Kaylee glanced at her watch. "Catch up with you guys later?" she said. "I have to get ready to meet my friend Agustin."

Pocky and I said goodnight. The kids were going out on the town, so we hailed a taxi to our hotel. On the way, however, we decided to stop at a well-known restaurant, the Parrilla Peña, for the traditional *lomo asado*. The Argentines know how to cook their meat. The ribeye cut was juicy, and cooked to perfection.

DESTINY AT THE SPEAKEASY

At breakfast the next morning, Nick told us what had happened the night before. He nursed his black coffee, his eyelids drooping with exhaustion.

Nick and Kaylee had gone to a speakeasy. Buenos Aires has some of the most adventurous and unique nightlife in the world. For some clubs, you must know the special passwords, which may be hidden on Facebook pages and Instagram feeds that change more than the speakeasies themselves.

Agustin had waited for them outside the club. A rock star and actor, he had movie-star looks and a perfect physique. He greeted Kaylee with a big hug, then shook Nick's hand.

As they entered the club, beautiful people surrounded them, all of them locked in friendly and passionate embraces, some laughing, others retiring to dark corners for privacy. The three found a quiet corner beside a fireplace.

Fans came by to talk to Agustin and ask him the usual questions. "What's it like to be on stage and perform with your band?" The girls gushed, fawning over him, their eyes wide with admiration.

Agustin answered them politely. "I love music." With a gleam in his eye, he added, "Every song brings a certain memory, thought, or person into my head."

Kaylee decided to help me out by asking Agustin what made him happy.

He grinned and slid close to her, saying, "This is a serious question with no serious answer, I'm afraid! Everything makes me happy!"

The owner of the speakeasy approached. He kissed and hugged Agustin.

"We'll need a few more of your magic elixirs, Victor, especially Kaylee's favorite white malbec. I'm in a very intense interview at the moment and my mouth is getting a little dry."

Victor smiled. "Absolutely. For you, my friend, it's on the house. Mi casa es su casa, hermano."

Victor disappeared behind the old school bar that was stacked from ceiling to floor with bottles of alcohol in all the colors of the rainbow.

"I like to connect with nature," Agustin said to Kaylee. "This makes me extremely happy. I feel like nature is there for us to enjoy, and it can heal us. Nature feels good no matter how bad we feel. No matter if we are depressed, angry, anything."

She nodded. "I feel that way, too. When I'm surfing, I connect with my spirit."

"Yes, like that! Exactly," Agustin said. "For me, I feel like I am one with the river whenever I jump in. I become a part of it, you know? I am no longer separate from its energy. I become a part of the way it flows and the way it turns."

Kaylee told him, "You have a passion for life, Agustin. I really admire the way you love everyone and everything."

She told Nick how Agustin had a gift for making you feel special no matter who you were, even if you didn't have anything in common.

Nick told us Agustin exuded an energy that attracted everyone to him. Especially young women.

The chef brought over a tray of appetizers, on the house.

Agustin continued talking about happiness. "My Harley Davidson Sportster makes me happy. I enjoy riding with my friends. Vacationing on the bike helps me experience the road in a different way. Nothing separates you from nature when you are on a motorcycle. I enjoy the speed, too!"

"So what's it like to perform with your band?" Nick asked him.

Agustin grinned. "I play guitar in my free time, but when I play with my band, it's even better. All of the instruments work together— this instrument is supposed to play at this time with this instrument, another instrument plays at this exact point in time to create this exact sound—and wow! When I perform in front of a crowd, it turns me on, you know? The music flows together, all the people enjoying themselves, and I become lost in all of it."

Agustin took a few obligatory bites of each complimentary appetizer. He asked Kaylee, "And what about you? What makes you happy?"

She said, "Seeing my family. I had no idea how much I missed seeing them until I actually got a chance to take them around my city."

"Listen to you. *Your* city," Agustin teased. "I love your passion for life, too. I love how we met."

Kaylee laughed. "I took that jujitsu class to meet people here. I had no idea I'd be sparring with Argentina's most eligible bachelor! It was destiny."

He grinned and gave her a hug. "Oh yes. In astrology we are studying our fates, and how our destinies are already laid out for us in the stars, or whatever," he said, using his hands to indicate the stars. He spread his arms as if he were conjuring the fates.

"Like, how do you mean?" Nick asked.

"There's a complex web where everything in your life and your environment and your situations and your friends and family is all related. Like everything is—what's the word?"

"Intertwined?" Kaylee suggested. "Like our meeting in jujitsu?"

"Exactly! Within this web, you must accept everything that happens to you. If you try to resist something, such as trying to escape the feeling of sadness or anger, the web is disrupted. Then it pulls one aspect this way, another one that way, and it gets all messed up."

He motioned back and forth across his body to emphasize the pull of escaping emotions.

Kaylee said, "Like that song 'Que Será, Será'—whatever will be, will be."

Agustin nodded. "This is exactly another way to describe the web."

"Then what about death? What do you think happens when we die?" Kaylee asked.

"In reality, we will never know," Agustin said. "I would like to think we come back as something else, or our spirit goes on and does something else, but we will never know."

"I guess a person has to believe in something," Kaylee said. "I believe that if this is the only time we have, then we have to make the most of it. We have to pay attention to our dreams."

Agustin said, "But it's not just about paying attention to the dreams. It's about *living* them!"

Kaylee would tell us later she would recall that moment forever, that moments like that didn't come around very often in life. How many times do you sit with your brother in a secret nightclub with a rock star, drinking white malbec and talking about destiny?

Kaylee joined us at the breakfast table, her eyes bright with excitement. As she told us her version of the story, I could see how Agustin's exuberant take on happiness confirmed the themes I'd been gathering on my adventure on the blue dot. He had spoken of the peace and healing found in nature, the joy of music, and the solace in thoughts of destiny and the afterlife.

As I thought about Kaylee's friendship with Agustin, I wondered if we met people by accident, or if they crossed our paths for a purpose. I believe destiny is shaped by the decisions we make. I wondered how my daughter's decision to live in Buenos Aires would shape hers.

A PARTY FOR ALL

When we finished our coffee, Kaylee led us to another fascinating neighborhood, La Boca, which means "the mouth." The neighborhood is found at the mouth of El Rio de la Plata, which was once a shipyard barrio that housed many Italians. Their homes were constructed from discards from the shipping business, such as wood planks, sheet metal, and corrugated steel. The neighborhood had an urban-bohemian feel, the streets tagged with graffiti.

Nick dropped behind us every few minutes to photograph the murals on the sides of the buildings. Kaylee showed us her favorites, bold art statements with passionate perspectives on love, life, and the human struggle.

We walked along the Caminito, a colorful artists' area by the waterfront. We looked at the murals there, many depicting political statements, others fun paintings—like the one of Homer Simpson eating a donut. Picasso-esque portraiture loomed large, too, as did paintings of the revolutionary Che Guevara.

Art appreciation is one of the hallmarks of a happy culture. The simple act of opening our eyes to what captivates us, stopping to smell the roses and appreciate their beauty, is a practice that leads to increased joy. This is something all of us can do.

I studied the graffiti. Even though the language was unfamiliar, the fat letters and colorful drawings fascinated me. When I got home,

I looked into the subject of graffiti and found a great explanation by Banksy, the infamous British graffiti artist. His identity remains a mystery after two decades on the graffiti scene, but his comments on the subject are insightful: "Imagine a city where graffiti wasn't illegal, a city where everybody could draw whatever they liked. Where every street was awash with a million colors and little phrases. Where standing at a bus stop was never boring. A city that felt like a party where everyone was invited, not just the estate agents and barons of big business. Imagine a city like that, and stop leaning against the wall—it's wet."

Buenos Aires was like a party to which everyone had been invited.

Kaylee introduced us to her favorite mate bar, a café where they serve the infusion along with snacks. Mate bars are a popular after-work tradition in Buenos Aires, the local choice for friendly get-togethers. Kaylee told us, "Mate bars are all over the city, but you can't find them unless you're in the know. Regular restaurants don't serve yerba mate because it is regarded as an experience, rather than just a drink."

The woman behind the counter gave us a kettle full of hot water, loose-leaf yerba, which was light green in color, a mate cup, and a *bombilla*, which is a long metal straw with a filter at the end. In the old days, the mate was served in a *calabaza*, a pumpkin or winter squash.

Kaylee ordered dulce de leche, too.

We took our seats in the crowded café. At each table, customers were passing the yerba mate cup from person to person, sharing the single straw. In our germophobic part of the world, this would never fly. Americans don't want to drink from the same cup. But the practice looked sacred to me, bringing to mind the idea of communion in church services.

Sharing sips of yerba mate with those I loved felt transformative. The tea was strong and flavorful with a taste of the bitter, symbolizing the journey of love—which is, of course, the ultimate adventure in happiness.

THE PRACTICE OF PASSION

We decided to see a tango show at a theatre in nearby San Telmo. The show would begin later that evening. So, after our mate break, we wandered around La Boca, continuing to discover the charms of the cobblestone neighborhood.

Strolling along Calle Defensa, we stopped to check out the beautiful antique shops. I leaned into Pocky and we held hands. The romance of the city had infused us with a feeling of careless sensuality, and we hugged more in public than we did at home. Kaylee told us how the neighborhood had been full of mansions until a yellow fever epidemic in the late 1800s killed over ten thousand people. The area then became a ghost town. But the twentieth century brought a new wave of European immigrants, mostly Italians and Spaniards.

Pocky said, "This place feels like the old country." He nodded to a group of men gathered on the corner. "Check out those guys."

The men all wore their shirts in the same style, half unbuttoned so that you could see their hairy chests.

"Go for it, honey," I said.

Pocky undid most of his shirt buttons and smiled. He walked a few steps, then buttoned back up again. We all laughed.

"Anyway," Kaylee said, rolling her eyes, "the immigrants had a lot of time on their hands, and love in their hearts, so they began to dance. They blended all the dances they knew with Argentine folk music, adding in Cuban habanera and African rhythms from the freed slaves. The early tango took place in the seedier parts of town, and earlier versions enacted the relationship between a pimp and a prostitute, or two men battling with knives over a prostitute."

"Let's tango" means "Let's *fight*," but the dance took on romantic themes. Today the tango is often described as making love in the vertical position, a perfect fit for this passionate country.

"That's my kind of dance," Pocky said in an Argentine accent. He imitated the man on the poster at El Viejo Almacen Theatre, which advertised dinner and the "dance of hugs." He stood tall, one hand placed at his waist.

I laughed.

He cozied up to me, and arm-in-arm, we followed the kids inside the intimate theater.

We sat at a quaint little table near the center stage and ordered a bottle of malbec. As we took our first sips, the dim lights brightened. An exotic-looking couple took center stage. Both slim with dark hair, the couple was dressed in tight red silk. They stared at one another, their bodies taut and their eyes piercing.

My heart raced and I reached for Pocky's hand.

The music began: two bandoneónes, a violin, double bass, and a piano. The two dancers moved in perfect harmony, their bodies attuned to one another. As the singers told a love story, the dancers acted it out in a riveting performance. Using cuts and ravines, the dance steps of the tango, the couple came together and moved apart, their bodies alive, so full of passion.

For a moment, I recalled why I had embarked on this adventure. I reflected on my clients, the people at home, the fear I had of becoming one of the walking dead. The performance was the opposite of robotic, the sensuality of the dancers filling me with passion for life.

I whispered in Pocky's ear, "It's getting hot in here."

He winked and gave me a peck on the cheek.

During intermission, I walked backstage. I approached a woman seated at a desk doing paperwork and asked her, "Do you speak English?"

"A little."

"I'm writing a book about happiness. Do you think a tango dancer would allow me to talk to him or her after the show?"

She smiled at me. "Maybe. I will see."

After the show ended, two dancers approached our table. The couple had agreed to speak with me. They seemed to float across the room toward us, as if the normal force of gravity didn't apply to them.

They introduced themselves. Natalia's long black hair fell down her back. Her backless dress showed her toned muscles, and her gold heels accentuated her flawless posture. Dramatic makeup highlighted her style and elegance. When Mateo held the chair for Natalia, she took her seat as if it were part of a dance move, perfectly graceful.

Mateo's dark hair was slicked back, and this accented his large dark eyes and sexy smile. They both sat straight and tall. Since they spoke little English, Kaylee translated.

"What makes you happy?" I asked Natalia.

She said, "I am in love with traditional romance. Where the man takes me out to dinner, offers me tiny surprises, and there is much attraction. I long for a love so deep, a love where we can communicate without words. There are a lot of chamuyeros—smooth-talkers—around, but that is not sexy. Many men—and women—are not looking for something enduring, something real. I believe truth, honesty, happiness, and family are the most important things in life. A man who agrees with this? This is what I find sexy."

How fascinating that she danced in a way that conveyed her own desires. I asked Mateo the same question.

Mateo's expressive eyes searched the room. Then he spoke very quickly. "I find happiness in my work. I enjoy being myself and doing what I love. A person must know themselves and their own body to be able to dance with confidence. To dance and live with the head held high."

Kaylee translated as fast as she could, and Nick took notes in his cell phone. I was glad to have their help as Mateo spoke rapidly. The theatre's cleaning crew worked around us as we talked.

Mateo said, "I enjoy preparing dinners with candlelight. I love the feeling of attraction between my partner and myself. I love the art of flirting, it is so much fun. Flirting is one of the great pleasures in life. Women like to feel they are special to their man, like no one else can replace them. I don't know why so many men fail to see this! The payoffs are amazing. It is a joy to know you can make your woman happy," he said with a sincere smile.

"And what makes you happy about dancing tango?" I asked them.

Natalia answered first. "It is like a passionate relationship."

"Yes, exactly," Mateo agreed, adding, "It is about the technique, the chemistry, and the hard work required by the most passionate of relationships. Sometimes our practices run for twelve hours! This is because we lose ourselves in our passion."

The management had begun to turn off the lights. The dancers' dramatic looks, their shiny hair, the elaborate makeup, and beautifully handcrafted outfits looked even more vibrant in the darkened theatre.

Natalia said, "I must feel the music in my body and in my heart. Just like people feel love. I must feel it in an uninhibited way and surrender to it, move with it, and become one with it. It's like a game. You chase each other, pull away, come together—the game of love and passion. In our tango, we tell real stories of love, betrayal, and passion."

Mateo said, "We enjoy the dance and try to improve a little whenever we can."

Natalia added, "We fully embrace another person, our partner, and learn from them. And we learn from the other dancers as well."

Everything they said seemed like a metaphor for love. Fully embracing our lover or partner, learning from them, surrendering to the feelings. Trying to improve. Playing the game. Working hard and enjoying the feelings.

"We have a passion for what we do, and that extends to our lives," Mateo said.

Natalia nodded. "Yes. I think it is important to live life fully by taking your emotions fully into your heart and body. To feel life, love, and beauty, not just notice them in your mind."

Natalia and Mateo stood up at the same time to say their goodbyes. They walked away, disappearing into the darkness together as gracefully as they had danced into the spotlight of our lives.

How strong their passion was. How fleeting encounters of love can be. But even when love might seem to disappear, each encounter leaves our hearts forever changed.

As we returned to the hotel, I thought about the dancers and what they had said about love and passion. How essential it is to feel our emotions, not just think them through. How essential it is to have passion—which is the opposite of being one of the walking dead, leading a life in which we deny our emotions, as we so often do in our world of to-do lists and continuous distractions.

Passion is a practice. To keep that level of energy in love takes a conscious effort. As we traveled through the brightly lit city, I pledged to help my clients rediscover the passion in their lives. I also decided I would flirt at will, love with abandon, practice passion shamelessly, and maybe buy a pair of gold heels.

Pocky loved the idea.

THE HAPPINESS OF WINE

We spent our last days in the foothills and valleys outside Buenos Aires, which are home to multiple bodegas catering to wine drinkers. We also went to the lovely town of Mendoza, a base for exploring Argentina's wine region. Located on the eastern side of the Andes, Mendoza has pretty streets lined with tall trees that are perfect to sit under with a glass of malbec.

We stopped at a bodega with a long bar. The room was modern but earthy, and our hostess was named Diana. In her mid-thirties, with long dark hair and a bright smile, she spoke excellent English as she poured a flight of wine for us to sample. "We cultivate more than eight hundred acres of vineyards in the Mendocinian districts of Vista Flores, Altamira, La Consulta, Maipú, and Santa Rosa. Our wines are characterized by their high quality and modern style."

We shared the tasting bar with several other visitors, and soon enough, we began to chat. When I said I was a psychotherapist, Victoria from Brazil told me, "My husband Felipe and I are also therapists!"

Pocky and Felipe shook hands. Felipe shook Nick's hand, too.

Pocky said, "My grandfather came to Argentina from Italy, so the country feels like home to me."

Felipe smiled. "Any place that serves wine like this feels like home to me."

We all laughed.

Diana poured another flight of wine. She told us, "Malbec was originally a French grape popular in the Middle Ages. The grape came to Argentina in the nineteenth century. This is our signature blend, perfect when paired with grilled meat. Like our famous asado dishes, which I'm sure you've all had the pleasure of tasting."

While the others were sampling and chatting, I took the opportunity to engage her. "What about you, Diana? Where do you hail from?"

She leaned on the bar to talk to me. "I came here from Mexico. My family is in the wine business. I love the experience of working in a different country. I find the people are happy here in Mendoza."

When I told her about my book, everyone joined in the conversation.

Victoria said, "You know when I'm happiest? When I'm learning new things. Like when I travel. I love to travel."

Felipe smiled and said, "Being with family, and playing and listening to music, these things make me happy."

A man standing a few feet away chimed in, "I love adventure!"

"Well, you've come to the right place," Diana said. "There are so many adventure sports here. Hiking, skiing, mountain biking. We have the Andes right at our doorstep."

He said with a wide grin, "I love to experience new things. I am Hugo."

Soon enough, Hugo was part of our party.

I asked Diana why the people of Mendoza were so happy.

"Because wine is a way of life here," she said. "It connects people socially." She lifted her glass. "To wine!"

We all joined her in this toast.

She kept our glasses full as she explained the various characteristics of the different varietals. We talked about the wine and everything else—including our homelands, favorite travel experiences, families, and happiness. We even touched on world peace.

The more we sampled the wine, the more we shared. This is the delightful gift of wine.

Diana told me, "I feel like simplicity is one of the keys to happiness. Like when people can gather together—family, friends, strangers—and have nice conversations, especially over good food and good wine. This is at the heart of pleasure and enjoyment, what it means to live the good life."

I agreed with her. In fact, Argentina had been all about the good life. Our wonderful, wayward days eating and drinking, wandering, observing the people and exploring the cities, the beautiful countryside. Relaxing and enjoying the company of family and new friends.

When our wine tasting ended, I said goodbye to Diana. The rest of our group had decided to find a place to eat lunch together. As we drove the hilly streets through the green rolling vineyards, I thought about the simplicity and wonder of our experiences in the region. How good it felt to slow down and listen to people tell their stories. This was a process that turned strangers into family.

We parked at a vineyard restaurant and headed for a large table. Set outside on the terrace, our big round table offered a stunning view of the vineyards gently cascading over the rolling hills. We joined diners from all over the world, and I overheard a wide variety of languages.

Bright sunlight streamed through a trellis choked with purple and pink bougainvillea as our servers brought out trays of food; fresh fruit, pastries, empanadas, grilled meats and vegetables, and dishes of colorful ice cream. Conversations about love and life seemed to change flavors with each course's perfectly paired wine varietals. I reflected on what Diana had said about simplicity, which reminded me of a quote I'd always liked: "Simplicity is the ultimate sophistication."

So often it is what we seek that we already have in large measure. Scratch the surface of any sadness, and the roots of happiness are already there, if only we would appreciate what we have. I thought about how I might keep it simple back home. To always look at what I have before listing off everything I lack. How often in my life had I lamented what was missing without regard to all that I had?

Argentina had seduced me, the country arousing all my senses while keeping my life simple—a kiss, a hug, a dance, fine wine, lingering around a lunch table, passionate conversation with family and friends. I realized this was the great gift I'd received on this adventure: a window into how to put a pulse back in my life.

I looked at the lush green hillsides, the red wine sparkling in crystal glasses on the white tablecloth, the shining faces of happy people around me. It seemed like the soundstage of a great romance movie, and for a change, *we* were the stars. The feeling was so beautiful, I wondered why we didn't always give ourselves permission to live the life of our dreams, casting ourselves in the starring roles our love lives deserved.

In my practice, I find married people often put romance on a back burner. Because of this, when problems and conflicts arise, romantically estranged couples often fail to get themselves back on track in the relationship. The glue is missing. Romance is the nectar of love. It's the wine, and it has to be cultivated and cared for like the best vineyards.

I took a last sip of malbec and leaned over to give Pocky a kiss on the lips.

Chapter 8

PERU: MYSTERIOUS LAND
OF THE INCAS

Seated at the departure gate at the airport in Buenos Aires, I stared at endless rows of talking heads on the TV screens hovering over the crowded terminal. Pocky, Kaylee, Nick, and I found ourselves with lots of time on our hands before our flight to Lima, Peru.

Lots and lots of time.

As we waited . . . and waited, I reflected on the timing of things, how life flows so easily sometimes, while at other times life seems stalled. We meet the perfect person at the wrong time, or a project, appointment, or situation interrupts our life in ways we never expected. We find ourselves . . . waiting, caught in the space between what we want and where we are.

My family and I had two options during the delay: to get angry about our lost travel time, or to have fun. We chose the latter, singing songs and playing with phone apps that allowed us to swap faces. A ready sense of humor had proven to be one of the most important things to pack on my adventures in happiness on the blue dot. We had plenty of time to shower Cara with lots of digital love through silly posts and text messages, too. Peru had already begun whispering its slow-time wisdom, even as we missed our connection to Cuzco.

I took advantage of the downtime and buried myself in a book about the history of Peru. Once known as the land of the Incas, Peru had been the capital of South America. The Spanish founded their empire in its lush green mountains packed with rich reserves of gold. The vast empire spanned over two thousand miles of the coastline from modern day Ecuador to Chile. Almost at the center of this empire lay the heart of the Inca civilization, the sacred site of Machu Picchu, which means "old mountain" in the Quechua language.

The allure of Machu Picchu had brought us to Peru, but I also was curious about the descendants of the Inca. The Inca had revered, feared, and adored nature, making sacrifices to Inti, the sun god, and Pachamama, Mother Earth and the goddess of fertility. I wanted to learn more about the Incas, and about the different peoples who made Peru their home.

BELLY BUTTON OF THE WORLD

Finally, we arrived in Lima, and took another flight to the charming city of Cuzco. Exhausted, we went straight to our hotel. A former monastery, the large stone buildings were rich with golden tones, and the smooth walls featured the artwork of local artisans. The lobby was adorned with exquisite handmade furnishings. A central courtyard held peaceful gardens and arched stone walkways that added to the feeling of grandeur. The historical ambiance offered a window into the country's majestic past.

We met with our guide in front of the hotel. Carlos, a short man with black hair, greeted us with a kind smile. He told us he had planned our driving and walking tours of Cuzco and the Sacred Valley. He explained that his family had resided in the Sacred Valley since the sixteenth century, when conquistador Francisco Pizarro landed on the shores of the northern coast of Peru.

We wandered through Cuzco, the gateway to the Sacred Valley. Situated in the Peruvian Andes, the city maintains some of the structures of the ancient Inca Empire. Residents wear traditional, brightly colored clothing made from Inca textiles.

As we walked past the native people in their remarkable dress, Carlos said, "Gold, when beaten, shines."

A wise and interesting Peruvian saying, one that made me reflect on Peruvian history. The people had overcome their oppression, retaining what lay at the heart of their culture that no invading power could ever take away—their joy. They were able to withstand the trials of life, suffering the worst kind of blows, and still, they shone. The lesson was clear: We too can shine if we allow our bad experiences to shape us rather than destroy us. No one can steal our ultimate treasure: our capacity for happiness.

Carlos told us, "You are walking among the descendants of the Incas. The name Cuzco means 'center' or 'navel' in Quechua, their original language, a language that survives today, and has little in common with Spanish. This was the belly button of the world in an empire that most likely had a population of twelve million at the time of the Spanish conquest."

He led us to La Catedral, which had been built on the site of Viracocha's palace. He said, "The construction of this cathedral was accomplished using pilfered stone from the Inca site of Sacsaywamán, which means 'satisfied falcon' in Quechua."

We admired the depository of colonial art inside the cathedral. These included devotional paintings, which used the colorful palette and iconography of the indigenous Andean artists.

Carlos said, "The Spanish conquistadors arrived in the Andes in the early 1500s, and began to convert the Peruvians to Catholicism. They built their cathedrals on top of the ancient Inca temples. All these years later, 90 percent of the population here is Catholic." He paused, then added, "But, like me, many still participate in traditional Inca ceremonies and traditions."

We walked outside, my mind obsessing darkly about how people always seem to ruin other cultures, but the happy colors of the people on the street instantly lifted my spirits. I spotted many women using richly colored fabrics to carry their children or groceries or other products on their backs. I remarked on this to Carlos.

"The llicllas are made of a special fabric, and can be used in a variety of ways. The women carry their babies and supplies the way their grandmothers and their grandmothers' grandmothers did before them," Carlos told me. He smiled. "I have nine brothers and one sister, and I can remember my mother carrying us around in this way."

I thought about how family traditions, like the Sunday night pasta dinners Pocky's family celebrates, can help to boost our happiness. Ovul Sezer, a researcher at Harvard Business School, reported the following: "Whatever the ritual, and however small it may seem, it helps people to really get closer to one another."

What a thrill to walk among a people whose lives and daily practices are deeply influenced by ancient tradition and ritual. I wanted to know more about Carlos and his traditions, as well as his thoughts on happiness.

While Nick, Kaylee, and Pocky roamed a market featuring the wares of Peruvian artisans, I had a chance to speak with Carlos alone. We sat together on a park bench with a view of the stalls and street vendors.

I said, "You mentioned you still practice some of the traditional beliefs of your Inca ancestors. Can you tell me more about those?"

He patted the material of his brightly colored vest. "I enjoy wearing our traditional clothing, and do so often. For me, it is a way to connect with my ancestors every day. I think about the long line of people who passed this weave down from ancestor to ancestor and finally to me. This feels sacred, and comforting as well."

"What other traditions do you follow?"

He said, "We celebrate Inca ceremonies like Inti Raymi, which is Quechua, meaning 'sun festival.' This occurs annually around the summer solstice."

"What do you do for this festival?"

He smiled at me, his dark eyes sparkling. "It is a spectacular event in which hundreds of actors portray our ancestors in homage to the Inca sun god. There are many events and festivals throughout the year, but the ones I enjoy most are personal. I like our Pachamama ceremony, what you would call a 'payment to the earth' ceremony."

"Can you tell me about it?" I asked.

He settled back in the seat. "We are a people who love and honor nature. A farming people, we have great respect for the cycles of nature. We once lived in great fear whenever Pachamama, or Mother Nature, would get angry. So we would appease her by burying certain items in the ground. Valuable items, like coca leaves and seeds, silver, and chicha."

"What's chicha?"

He grinned. "A traditional alcoholic beverage made from maize, wine, animal fat, jams, and something we call huairuros, a mixture of red and black native seeds that are a lot like beans." He leaned in, his face serious. "It is believed these seeds have miraculous powers of healing, and provide protection from evil spirits. We wear the seeds in the form of necklaces and amulets, also for the purpose of protection."

Cool. I said, "So you still make these offerings because you seek protection?"

He shook his head. "It's more than that. We have a logic of reciprocity in the Andean culture. And these pagapus—or payments—are the way we honor and give gratitude to the good spirits who control and direct all the natural forces. We give from our bounty to receive the bounty of nature."

I loved this approach. It reminded me of many religions, and of philanthropy, through which we give to others in the hopes we will be rewarded after death. Or at least remembered. And here's the best part: Giving makes us happier.

A study at the University of Zurich found that when we give, we stimulate the areas in the brain that are associated with feelings of altruism and happiness. People who give feel happier than those who don't. "At least in our study, the amount spent did not matter," said lead author Philippe Tobler, associate professor of neuroeconomics and social neuroscience at the university. "It is worth keeping in mind that even little things have a beneficial effect—like bringing coffee to one's officemates in the morning."

Or burying coca leaves in the ground.

The study showed the health benefits associated with generosity, and that people who made a regular habit of giving time, talent, or money experienced a longer life expectancy. The researchers believed this occurred because helping others reduces stress, and they found generosity as effective as meditation or exercise in lowering blood pressure.

Modern science often supports what the ancients instinctively knew.

Carlos said, "My people believed Pachamama needed to be satisfied, so they fed her and quenched her thirst with their offerings, wanting to give to her the strength and energy she had given to us."

I nodded. "So you believe you receive the energy that you give through your offerings to Pachamama?"

"Exactly," he said. "Pachamama presides over planting and harvesting. And earthquakes, which we have a lot of in this part of the world. So appeasing Pachamama is essential to life. You can see shrines erected to her out in the countryside. We will visit the countryside tomorrow and I will show you. Some of these shrines are made in the trunks of trees or hollowed out rocks. Sometimes people sacrifice guinea pigs or burn the fetuses of llamas as a sacrifice to Pachamama."

I would look forward to seeing the shrines. I said, "The power of life and death is a mighty motivator for reciprocity."

"Yes, and her power is needed at different times for different reasons. August is cold, and there are illnesses at that time of year. On August first, many families cook all night to prepare gifts for Pachamama. We fix her a plate before we eat."

Nick waved to us from the marketplace. "Hey, come check this out!"

A group of street artists were playing flutes that sounded like the wind. Pocky and Kaylee waved to us from where they were all enjoying the music.

I waved back, then asked Carlos, "So what makes you happy?"

He smiled at me. "I love my life here, in this beautiful place, so unique in all the world. I love our traditional celebrations, and the dancing, too. I am deeply connected to the natural world, so I love living in the Andes. The mountains have provided for me beyond my dreams, and satisfied my family for generations with food, shelter, and spiritual satisfaction. I am happy when I honor the mountains and worship them. I love my job, too, because I enjoy sharing Peru's rich history with people from all over the world."

I smiled at him. What a rich, full life he had. "You have a talent for bringing culture to life," I said. "I never thought of mountains as living, breathing providers. Obviously, this is what they are, and have been since the beginning."

He agreed. "Cuzco was the center of the earth for the Incas. In a way, it is still the center for spiritual seekers and adventurers, artists, and poets. Because of this, the whole world comes to me! I love the cultural diversity, and it makes me happy to see the freedom we have found in the various customs that fit our ancient beliefs."

We sat silently, both of us looking out at the busy marketplace, the bright colors worn by the people, the sounds of their flutes, their laughter. And the majestic beauty of the Andes looming over the crowded streets.

"I also love drinking coca tea with friends," Carlos said. "Let's go have some."

We walked over to join my family, and it didn't take much convincing to get them to agree to join us for some coca tea. Carlos led us to his favorite local café and ordered for us.

We'd only been here for a day, but already the Andes and the Sacred Valley felt a part of me. These places were sacred, spiritual in a way I had not experienced on my other adventures. The fact that the people actually worshiped the land took my breath away.

There is a lot of scientific research to support the link between nature and human health and happiness. As a kid, I was always outdoors playing. I loved running through the neighborhood with my sister, and feeling the wind on my face as I sped down the street on my bicycle. These simple pleasures made me feel more alive. Even as a child, I craved that connection to the outside world.

It is healthy, life affirming, and spiritually uplifting to move out of our distracted, busy lives into Mother Nature's flow. After my conversation with Carlos, I decided Mother Nature and I would get reacquainted. I'd please her by making sure to reciprocate the delights and surprises she constantly showered on me.

The tea was delightful, we all agreed. It tasted like green tea, but it offered quite an energy boost. Just another one of Pachamama's gifts to us.

SKULLS ON THE MANTEL

The next day, Carlos drove us through the countryside. He stopped several times so that we could pet and feed llamas and alpacas, some of the most adorable, expressive creatures I've ever had the pleasure of meeting. Their big eyes shone with affection as we spoke to them and allowed them to nibble treats from our open palms.

Carlos parked his car in one of the small villages. We all piled out to follow him as he walked along a dirt street. Before long, we encountered a lady sweeping the stoop outside her home. Carlos asked if we could enter. She smiled at us and motioned us inside her little adobe house.

There was no front door, just an archway in the adobe. This gave the home an indoor-outdoor feel. The single room had a tiny fireplace, a single bed, and a couple of wooden chairs. In the corner were some small animals, and they scurried about. They were not caged, so I wasn't sure if they were wild or pets. My heart raced when I saw they were rats.

Then I spotted three human skulls sitting on the stone mantel over the fireplace. Above them sat a spray of fresh flowers.

What was *that*?

Carlos introduced us to a short woman with a complexion like a weathered map, full of crisscrossed lines. She was ancient, and proud of that, and I found it refreshing to admire the raw beauty of this self-assured woman, to see the strength of character reflected in her face. How rare it is to see this kind of beauty back home, where people wear plastic masks made from Botox, surgery, heavy makeup, and the latest wrinkle cream. This woman was proud she had survived, and she wore this like a badge of honor on her face.

She was warm and accommodating, inviting us to come in and get comfortable. She smiled proudly, indicating the altars in the windows made from little branches and food offerings.

"Are the rats her pets?" I asked Carlos.

He said no, they were guinea pigs, a staple in the family's diet. "Guinea pig is considered a delicacy in this part of Peru," he said.

"And the skulls?" I asked.

The mantel held a candle that had obviously been burning for many hours, the melted wax layered on top of the stone. Around the skulls, the rocks that made up the mantel were painted purple. Other artifacts on the altar included a male doll smoking a cigarette and holding what appeared to be wrapped packages. The doll reminded me of Santa Claus. There were several carved stones in the shape of animals and fertility symbols. And fresh flowers, ceramic ashtrays, female dolls, a bell, and small bowls containing seeds, eggs, flour, and roots.

"Those are the skulls of the grandparents," Carlos said.

Wow, such a shocking and sacred way to honor love and death in one's family!

I walked over to the mantel and examined each of the artifacts, then stared at the skulls. I reflected on my own parents, and how I had not visited their graveside very often over the past decades. I thought about how bringing the eternal into everyday life could provide comfort in the face of losing the ones we love. Sharing the reality of the departed with tangible items such as skulls could transform the ambiguity and uncertainty of death into a concrete part of our everyday life.

Carlos pointed to the little branches on the windowsills. "These are the daily offerings made to the ancestors. Every morning, they set out food and other offerings. This is intended for the relatives who have passed away. The offerings face the mountains."

When I asked him why, he said, "To honor the mountains for bringing them sustenance. And for protection."

The relatives who had passed on still had meaning in this part of Peru. The deceased gave meaning to daily life for these people. The beautiful tribute paid each day gave the dead a presence among the living.

We thanked the woman for sharing her home. As we drove away, I thought about how every day of her life she honored and remembered loved ones who had died. The short visit in her simple home would have a big impact on my views on death.

FRUITS, VEGETABLES, AND HARD WORK

We returned to Cuzco and had dinner at a local place, then visited a nearby market. The stalls were a riot of bold colors and textures, and I wanted to buy everything I saw.

Many of the indigenous Quechua vendors had traveled from the surrounding highlands in order to sell their produce and stock up on supplies. I met a woman named Evangelina at her fruit and vegetable stand. She looked very weathered. Eighty-five years old, she seemed both young at heart and worn out by the hard experiences of a life of physical labor. Short and small boned, she exhibited an amazing strength of character.

Evangelina told me she had been coming to the market to sell fresh fish, vegetables, and coca for the past sixty years. I was intrigued. Carlos translated, and I asked her if she would be willing to talk to me about happiness.

She looked at me, her face serious. "Happiness is selling lots of fruits and vegetables. I sell so many my friends get jealous. It makes me feel good every time I sell something, so when I am here, the happy feeling keeps coming."

"Are you married?" I asked her.

Still unsmiling, she recounted, "My husband lived a long time, and I was much happier with a man in my life. He lived to be ninety-five years old, and we were married for sixty of those years. We met at a party near this market. He was a farmer and a sailor, and we worked together well. He farmed, and I sold." She paused. "I think selling is beautiful. Together, we made enough money to support our large family. We didn't make much, but it was enough to feel happy."

"How large is your family?" I asked her.

"We had eight children, but most of them have moved away now. I have forty-eight grandchildren and great-grandchildren, and that makes me happy and proud. I am happiest when they visit. I also love when my friends and I celebrate our religion together at parties. We enjoy eating lots of food, dancing, drinking, and wearing our traditional costumes."

She smiled for a moment, then sadness darkened her face. "I miss my husband very much. He was so loving and understanding with the children. More than I could be. Since he died, they don't come around as often. He was the one who brought us all together."

I remained quiet with her in the silence that followed. Her eyes raised to the mountains in the distance. They were shadowed, shrouded with the onset of evening.

Finally, she said, "I believe his spirit is still in the mountains. So I give thanks to him for his life with me by putting food and drink by my door facing the mountains. People buy my coca leaves. Also, I blow them toward the spirit of the mountain."

I told her, "I admire the Inca traditions you use to honor your departed husband. Can you talk to me about your spirituality?"

She nodded, her dark eyes glittering. "I follow the Catholic faith, but I also believe in my Inca gods. I feel a special connection to the Earth Mother. For me, spirituality is the same as intuition. This deep knowing is like a connection to nature, it is something we receive in the spirit world. I believe people pass on to a different life after this one, but with the same spirit. Dead ones watch over us and connect us with others alive in this world."

What a lovely thought. I thanked her for her time, and gave her a hug. Evangelina had touched me deeply. Her bitterness was tempered by an iron will. Hurt by the abandonment she felt after her husband's death, she still found pleasure and purpose through friends, religion, and selling at the market.

During my adventures, I found one truth over and over: Happiness and friends and family go hand in hand. But in Peru, the connection entered the spiritual realm as the living included the departed in their everyday life, holding them close to their hearts. For Peruvians, happiness included a spirit world alive in the natural world all around them.

Evangelina's marriage hadn't ended with her husband's death. Instead, she'd maintained the relationship, connecting to her dead husband's spirit she believed was alive in the mountains. How beautiful.

As we left the market for the hotel, I thought about the research conducted by Harvard psychologist Dr. Daniel Gilbert. He published a fascinating study on the predictors of human happiness, which he found to include the quality of social relationships—including the relationship with one's spouse. He concluded, "It's not marriage that makes you happy, it's happy marriage that makes you happy."

Evangelina's life provided a perfect example of the results of another study on the link between retirement and early death. She was still selling produce after six decades, and it still made her happy. Professor Karl Pillemer, a gerontologist and director of the Bronfenbrenner Center for Translational Research at Cornell University, has studied retirement and concluded it is not all for the best. "At first, there is a honeymoon period where people go on vacation and spend time with their grandchildren," he said in one publication. "But it wears off. In general, people who engage in organized work have a higher age of mortality." In other words, those who work longer, live longer. Happily peddling fruits and vegetables for sixty years, Evangelina was living proof.

NO ROOM AT THE INN

When adventuring, weather can play a major role. For days and days, the rain had been coming down in torrents, ruining our plans for a hike to Machu Picchu. Finally, we decided to take the train up the mountain to the ruins.

We sat together in the cozy and mostly empty train car and admired the view out the window. The lush jungle was a rich green from all the moisture, and the flowering plants were amazing. Suddenly, a man dressed in a ferocious mask danced down the aisle, passing right by us. He looked like a mythical creature, part leopard, part mountain goat.

The colorful beast was followed by other costumed dancers who pranced by us as we rode up the mountain. The indigenous dancers were sharing the local folklore while entertaining the tourists on the train.

There weren't many of us due to the inclement weather, and the fact that it was Christmas Eve day.

At the top, it seemed like we had Machu Picchu to ourselves. The rain stopped as we approached the sacred site, and we experienced both beautiful weather and an almost private tour. We hiked around the Inca ruins on top of the world as the sun cast glorious light over the emerald green mountains below.

We hiked over to Inti Punku, or the Sun Gate, which at one time served as the main entrance. The entire sanctuary was laid out below, bathed in sunlight. The fifteenth-century Incan city made of stone, rising out of the mountains, was a haunting and majestic sight. In that moment, I stood in absolute awe of the power and beauty of Machu Picchu. The spiritual energy was palpable, and I felt a deep connection.

We discussed the incredible feat of construction, wondering how the Incas moved all the heavy stones to create a palace for the emperor Pachacuti. They had pieced the heavy stones together without using mortar. And this was a good thing. Over the years, many earthquakes had rattled the region. Since the rocks could move freely, the site had remained intact for more than five hundred years. I tried to imagine what it would have been like to live here many years ago, and wondered what stories the ruins could tell.

By the time our train arrived back in Cuzco, darkness had fallen. A full moon lit up the sky, welcoming in Christmas Eve. We took a drive up into the hills to see the lights of the city and soak up the sight of the mountains bathed in moonlight. This was a holy moment for my family, and I thought it was the best Christmas present ever.

When we arrived at our hotel, Pocky checked in at the reception desk. We had booked the rooms weeks earlier.

"I'm sorry, sir, we have no more rooms," the young man said.

"What? Are you telling me there's no room at the inn?" Pocky said.

He gave me the chin, pointing across the lobby to where a giant Christmas tree towered above the couches and chairs. Below the well-lit pine tree was a crèche scene with Mary, Joseph, and the baby Jesus. Far away from home, strangers in a strange land had been told the same thing thousands of years before.

If it hadn't been so serious, I would've laughed.

"There must be some mistake," Pocky said to the clerk. "We've had this reservation for quite some time."

We finally went in the dining room, unsure where we would be laying our heads that night. "Let's just have a wonderful Christmas dinner," Pocky said. "I'm sure it will all be straightened out by the time we finish our meal."

I loved when he spoke in his everything-is-going-to-be-all-right tone. He could make my whole body relax in a way nothing else in this world ever had. I wondered if Mary had experienced the same sort of calm with Joseph.

We enjoyed many Peruvian delicacies that night. We also drank some excellent wine. The chef invited us to his table to help him make trout sashimi. The boys abstained, but Kaylee and I helped the chef, then tried the results of our efforts. Very tasty. All in all, it was the perfect Christmas Eve dinner.

As we polished off the delightful anise pastries, the front desk clerk appeared at our table. My heart sank when he greeted us with a solemn face. He then said, "Mr. Marranzino, we've found your reservation. When you are finished with dinner, we'll escort you to your rooms."

Pocky smiled at me.

As I lay my head on the fluffy pillow that night, I said a silent prayer of gratitude for the nice room. Another wonderful Christmas present. It had been a day filled with gifts, the incredible sights and natural wonders of Peru. I also said a prayer of comfort for all the people in the world who are told there is no room at the inn.

Early on Christmas Day, we made our way to the airport. Of course, there were delays. I wanted more time in Peru anyway, more time together. I hated to say goodbye to Kaylee.

When she told me she needed to hurry off to her terminal to catch her flight to Buenos Aires—"her city"—I recalled the conversation with Miguel and Natalia about the flow of passion in life. I hugged her tightly. In our embrace, I allowed my passion as a mother to flow freely. I also embraced the emotion of letting her go, setting her free to continue to spread her wings. I did this with pride, then let the tears flow after she walked away. I was proud of her, and grateful to have such a passionate daughter.

What a treasure it is to love someone so deeply, to be so strongly connected. The sadness I felt in this moment bestowed on me a gift of pure gold. I became acutely aware that the opposite of passion is not sadness, but indifference. The heartache I felt was part of the flow of our loving relationship and the passion we share for this life.

HOME SWEET HOME

On the flight home, Pocky and Nick became sick to their stomachs. I was grateful they hadn't tried the trout sashimi I'd helped the chef prepare. I didn't want to be the one who had given them food poisoning. I felt fine, but the long journey was uncomfortable for all of us. We were all happy to land in Denver, grateful to be home again.

Part IV

AFRICA: NATURAL RHYTHMS

Chapter 9

SOUTH AFRICA: THE NATURAL ORDER

The only man I envy is the one who has not yet been to Africa, for he has so much to look forward to.

—Richard Mullin

Africa is a state of mind. Its solace and natural rhythms changed me more than any other place in the world.

My adventure in happiness on the blue dot took me from South Africa to Zambia and Zimbabwe, with an unexpected trip to Botswana. Poverty, corruption, unemployment, a poor economy, and a lack of quality education was the backdrop for the only person I met on my travels around the world who told me straight out that she was unhappy. Yet the other people I met in Africa had found happiness. I felt so many emotions on this trip—hopelessness about abject poverty, excitement and peacefulness in the bush, and inspiration from the color and vibrancy of the local tribes and traditions. While some of the people I met had little hope, they also had a deep gratitude for the basics of life.

Africa is the cradle of civilization. In a sense, a trip to Africa brings us home to where we all began. According to William D. Wright in his book *Black History and Black Identity: A Call for a New Historiography*, the name Africa was derived from the Egyptian word *afru-ika*, which means "birthplace," or "motherland."

But words cannot do Africa justice. The vast savannah, rich natural beauty, and breathtaking wildlife can only be captured in the wilderness of the heart.

THE CALL OF THE WILD

After the longest flight of our lives, Pocky and I finally arrived in Cape Town, South Africa. We rented a car and drove to the Franschhoek Wine Valley, an area known for its culinary delights and the region's favorite pinotage, a delicious dark grape.

We needed to take a walk to get grounded again, so we parked and wandered around Stellenbosch, a well-reserved historic village. This seventeenth-century university town is known as the City of Oaks. The many green trees provided ample shade for all sorts of boutiques and cafés. The town was surrounded by mountains with wine estates and vineyards. Historically, the area was once the home of thriving rivals as British and Dutch settlements vied for dominance in this essential stop on their spice trade routes.

Too jetlagged for wine tasting, we drove on to the hotel, passing through the beautiful vineyards nestled in the Hottentots Holland range. The deep green vistas reminded me of Napa and Sonoma, only more historic and dramatic. We enjoyed the endless mountain views and a captivating orange sunset before arriving at the hotel.

That evening, we had dinner with friends of friends, a couple who live in the area. The four of us sat in the middle of the hotel courtyard and dined on haute cuisine, with perfect wine pairings. They told us about living in South Africa, and provided a few items they thought we would find useful. This included a lemongrass spray they said was the best form of protection against mosquitos. They also gave us a huge batch of the local delicacy, *biltong*, a dried meat sort of like beef jerky.

A tour bus picked us up the following morning. The air was crisp and cool. We settled in our seats, excited to be going to see the Cape of Good Hope.

The tour guide informed us about the area as we drove to the coast. "You are in one of the most important centers of human evolution. This area was permanently settled by the Dutch in 1647 after the shipwreck of *Nieuwe Haarlem*, which means 'new place.' The shipwreck survivors built a little fort and called it the Sand Fort of the Cape of Good Hope."

I felt a tap on my shoulder.

The woman who sat behind me said, "The shipwrecked people lived there until they were rescued by a fleet of ships two years later. They had nothing. Hard to imagine these days, right? No internet, no phones, with the sea as their only freeway!"

I had to agree.

The woman introduced herself. A tall blonde with blue eyes and a sturdy build, Ruth was in her seventies. Her South African accent was beautiful, and her vibrant smile lit up the bus.

We arrived at Good Hope Nature Reserve and got off the bus. The wind off the ocean was strong. The tour guide led us on a hike up a cliff. A steep cliff. A cliff at the end of the world.

The blustery trek led us up to Cape Point, which is located on the southwestern tip of the continent. The cliff there overlooks treacherous reefs and wide sandy beaches. I stood for a while, staring into the savage sea below. The waves clawed at the sand, breaking in loud roars of tidal power. It reminded me of scenes in movies where an old-fashioned lighthouse would guide listing ships safely into harbor.

Ruth came up and stood beside me. "I can just see the *Flying Dutchman* out there, pitching and tossing where the two seas meet—one hot, the other cold. Legend has it, she floundered when her crew got lost at sea, and eventually there was no one left alive onboard to navigate. Legend says the sight of her ghostly golden sails all aglow dooms those unfortunate enough to see them."

We stared at the waves together, imagining the terrifying drama of being lost at sea in these rough waters. Suddenly, a rustling sound startled us, and a baboon scooted by.

I stepped back and lost my footing for a second, but Ruth held my arm to steady me.

"Thanks!" I said, my heart racing. Ruth was good to have around, I decided.

As we continued walking, Ruth shared a lot of what she knew about the local history. Her enthusiasm about the area was contagious, and I enjoyed her stories while the bus drove us to Boulders Beach.

As we climbed out of the bus, I looked down at the beach below. Penguins scattered across the wet sand. Baby penguins appeared to be playing hide-and-seek with their mothers. I watched as they waddled around together. Since I'd thought penguins only lived in ice and snow, I couldn't believe my eyes.

When our tour guide said we could spend a half hour on the beach, I decided to interview Ruth about happiness. I invited her to sit with me on a wooden bench. We sat side by side, taking in the stunning view of craggy rocks and endless ocean at the end of the world. On the other side of the ocean lay Antarctica.

When I asked her about her life in South Africa, Ruth said wistfully, "I met my husband on the beach. We fell in love instantly." Her smile so sweet and girlish, she seemed to grow younger before my eyes. "When I told my mom about the boy I'd fallen in love with, she immediately asked me if he was colored." Ruth shook her head.

The term "colored" made me squirm. But as I would soon learn, talking about taboos in South Africa was the natural state of things.

Ruth continued, "When I said no, he wasn't colored, my mother breathed a huge sigh of relief and said it was good that he was not. That's the only time I remember her saying anything prejudiced. Ever, in my entire life. My family accepted colored people, because one of my aunts had married a colored man, although he got papers stating otherwise and told everyone he was white."

"What? I don't understand," I said.

She looked at me, her brows raised. "Back then, people often lied about their race. It's just how it was."

How could anyone lie about that? For most people, race is obvious. Curious, I asked her, "What do you remember about apartheid?"

"Apartheid is a Dutch word. It means 'separateness.' The Dutch were traders first, and settlers second. Believe it or not, apartheid came out of their desire for efficiency, practicality, and self-preservation back in colonial times. The colonists believed separateness was the only way to maintain their Dutch identity and be able to rule the colony, the only way to avoid becoming overwhelmed by the sheer numbers of native Africans."

I asked her, "So what did it look like for you personally?"

She stared out at frothy waves. Sun lit up the dark blue sea with pinpricks of silver. "When I was young, black people had to live in specific areas of the cities and towns. They had to use separate restrooms. The government did not permit blacks and whites to marry, and they were not supposed to have sex. I remember hearing about Nelson Mandela and the demonstrations against apartheid that turned violent."

"Life and love are hard enough without the government getting involved," I said, shaking my head. I thought about one of my favorite quotes from Mandela's book *Long Walk to Freedom*: "No one is born hating another person because of the color of his skin, or his background, or his religion. People must learn to hate, and if they can learn to hate, they can be taught to love, for love comes more naturally to the human heart than its opposite."

Ruth pointed to several penguins sliding off a rock into the water. She laughed at their antics. I wanted to be as happy-go-lucky as the little fellas in front of us. They were black and white, the colors at the heart of the difficult past of South Africa.

Watching her laugh, I asked, "So, what makes you happy?"

She turned to me with a sad smile. "My husband made me very happy. But he died when we were in our forties." A peaceful expression came over her face. "I'm not interested in marrying anyone else."

My heart warmed. How wonderful to have found a soul mate, a love so profound she wouldn't consider remarrying.

Ruth said, "I'm happiest now when I go hiking like we are today, and when I go camping. I enjoy meeting people like you and sharing stories. This is what I do on my travels in Africa, and all over the world. I grew up during segregation, but I believe in diversity. Being exposed to all kinds of people makes life more interesting, doesn't it?"

"Absolutely," I agreed. "That's why I'm here."

Ruth said, "I love studying birds and other wildlife. I love doing photography and working in my garden. I enjoy the balance between having time to myself at home in my garden, and spending time with friends and family."

Pocky walked up to us, imitating the waddle of the penguins. Ruth and I laughed.

Happiness isn't about the *what* of life but the *how*. How we are able to balance our time alone with our time with others. This is how we recharge our brains and bodies to bring tranquility.

After the tour ended, I said goodbye to Ruth. Then Pocky and I had dinner at a restaurant overlooking the Cape Town harbor. We stared out at the cruise ships, lobster boats, and wartime vessels, the sailboats and schooners. The diversity was amazing. We shared a bottle of the best local wine as the lights came up.

I imagined arriving by ship at the Cape of Good Hope on *The Flying Dutchman*, and I thought about shipwrecks and lost travelers. I thought about the early Dutch settlers, their desires and fears, the hardships they faced in the new land. I remembered Ruth's reflections on growing up during apartheid. How brave we must be to release our fears about those different from us. Yet we must stop being fearful of *the others*. We have to open ourselves up in order to understand other people, to learn from them and enjoy them.

"Variety really is the spice of life, isn't it, honey?" I said to Pocky.

He raised his glass of African wine and smiled in agreement.

With each sip of wine, I savored the diverse charms of Cape Town—from the harbor to wine country, mosquito repellant to biltong, phantom ships to undying love, baboons to penguins on the beach.

NATURE IS INSTINCT

For months before the Africa trip, I'd been obsessing about my phobia of small planes. Worried about taking charter flights, I'd soon face my biggest fear, a charter to the Sabi Sands Game Reserve. I worked hard to talk myself out of my panic, but my fear soared when we stood in line to board the tiny five-seater.

I had not let my irrational fear of flying stop me from traveling around the world. But this plane was small. *Really* small.

As we climbed on board, I told myself the charter flight was just another exciting adventure. And that worked pretty well until I found myself sitting alone in the tail section of the plane, staring out a miniature window. Due to the plane's small size, the pilot seated the passengers according to weight. Being the lightest passenger had determined my fate. I didn't even have Pocky to hold on to because he had to sit up front with the pilot.

My hands shook and my heart pounded.

Once airborne, however, I did what I always do when fear grips me. I focused on relaxing, making a light tap here, and a soft tap there on my thighs, as I counted back from a hundred by threes. My mind released the fear, and I settled into a curled-up position that enabled me to look out the little window.

My phobia had come out of nowhere after I'd given birth to my daughter. But since that time, I'd traveled around the United States, to Asia and Europe, to Mexico and South America, and now to Africa. So I knew I could do this. I would be okay.

As we flew over the wild savannah, I watched wind patterns ripple the long brown grass. There was nothing around for miles and miles, and the endless views of wilderness spurred my imagination. I thought of all the wild animals running free on the beautiful earth below and it made my heart soar.

The turbulence increased as we landed due to the heat of the savannah whipping up warm wind currents. My pulse raced as I made my way to the front of the plane. But when I stepped out onto the dirt runway, I instantly felt grounded. Breathing deeply in the hot humid air calmed my pounding heart.

A jeep arrived with our guide and our tracker. We climbed aboard. We were going on a safari! Just the idea of being in the bush heightened all my senses, and my everyday worries instantly faded away.

Michael told us he was from southwest Zambia, and had been a safari guide for seven years. He grew up on a tobacco and beef farm in a wilderness-oriented family, with two older brothers who'd also been guides. Tall and dark, his startlingly attractive looks highlighted a sensitive demeanor and great sense of humor. He spoke with a British accent and exhibited the same shining spirit as my daughter Kaylee. I thought he'd be a perfect adventure partner for her.

The tracker was Tito. He told us he was forty-two years old, and would soon be ordained as a priest in the Zion Christian church. From the Tsonga tribe, he told us how his people rely on God, and don't drink or smoke. He said, "My people used to wear animal skins and dance with a stick. If you like, I can teach you our tribal dance called mchongolo."

I knew that my life would be in these two men's hands while in the bush. I felt comfortable with them, and hopeful they would keep us safe.

The jeep pulled into a dirt lot and parked. The camp was in the middle of eight-hundred-year-old trees, and consisted of a lodge on the banks of the Sabi River surrounded by tents and wood viewing decks. The place struck me as a kind of fairytale locale, with luxury tent accommodations, open-air common areas for gathering and dining, and nighttime skies filled with brilliant stars. Safaris took off each morning at sunrise, with a break midday to escape the hot weather. The safaris continued in late afternoon until sunset.

During our time on the reserve, we spotted the "big five"—elephants, lions, rhinos, Cape buffalo, and leopards. We also saw lots of other wildlife. We heard the call of the wild long into the night. The roar of the lion, we learned, could be heard from five miles away.

As soon as we had unpacked in our tent, we went out on a late afternoon safari. Only a few minutes into the drive, I spotted a female leopard standing in the bush. She was tall, her fur thick, her muscles taut.

Michael parked the jeep and we watched her. He told us, "Leopards can leap twenty feet."

We were closer to her than that.

I held my breath. Maybe the leopard didn't care that I sat within striking distance, but I sure did. I watched her slink toward us, elegant and graceful. She walked right in front of the jeep, pausing to look directly at us. I stared into the raw beauty of her impossibly green eyes. When she continued her stroll, I shivered.

Nothing separated us from the animals. Out on safari, there were no cages or bars. Just us and the call of the wild.

"Stay in the jeep and be still," Michael said. "The animals will pass us by."

He spoke with confidence and ease. Both Michael and Tito had the utmost respect for the animals, making sure humans didn't disrupt the natural order of life in the animal kingdom.

Michael told us, "Animals are not intentionally mean. They always have a reason for aggression. If you are in danger, odds are, you put yourself there. You must understand, the instincts of animals are not to harm us, not unless we are a perceived threat. Nature is instinct; we all come from it. The bush is the most real thing in this world."

He was right. I sat there watching the animals roaming around us, ignoring our nonthreatening presence while they followed their instincts.

Tito called out, and we drove over to where he indicated. With his keen eyes, he'd discovered several lions hidden in the bush a few yards away. The male lions huddled together feeding on a wildebeest. I winced as their sharp teeth tore at the dead animal's bloody flesh. But I couldn't help but watch the raw, natural beauty of the violent feast. In the dusky twilight, the scene was quite dramatic.

Michael told us male lions defend their territory while females do most of the hunting. Then the males eat first.

We drove on through the savannah until Michael spotted something else in the distance. He stopped the car and got out.

"Stay here. I'll be back," he said.

My heart leapt out of my chest. I felt more vulnerable without Michael there, concerned for his safety. Michael turned and motioned Tito to drive closer, then to stop when we got close. A hippo lay on its side in the mud. The animal was so large and so still, it looked like a huge mound of mud.

Tito whispered, "Hippos are one of the most dangerous animals in the reserve, killing more humans than any other species in Africa. They are fast, too, contrary to the way they look. Hippos can weigh as much as nine thousand pounds. Still, they can run nineteen miles an hour."

Tito stopped the jeep long enough to pick up Michael, who said, "He's dying of thirst."

"Can't we give him some water?" Pocky asked.

Michael shook his head. "That would disrupt the natural order of things. Apparently, it is this hippo's time. Once he dies, his remains will provide nourishment to others in the bush. Death fuels life here. Animals, like ourselves, all die. We all become part of nature again."

Tito added, "There is no waste of life and death in the bush. The dead hippo gives nourishment to other animals like hyenas and lions, who feed on its belly."

I appreciated the beauty of coming face to face with the cycle of life. Everything made sense in the bush—the way camouflaged animals followed their instincts, deciding what they should and shouldn't eat, knowing when it was time to die. And there we were, right there in the bush with them, just another animal.

As the sun set, we stopped for cocktail hour. I took the opportunity to speak with Michael as he set up a fantastic spread of appetizers including fresh fruit, various cheeses, and sliced meats. He set out beer and wine, and got to work making a fruity cocktail. At what might be the most exotic happy hour I will ever attend, I told him about my work on a book about happiness.

Michael said, "Happiness? Well, I feel peace and happiness by connecting to the simplicity of life, which I find out here. When you take a good look at nature and animals, the process that takes place is instinctual."

I thought about instincts, and how little we tap into them in our civilized culture. In my experience, I've found that most of us make major life decisions based not on instincts but on the avoidance of fear—fear of failure, fear of rejection, even fear of success. Decisions based in fear can cut off the process of instinct, which naturally draws us to the people, places, and things that make us feel expansive. Like when you know something or someone is truly right for you. Or when you hear a little voice telling you to walk down a certain path. When fear rules over instinct, we don't listen to that voice. Instead, we avoid expansion and limit our experience of life.

In the wilds of Africa, animals follow their instincts. I took inspiration from their pure, simple way of living.

Pocky was joking around with Tito, attempting to follow our tracker as he demonstrated a few steps of his tribal dance. Pocky has always had great instincts, but not great rhythm. I smiled, watching him practice the steps as zebras walked behind him in the background. My husband had always encouraged me to follow my gut more, and I knew I needed to take him up on that.

I turned to Michael. "I love what you said about instincts. Can you tell me about the lessons you've learned from studying them?"

"Well, let me see," Michael said, staring at the red-orange sunset. The fiery sky painted the brown savannah around us in golden hues. "I think we are all linked in the ways of nature, but humans jump in and out of that link. For example, we become too complicated in our minds, and too attached to all the stuff we accumulate, which can cause us to make a mess of the natural order of things. When we get too far away from our instincts, and too much in our heads and egos, this can lead to stress. And this kind of stress brings on so much unhappiness."

He handed one of the cocktails to me.

"I bet you learn a lot from the animals," I said, sipping my drink.

He nodded. "Simplicity is the greatest lesson they've taught me, and how that leads us to stay in touch with what comes naturally. Elephants are extremely intelligent, with big brains. Sometimes I think they are more intelligent than us in certain ways. They don't have to deal with all the mind chatter we have going on in our heads. They know how to survive and care for one another in a very pure way."

I pointed to my drink, which was delicious. "What's in this?"

He grinned. "We call it safari juice, it's very refreshing. A bit of vodka, orange, melon, and a dash of pomegranate. Highly drinkable."

I held up my cocktail. "To Africa."

Pocky saw me. He raised his glass in the air and we did a long-distance clink.

Michael said, "Besides honoring the animals, I believe my purpose in life is to have good intentions every day. That's something my mother always said. Pure intentions bring happiness," he said with a smile.

I had to agree. In my work with my patients, I'd noticed how the people who were aware they were well-intentioned tended to question themselves less frequently, and were less defensive. How easily we forget that those around us are usually well-intentioned too.

I said to Michael, "Your thoughts about death when we came across the dying hippo intrigued me."

He nodded. "I've been close to death myself a couple of times. What I worried about most in those moments was my own unfinished business, and the loss I'd represent to the loved ones I'd leave behind. I do not fear my own death because it is a natural part of life, but I do fear losing the ones I love. My brothers have had a few close calls with the animals. A bout with malaria as a kid is as close as I came to death. That, and a near miss with a hippo."

Tito joined us, saying, "But somehow we survive. Right, Michael?" He took a long drink of water, glancing at the heavens. "Most people who die in the bush didn't understand or respect the animals."

"What do you think about life after death?" I asked him.

He shrugged. "The truth is, I don't know about life after death, so I don't say that I know."

I found his vulnerability refreshing. Even though he was a devout Christian on the path to priesthood, he didn't pretend to have an answer to what happens after we die.

"Do you mind if I ask you more about your path to the priesthood, Tito? Does your faith make you happy?" I asked him.

He said, "I believe in God and Jesus—the Way, the Truth, and the Life. The same way my people believe in the truth, not in speculation or half truths. But sometimes people don't understand my way."

"How so?"

"Well, I am very direct and straightforward. I speak the plain truth, and don't see the point in exaggeration. This sometimes surprises people. The people in my tribe don't talk a lot, and are skeptical of people who do."

Interesting. I wondered how much clearer our communication might be if we all measured our words and only spoke the plain truth. But I also wondered what would be lost, especially the depth, color, and humor of conversations.

In the distance, I watched a gathering of zebras. They looked like ponies in jailhouse stripes.

Tito said, "I believe our integrity is shaped by how we treat the people who are different than we are. I will never understand how kids still die in racist tragedies. In 1975, I was finally allowed to watch TV for two hours a day. In 1976, I saw an uprising on TV where kids were killed by our government. Seeing this portrayed on television was new for me, and I realized the severity of the problems plaguing our culture. For example, how the African education system favored white kids over black kids, and how black people were not allowed to rise to levels of authority. Upholding truth and respecting all living things are keys to a good life. It is important to treat others with dignity," he concluded.

I nodded in agreement. If only we all thought this way.

The zebras stood in a circle facing the center, heads toward one another. They had an air of dignified vigilance. You would think zebras would stand out in the bush, but they camouflaged perfectly among the trees without leaves and the tall grasses.

Michael told me, "Zebras form a circle to protect each other, all of them on the lookout, each one keeping watch over the back of the zebra in front of him or her. This form of protection is as natural to them as breathing."

After happy hour ended, Pocky and I returned to our tent. White-hot stars clustered in the big black sky. As we got ready for the evening, elephants passed by our patio, as common as sparrows flying outside our windows at home. To be one with this kind of nature—the beauty, agony, wisdom, and peace—brought me such joy.

Pocky and I had a romantic dinner at the family-owned lodge. We dined outside underneath the canopy formed by huge trees. The bush was alive with the call of the wild, a symphony of sound.

Nelson Mandela's words echoed in my mind: "Love comes more naturally to the human heart than its opposite."

Chapter 10

ZAMBIA AND ZIMBABWE: ANGELS IN FLIGHT

Scenes so lovely must have been gazed upon by angels in their flight.
—Dr. David Livingstone, writing about Victoria Falls

After our incredible big-five experience in Sabi Sands, we hopped aboard another small plane. Once again, I swallowed my fear and curled up in the tail, this time to fly to Victoria Falls on the border between Zambia and Zimbabwe. When I stepped off the plane, relieved to feel my feet hit the ground again, the air was hot. We were booked at the iconic Victoria Falls Hotel, originally constructed to house workers on the Cape-to-Cairo railway.

The hotel intrigued me. It spoke of the colonials' attempt to tame the vast wilderness, as well as the courage needed and sacrifices made to explore Africa's mysteries. The colonial-style hotel faced the waterfalls roaring in the distance. My heart instantly connected to nature's abundance, the endless pounding of water, the lush refreshment and the energy it provided.

We toured the falls on foot. A viewpoint accessed along a rickety and wet footbridge exposed a dramatic vista called the Knife Edge. I stared in awe as thunderous water cascaded down the jungle-rimmed cliffs.

We descended to a whirlpool known as the Boiling Pot, where spray fell all around us in thick bands. I closed my eyes and surrendered to the soaking.

Pocky slid an arm around me. He gave me a squeeze and I opened my eyes. He stood with his head back and his mouth open, drinking in the falls. I laughed at him. Then I laughed at how drenched we both were, and how good that felt in the heat of the day. I thought about how in a matter of days we'd be celebrating our twenty-second anniversary. We hadn't taken the trip to celebrate the event, it had just happened that way.

Once again, everything in the bush flowed naturally and made good sense.

MANI, PEDI, AND FAITH

The falls were one of the most awesome spectacles I'd ever seen in the natural world. I was stunned by their immense beauty and power. But as I dried off, I noticed how unkempt my nails had become after so many days of travel, so when we returned to our hotel, I decided to go with the unnatural and get a mani-pedi in the hotel spa.

As I entered the small salon, a petite woman greeted me. Her name tag said her name was Faith. Thin, almost frail, she wore her faded blonde hair in a loose ponytail. Her gaze had an intensity tinged with deep sadness.

"Pick your color," she said robotically.

"My name is Lisa," I said with a smile. "Hi, Faith."

A look of surprise filled her blue eyes. She seemed to appreciate my overture. I suspected she'd long been relegated to the background of life.

She motioned me over to the nail color selections. The busy salon buzzed, with only the one empty manicure/pedicure chair.

I perused the colors, listening to the chatter of the women getting their hair styled. Then I sat in the empty manicure chair. The casual way Faith captured and flipped over my hand spoke of her lack of enthusiasm.

She worked on my nails silently, her eyes downcast.

"So do you live around here?" I asked, trying to break the ice.

The question caused her to bristle a little. "Yes." Her small hands took care of business, pushing down my cuticles, cutting and filing my nails. "It's a new place," she added.

I picked up the thread, pleased to be able to connect with her. "Oh, so how do you like it?"

"It's okay," she said in a monotone.

I decided to invite her into my world. "I'm writing a book about happiness and I'm talking to people all over the world about it. You care to talk with me about this? Like about whatever makes you happy?"

She looked up. Her gaze met mine, her face opening to me like a fast-blossoming flower. A very sad flower. "I'm not happy," she said frankly.

I didn't know what to say. Faith was the first person to respond to me in this way. Not that everyone I'd interviewed had been wildly happy with their lives. But they all seemed to be able to find aspects of life that made them happy. Rose wasn't very happy when I spoke with her in Vietnam, but she didn't admit to this right out of the gate like Faith had just done. And Rose had things in her life that brought her happiness.

Not sure what to say, I asked Faith how old she was.

"I'm twenty-one. I'm a single mother. I have a two-year-old daughter." Her sad voice and exhausted expression spoke of her fatigue and hopelessness.

During the silence that fell between us, I thought about my clients. One of the most frightening signs I saw in some of them was hopelessness, the feeling that their current painful state would not improve. Helping my clients take things one step at a time down a clearly identified path could help. But they told me how even the smallest steps felt like heavy lifting. The hopelessness they felt zapped all motivation and became a self-fulfilling prophecy.

I didn't want to push Faith, so I told her about my own life. How I had been divorced at a young age and was a single mother with a young child. How hard that time in my life had been.

That broke the ice.

Faith held my hand in hers. "I left my abusive parents to marry my husband. But he was abusive, too. After he abused my daughter, we fled." She filed my nails in short sweeping motions. "Now I work seven days a week, eight hours a day, to pay for our freedom."

Her shell was hard. Now I understood why. If you've been abused by those closest to you, how can you ever trust anyone again? She would only lift the lid off her story a little bit. Unlike Rose, Faith wasn't ready to take that lid all the way off. Not yet, anyway.

"So what are your dreams now that you're free?" I asked her.

"Dreams?" She stopped filing and gave me a blank stare. "I don't think about dreams. Maybe someday I will. But it's too hard to think about dreams right now. Dreams will just get my hopes up, and I need to focus on doing the best with what I have."

This made sense, but it also made for a bitter and difficult life. I didn't try to be her therapist, but I felt compelled to bring some positivity into her life.

I said, "It seems to me you must have a lot of strengths. You got this job. You're intelligent and hard-working. And what strength you must've mustered up in order to win your freedom and save your child."

She said in a soft voice, "My siblings are strong, too. They help me take care of my daughter."

It was good to know she had support. "So when was the last time you remember being happy?"

"The happiest time in my life?" She stopped filing my nails and stared at the ceiling for what seemed like a very long time. "I guess when I was in school. I was happy each day after I got out of school, or when I would leave my parents' house on my way to school. These were times when I would be on my own for a while. When no one was telling me what to do."

Upon first meeting her, I had seen Faith as small and frail. But as I got to know her, I could see she radiated a certain power, a mixture of strength and anger. Faith didn't have the advantages others do. But she did the best she could with what she had—for herself and her child. Isn't that all any of us can ask of ourselves?

Faith did a beautiful job on my nails.

When I stood up to leave, she said, "I guess if there's something to be happy about, it would be that no one harms me anymore, or tells me what to do."

I smiled at her and she smiled in return. I had faith that she would continue to handle her challenges with remarkable grace.

BLIND TRUST

After I left the salon, I went outside to a bench overlooking the lush grounds of the hotel. Huge old shade trees and manicured bushes were scattered around the lawn. Warthogs were snuffling in the grass. In the distance, I could see the falls.

I sat in the sun for a few minutes. I was feeling grateful—for the thunderous rainbow-filled waterfalls, for not dying on tiny airplanes, and for being able to talk about happiness with Faith—when a bee landed on my foot. I looked down at it. Instantly, it stung me on the ankle.

I have experienced bad reactions to bee stings in my life, and I didn't want to think about all the ways the trip could go wrong due to that. So I went up to the room to get some salve to put on the sting.

I elevated my foot and hoped for the best. But Pocky kept looking at my ankle, saying things like, "Um . . . it's swelling up. It's getting really big." And, "It's getting a lot bigger."

Pocky couldn't ignore the elephant foot in the room. He wouldn't let me do that either as my ankle grew very swollen very quickly. Soon we were having our next adventure as we went to the African pharmacy and hunted for someone who spoke English.

The pharmacist gave me some pills to take and a salve to put on the sting. I would have to trust the swelling would go down and everything would be okay, even though I couldn't walk on my swollen foot.

After icing the foot for a few hours, we got some unexpected news. We were supposed to move to our next hotel, but they had mixed up our reservations. So we had nowhere to stay for the night.

Pocky reached out to our travel agent, who booked us an extra night in Victoria Falls and a river safari in neighboring Botswana. Everything happened really fast—the bee sting, the swollen foot, no place to stay in Africa, and the offer to go on a river safari, which, it turned out, left right away.

Whirlwind!

The next thing I knew, I, my elephant foot, and Pocky were driving to the border in a jeep with our guide.

Dark and clean cut, Farai was dressed in crisp white linen. He warned us that whenever you cross borders in Africa, you never know whether the experience will be smooth or difficult. At the border, he asked us to hand him our passports, which he took to the customs people in a small building under a tall bare tree.

Pocky leaned toward me. "We are off our itinerary now. You know there isn't one person in the world who knows where we are, right?"

The hairs on the back of my neck stood up.

We hadn't even planned to go to Botswana. Except for our travel agent, we hadn't spoken to anyone about visiting that country. Nobody would guess we'd be headed there. I asked myself a lot of questions in that moment. *Are we crazy? Are we taking a huge risk? Will we be in danger? Will we be okay?*

This would be a day filled with the unexpected, requiring a kind of blind trust.

I stared at my husband. We were in Farai's hands. We would have to trust him. We had to do just what we'd done in the pharmacy; that is, trust that everything would be okay.

I stared down at my fat foot.

Farai returned to the jeep. "Come with me," he said.

My stomach dropped and I felt queasy. I hobbled along, leaning on Pocky as we made our way up the dirt path to the makeshift building. Farai told us we needed to step in a tub of clear liquid. This was supposed to kill any hoof-and-mouth disease we might have picked up on our shoes.

I realized we were in good hands.

Farai drove us across the border and into Botswana. Soon we arrived at a wood dock on the Chobe River where several small motorboats were tied up. We walked down to the dock and met our driver, a lean and friendly man with a laid-back vibe. We climbed in his twelve-foot motor boat and took our seats.

"See you on the other side," Farai said, giving us a playful wave. To calm the uncertainty he found in our eyes, he added, "I'll meet you in a few hours, and you can tell me all about it."

We set sail, drifting deep into the wilderness. The boat floated so slowly down the picturesque river we could see all kinds of animals along the bush-lined riverbanks. Elephants took mud baths and tossed water around with their trunks. Hippos lurked in the water. We saw exotic birds catching fish, and crocodiles sunning themselves. I couldn't take my eyes off the giraffes.

"Disney does some amazing work, huh, honey?" Pocky joked, as if we'd taken a vacation to Disneyland and had seats on the Jungle Cruise ride.

I laughed.

The little boat sailed up so close to the wildlife that we could appreciate the size of the animals. The giraffes stood as tall as two-story buildings. They hooked their necks around one another and bobbed up and down playfully.

"Look, they're necking," Pocky told me with a grin.

I wasn't sure whether they were fighting or showing affection. One would nudge another, then they would end up in this funny neck dance.

Their feet stayed still, but their necks hooked up and hugged in flirtatious ways.

The river boat captain told us the giraffes were actually getting ready to do battle. He said, "See their spots? The fur patterns are unique to each giraffe, just like human fingerprints."

We watched as a giraffe drank from the river. Their heads were so high up they had to bend over in a kind of curtsy, twisting their legs to get low enough to take a drink.

Pocky whispered in my ear, "I guess you could say giraffes have a drinking problem."

I laughed, but I was impressed by way the animals embraced their awkwardness so gracefully.

Just beyond the giraffes, massive Cape buffalo roamed. These African bovines could weigh as much as 1,300 pounds. Birds landed on their backs to eat the insects that lived on them.

Farai greeted us after the safari ended and our boat docked. Pocky and I couldn't wait to thank him for helping us have such a beautiful experience. We shared some of our stories as our captain tended to his boat. Farai laughed and nodded with excitement as we told him what we had seen on the river.

A delightful person, I wanted to learn about Farai's take on happiness. When we returned to the jeep, I asked him what he did for fun.

"I love to sing gospel music," he said, turning over the ignition. "I like to play music and dance, too, especially when I call up the spirits of my ancestors while wearing our traditional dress."

"I'm writing a book about happiness around the world," I told him.

He smiled. "Really? How interesting. Well, what makes me happy is working hard so my kids can have a better life and get a good education. I have two daughters. One is two years old, and the other is five. Every day I try to be a good person. I am Christian. All these things make me happy."

I nodded in agreement. "All wonderful places to find happiness."

He drove slowly. "Yes, but it's not easy. It's hard to make money in Zimbabwe, and the political system is corrupt. No matter who is in power, corruption exists. They use methods like withholding food and supplies in order to get votes. Most people I know are not happy because unemployment is high and the quality of employment is low."

He headed the jeep back toward the border. "We once looked to the ancestors for guidance. My tribe and my family had many interesting rituals they could use in order to consult the wisdom of our ancestors. For instance, if there was a problem in the family, we would sacrifice a goat and visit the grave of an ancestor to ask them to please hear about the struggle and give us guidance."

"That's fascinating," I said.

"I haven't gone with my family lately, but the last time we all went as a group my parents wanted advice because one of my sisters couldn't have kids."

I sat forward. "And what did the ancestors say?"

"Don't worry, be happy," he said with a smile.

I appreciated the way Farai could blend Christianity with his ancestral traditions. It reminded me of the Peruvians, who kept their traditions alive within their Christian beliefs.

"And don't point," he said.

Pocky and I looked at one another. "What do you mean?" I asked Farai.

"We believe that if you point at the grave of an ancestor, it brings you terrible luck."

"Oh, I see," I said.

I must have looked scared because he said, "Don't worry, we believe to counter the bad luck all you must do is bite your fingers." He demonstrated, then laughed.

I laughed, too, his playful nature contagious. "Thanks. Great advice. I'll be sure to watch my finger pointing from now on."

Like Faith, Farai was thankful to have a job. For him, the job and the chance to improve his daughters' lives created happiness in his life. Unlike Faith, Farai held out hope for his children's future. He had a sweet gentle spirit that seemed like an enduring light, impossible to extinguish.

I sat back in the seat and stared at the beautiful countryside. The day had been so much different than we'd expected. Yet it turned out to be one of the best days of the African adventure.

Life isn't always about executing the perfect plan. It's also about trusting the day will take us where we most need to go.

JUNGLE CRUISE ZIMBABWE

We flew in another small plane to Hwange. I was still frightened, but once again, I managed to curl up and relax in my usual seat in the tail.

After a bumpy landing, we drove to where we would be glamping. I sighed with happiness when I saw the reserve, which was the kind of place I thought only existed in fairytales and dreams.

A thousand acres filled with teak forests, palm islands, Kalahari scrub, and acacia woodlands, the reserve was a legendary spot for herds of elephants and some four hundred bird species. The camp offered an intriguing mix of sophisticated interiors and old-world safari spirit. Our tent looked out over a watering hole where elephants interacted with anteaters. I found waking to the pre-dawn call of the animals the best alarm clock for sunrise safaris.

Out on safari one morning, we came upon a group of elephants walking single file, so perfectly camouflaged they seemed to appear out of nowhere. The huge animals blended into their surroundings.

The elephant leading the pack was enormous.

A woman traveling in the jeep with us wanted to photograph the leader. She abruptly stood up to take a picture—a safari no-no. The elephant slapped his ears, a sign of aggression. Tawanda, our tracker, gently reminded the lady to sit down. We were supposed to remain still, the number one safari rule.

The big elephant walked over to the jeep. He went right up to Pocky and looked directly at him. Pocky instinctively remained seated in a stare-down with the enormous beast. I could only see one eye since the elephant's head was so huge. That eye held so much intelligence, and the thick gray hide surrounding it was crisscrossed with lines.

Pocky said later that he could see his reflection there. Yes, the elephant had been that close.

Elephants are fascinating creatures. They have honor rituals around death, one of the few animals that do. Elephant researcher Martin Meredith talks about such rituals in his book *Elephant Destiny*. He describes how the family of an old female elephant gently caressed her dead body with their trunks. He reports on how the herd screamed and wept, then silently threw leaves and branches to cover her body. The herd then stood over her for two days.

Amazing.

As the elephant left Pocky to lead his herd away, my husband heaved a sigh of relief, tinged with awe. He'd been honored by the lead elephant.

Tawanda provided a strange counterpoint to our soulful day on safari. He told us he had once worked at Disneyland on the Jungle Cruise ride.

"And what did you think of it?" I asked him.

He shrugged. "Many people here in South Africa are content to do the same thing over and over. Not me. I wanted to get away, you know?"

I nodded.

"But watching game animals and being in the bush, this is always what we long for. The bush is a part of our heart. When we leave it, nothing feels real or right. Africa is the happiest place on Earth. For me, nothing is more real."

As we drove through the bush, it felt like we were in a Disney movie, or somewhere equally magical. It felt unreal to me, but also natural and happy.

At sunset, we visited a watering hole. We parked far enough away so we wouldn't bother the animals. At first there were no animals around, but then the elephants began to arrive, hundreds of them coming from every direction. Silhouetted by the setting sun, they walked single file toward the water. The beauty of their instinctual drive to visit this place at the same time each day gave me chills. I felt like I was spying on a private happy hour for elephants.

While one group drank, the next group arrived on the edge of the watering hole. No fights broke out; everyone waited their turn. There wasn't any drama about it. After they got their fill of the water, the adolescent males played around while the females tended to their babies. The beautiful scene seemed very human-like, only the elephants were better behaved. The massive animals appeared to be nicer and more respectful of each other than most humans.

As I watched the elephants, the peacefulness of the bush washed over me and the wisdom of Africa's rhythms soothed me. I thought about how everything in nature so gracefully falls into place. The curious elephant that went eye to eye with Pocky didn't seem afraid. To have the opportunity to stare an elephant in the eye had brought me an intense moment of connection. For just a fleeting moment, it felt as if he understood me and I understood him.

IMPOSSIBLE LOVE

Pocky and I had an accidental anniversary celebration in the bush. We'd ended up in the most romantic camp imaginable, a place that seemed like a movie set in our own personal version of *Out of Africa*, dropped in the middle of a vast savannah, complete with exquisite camp furnishings, gourmet food, fabulous wines, and wildlife viewing at every turn. If we needed anything in the middle of the night, we simply rang a bell. We weren't supposed to go out, as danger lurked around the camp after dark. We were told to stay in our tents until dawn if unescorted. No fences had been erected to protect us from the animals, a job left to our gun-toting escorts. In a heartbeat, we could become a midnight snack for a hungry animal. In this way, the experience had a thrilling *Survivor* feel to it.

Such danger can be quite erotic.

I loved the feeling of living outside. The way we awakened to animal calls in the morning, exotic sounds I'd never heard before and would likely never hear again. Our adventurous days spent on safari ended in breathtaking fantasy dinners under ancient trees and millions of stars. The camp had become as much a part of our experience as the savannah. I felt nestled there, like a lion cub protected by its mother.

On our last night in Africa, we attended a relaxing happy hour. The open-air bar was small and intimate, and overlooked the outdoor fire pit, with a view of the bush beyond. The bartender invited us to take in the view while he mixed our drinks.

Pocky gave me a sideways hug while we watched the elephants drinking from a pool about thirty yards away.

"It never stops taking my breath away," I said.

"Me neither," the bartender said.

And then it hit me: This was his view at work—every day! What an amazing thing, to have wild elephants as the backdrop of your life.

Pocky and I took seats at the bar next to another couple and we all shook hands. They'd been out on safari with us earlier, so we'd met them briefly. Phillip was an artist originally from Zambia, and his wife Janie was American. He shared some photos of his wonderful paintings of animals.

When we told them it was our anniversary, they toasted us. Then I asked, "So how did you two meet?"

The artist looked at his beautiful young wife and beamed. "A wedding," he said.

Pocky's eyes brightened.

"I was a groomsman," our new friend said.

"I stood up for my twin sister as maid-of-honor," his wife added.

"It was love at first sight," he said.

"And second sight, too—but the bride was taken," Pocky said with a smile.

We all laughed.

The woman said, "Our relationship had a few challenges, with him living in Zambia and me in LA. But we share a passion for travel, so our romance was that much sweeter."

He grinned.

"We live in Bangkok now and hope to live in the States someday," she added.

"But I'll always come home to get my safari fix," he said.

"My husband's artistic inspiration comes from the animals of Africa. It's a special place for both of us."

It occurred to me how often small differences become big deals in our relationships. This untraditional couple didn't have to be from the same culture to be together. In fact, the vast distance had enhanced their romance.

The hostess took a seat at the bar. She said, "I know what you mean about romantic challenges."

"This is my fiancée, Suria," the bartender explained, placing a glass of water in front of her. "She is from the coast, and I am from the mountains," he said with a shy smile.

"You two are from different cultures," Suria said to Janie. "Mulilo and I are from different tribes."

"How did you meet?" I asked her.

"We met here at the camp and recently became engaged," Suria said with a happy smile.

"It is an alarming process, and difficult, too," Mulilo said, washing a glass.

Suria gave him a compassionate, apologetic look. "The process has been hard on us, and on our families, too."

Process. The word made an impression on me. I had never thought of getting engaged as a process.

Mulilo said, "I must pay the dowry to Suria's family. This is our custom. It all started when I met her aunt's side of the family. After that, they decided who would present me to Suria's parents. In the end, Suria's mother's eldest sister took on the obligation of the introduction. This aunt also negotiated the dowry between her family and mine."

Complicated!

Suria said, "I was nervous for Mulilo because my father didn't want me to marry outside our tribe."

I asked Mulilo, "What type of dowry is required?"

He looked solemn. "It is different for members within the tribe. But for someone like me, an outsider, I have to pay more."

Suria said, "Cows are definitely part of the dowry, and they talked about offering a goat for the wedding feast."

Mulilo said, "Money, too. I need to make a payment. We are still in negotiations on this point."

Suria caught his gaze and his tough exterior instantly softened. He said in a soft voice, "Right now we are waiting to hear whether Suria's father and brothers will accept me."

She looked at me. "It is delicate because my dad is from the Shona tribe, which means 'those who disappear' in English, and Mulilo's family is from the Ndebele tribe, which means 'strangers from the coast.' We might as well be from two different countries! Our tribes speak different languages and we have different customs."

"When they do accept me, I need to procure special gifts for her mother and father, including clothes," Mulilo said hopefully.

Suria nodded. "On our wedding day, right before the wedding, my mother and aunts will talk to me about how to be a good wife. This must take place before I am allowed to join the wedding reception," she said, her eyes bright with hope. "They will tell me all the things a woman should know."

I took heart as I listened to the twists and turns of their true love. It impressed me how they both regarded one another's place in the family to be as sacred as their journey together down the aisle. I recalled the couple we built the house for in Tijuana, and how the husband had to pay what seemed like an impossible amount of money to his wife's family before he could marry her. He had not expressed any regret.

Mulilo said, "We are counting our blessings as we wait for the approval of her family. We're both happy to have good jobs, and hold on to the hope of one day being husband and wife."

"We don't know how everything will turn out, but living in hope with Mulilo like this is good, too," Suria said.

The divorce rate in South Africa is lower than in the United States. I wondered how couples in America might benefit from a long engagement. The engagement "process" in America may not involve cows and goats, but the exchanging of gifts and talks with future in-laws could help to ground a couple. It might give them a greater awareness of their compatibility—or lack thereof. If family became more involved in the selection of our future partners, might our marriages be happier?

I wasn't sure how much I liked the thought of families selecting one's spouse, but I do love the idea of family traditions. Such rituals can help to ground societies, especially in times of transition. Nostalgia can enliven the senses, and create fun and comfort.

I had married into an Italian family. Pocky's parents would regularly have big Italian dinners and invite all the cousins, aunts, and uncles. Their little house became so full of people, all the windows steamed up. There were traditions, including the order in which the food was served—pasta first, then meat, then salad, and finally dessert. And they served lots of wine. To this day, Pocky and his sisters will talk about the family's dining traditions. Listening to them tell their stories warms my heart.

THE EYE NEVER FORGETS
WHAT THE HEART HAS SEEN

During our time in Africa, I could feel nature at work while everyone stood out of the way. The natural rhythms were strong, rich, and beautiful. Living among lions made me grateful to be alive, awed by nature's incredible diversity and power. This lightening of spirit left me free to have blind trust in Botswana, and a memorable encounter with a strong, unhappy woman with little faith. I felt free to enjoy the thrill of a leopard's powerful, restrained approach and to stare into an elephant's brilliant eye. Each night, I'd fall asleep to the call of the wild.

I saw Africa through my heart. I saw Africa in exhilarating and surprisingly sensual ways. The well-ordered natural world brought me a deep sense of peace. It gave me new ideas and important revelations. Along with an elephant foot, I had a new favorite way to see the world: peering out a little window as I flew over the vast savannah, crouched in the tail of a five-seater plane.

Part V

THE MIDDLE EAST: FINDING GOD

Chapter 11

QATAR: LAND OF ABUNDANCE

The early morning sun painted the dunes below in changing hues of pinks and purples. Qatar appeared to be an endless land of constantly shifting, windblown sand. Suddenly, an ultra-modern city emerged, and we began our descent into the capital city of Doha.

Arabia. The word conjured exotic scenes in my mind, mostly from movies and legends. On our way from South Africa to Denver, this layover in Qatar would be my first trip to the Middle East. I thought of the area as a place of tribal people, some nomadic, who knew no borders until the victors of World War I artificially drew them. This occurred in response to the collapse of the Ottoman Empire and discovery of oil in the Gulf region.

When our delayed flight turned into a much longer layover, I received another one of those gifts I often got on my travels on the blue dot. This time it was the opportunity to learn about the people of Qatar. One of the richest countries in the world, Qatar has no income tax and almost no unemployment. So, were the people who lived here happy? I wondered. I wanted to find out.

While walking around the airport, I noted that most women covered themselves from head to toe in the fully enveloping traditional attire called burkas. I suddenly became self-conscious about my appearance as a Western blonde in sweatpants and a T-shirt. I wanted to talk to these women, not blend in with them. However, I wasn't sure how to approach them, and I had some fear. Did they hate Americans? Were some of their views in line with the area's terrorist agendas? I would have to overcome such thoughts if I wanted to ask about their lives.

THANK YOU, GOOGLE TRANSLATE
(شكرا لك ترجمة جوجل)

Even flying on Qatar Airlines felt like a lavish present. When one of the strikingly beautiful flight attendants had asked if I wanted a tuck in, I said yes, please. She placed a crisp, clean sheet over me and then a blanket before tucking me in nice and tight. This made me feel safe and secure. As I drifted off to sleep, it occurred to me I hadn't been tucked in like that since childhood.

In the airport, the gracious bathroom attendants stood ready to open doors. They offered toilet paper and handed out fresh towels. As Pocky and I walked through the terminals, we noticed the pricey high-end shops and restaurants. I wondered if an airport could be too opulent, something I'd never considered before. It looked as if more people were there to clean, serve food, and man the gates than there were travelers shopping at the Duty Free. No wonder the unemployment rate was so low, I thought.

I spotted a good-looking young man sitting alone at an empty gate. He was dressed in the traditional white robe called a *dishdasha*, with a red-and-white-checked turban. I thought he might not mind speaking with me as he waited for his flight. Still, he might be offended by the approach of a strange Western woman in sweatpants who wanted to talk about happiness.

I took a deep breath and approached. When he looked up from the newspaper he held, I told him I was from the United States and was working on a book about global happiness. I asked if he might spend a couple of minutes talking to me.

In excellent English, he bid me to take a seat. Abdulrhman told me he was a local and, at age twenty-four, a student at a tech school in Doha. He seemed poised, and sported a Rolex on one wrist.

He flashed a dazzling white smile as he said, "I like the USA and its people because you are more open."

"Thank you, I'm happy to hear that," I said, taking the seat next to his. "I think maybe our openness comes from how many diverse people live in our country."

His smile faded. "Yes, but that comes with a price. I have heard stories about struggles between blacks and whites in America."

I nodded that this was true. Then I asked, "What do you do to be happy?"

"I'm happiest when I spend time with my friends. I enjoy watching and playing sports. I also love to shop in Doha for lots of things."

A Muslim, he said he prayed for five minutes, five times a day. He also said he looked forward to completing school. "I will likely marry after I finish school, and will probably choose a Muslim woman who is twenty-two or twenty-three years old with a good face and body."

We talked a bit about how his family would need to approve the marriage. This was a familiar conversation, as I had spoken to so many couples about this on my travel adventures.

I'd been nervous when approaching him, even though I worked with Middle Eastern clients in my practice. Understandably, I had reservations about how he might view Americans, specifically an American woman asking him random questions about his personal happiness. He must have sensed my apprehension, because as we said our goodbyes, he added, "The Koran doesn't say to fight, so I believe in peace."

His words calmed my spirit. I realized how much fear I had about the Middle East and its people. How senseless it was for me to make judgments about people I knew so little about. There had been nothing to fear here. Nice and friendly, Abdulrhman gave me the confidence I needed to happily continue my adventure in Qatar.

Pocky was drinking coffee at a gate nearby. As we continued our walk around the airport, passing Swarovski Crystal stores, gold-plated coffee kiosks, and men who looked like Arabian princes, I thought about the young man I had just met. How many young men around the world would answer my questions the same way he had? If they were as lucky, most of them would say the same things Abdulrhman had, I decided.

WHEN ARAB EYES ARE SMILING

After my interview with Abdulrhman, I was more certain people would speak to me. Now I felt confident enough to approach the women.

When I spotted two women in black burkas waiting at another gate, I walked toward them. As they turned to look at me, the narrow horizontal strip within their veils revealed their big dark eyes. Their beautiful, expressive eyes seemed to be asking, *What the hell is this blonde lady doing?*

Face to shrouded face, we stood across from one another, all of us perfectly silent. I wondered if they experienced marginalization or oppression. I wondered what their lives were like at home. I wondered what they thought of me. Perhaps they hadn't met the likes of me before, and in that case, we were all in the same boat.

Taking a deep breath, I decided to keep it simple and not use a lot of words.

I said, "I'm American and I'm writing a book on happiness." I spoke slowly. But the economy of words ended up making me sound strange, like I was communicating with the hard of hearing.

Their eyes conveyed their wonder, and they stared at me for what seemed like an eternity. Then they turned to each other and began to whisper. I imagined their dialogue went something like this:

"What is this mad American woman doing?"

"I don't know, but she looks stressed out."

"Long flight, I guess."

"What's she wearing?"

"No idea. It's not attractive."

I felt so awkward, I wanted to flee. But then one of the women looked at me and said, "Okay."

It was a start.

I asked if they spoke English. One of the two women pulled out her cell phone and clicked on an app that enabled us to communicate.

Thank you, Google Translate.

It is said the eyes are the window to the soul. And since that's all I saw of these women, this encounter would be one of the most unique interviews I'd have on my worldwide adventures. But it didn't take long for the process of communicating by app to become great fun. We all waited in anticipation for each translation and got really excited when we figured out what the heck we were saying to each other.

I watched their eyes, for their eyes told their stories—sparkling in laughter, shifting in skepticism, rolling in mirth. In the West, it is considered impolite to stare. So, even though we were engaged in conversation, I was trying not to stare at them. But I had to. And while focusing so intently on their eyes, I found I was more present in our conversation. I paid much closer attention than I did in conversations with people not dressed in burkas.

The two women told me they were from Oman and asked if I'd heard of the sultan of Oman. When I said no, they told me that Qaboos bin Said al Said was their ruler, and a very good man.

"We are waiting to fly home after a vacation in Saudi Arabia. We spent twenty-five days praying there," the woman named Ayah said.

"Lots of Muslims gather there to pray," her friend Mira said. She told me she was twenty-four.

"Are you able to work in your country?" I asked them.

"We work together in a warehouse for a company that provides engineering services," Ayah said.

"Things have changed quite a bit, so now both men and women can study and work," Mira explained.

"Do you wear your burkas at work?" I asked.

"We call them abayas. And yes, we wear them everywhere we go. But not in our own homes," Ayah said.

"Do you find them difficult to wear at work?" I said.

"Not at all. We enjoy our Muslim traditions," Ayah said.

"We are happy to honor our traditions because they add meaning to our lives and make us feel special," Mira said.

"Thank you for sharing your traditions with me. So what do you think about American traditions?" I asked them.

They looked at one another, then at me. Mira said, "We don't know much about America, or American traditions. We don't watch American TV. But our sultan liked President Obama when he was in office."

"Can you tell me more about your time in Saudi Arabia?" I asked them.

"We visited the Saudi Arabian city of Mecca for Hajj, a spiritual pilgrimage meant to cleanse us of sin and bring us closer to God," Ayah said.

"All Muslims are asked to do this at least once in their lifetime—if they can afford it. Before that, we spent a month fasting in order to prepare for the journey," Mira said.

I had heard of the Hajj, but didn't know much about women's role in the pilgrimage to Mecca, the fifth pillar in the Islamic faith.

They told me they couldn't travel to Saudi Arabia alone, so an uncle had accompanied them. This man was called a *mahram*, or chaperone, a male relative who would keep the women safe from *khulwah*—that is, being alone with someone of the opposite sex.

"These Islamic traditions make us very happy by bringing us closer to Allah. We enjoy them because they give our lives meaning," Mira said to me.

Their apparent contentment made me think about the relativity of happiness. These women probably didn't have much awareness of all the freedoms the rest of the modern world affords to women. Since they didn't know any other way, they simply did what they were told, and met the expectations under the rules of their society. This point was later underlined for me upon my return home when one of my clients compared her experience of being a Muslim woman in the Middle East to living under a "big black umbrella." She said when she moved to America, it was like the cloudy skies had cleared and she finally felt the sunshine and light.

While the young women seemed to be content, I wondered if they'd still feel as happy if they knew what life could be like in another culture. It was hard for me to imagine they wouldn't want something different if they had that option.

I asked them, "Are you married or single?"

Ayah said she was twenty-three and married with two children. Mira was single.

"Can you tell me more about your traditions concerning marriage?"

Ayah said, "I was expected to marry into my tribe. There are many rivalries between tribes. Usually a dowry is paid to the bride and, because I had been educated, my dowry was higher. During Islamic weddings, the men and women remain separated, but we all dress up."

Mira's eyes lit up.

Ayah continued. "Our ceremony was held in the mosque with my groom and his male friends and relatives, while my women friends and I gathered for a party with food and dancing. This was held at the home of one of my friends. Later, my husband picked me up as his bride and took me away."

"I'm surprised the men and women are separated during the ceremony," I said. "Men and women participate together in wedding ceremonies in America."

"We love it our way," Ayah said. "Because when the men aren't around, we can be uninhibited—and that's when we have our fun."

We laughed together in the common bond of sisterhood. Even though we were from different places with different cultures—about as different as you can get—we had a shared sense of humor. I enjoyed our conversation as if it were one I might have during a girls' nights out back home.

They told me their flight was boarding, so I bid them goodbye. If I ever saw them again, I would not be able to recognize them. All I could see were their eyes, but they had both told me all I needed to know about their beautiful spirits and the way their traditions brought them comfort, community, and fun. I loved how they'd been brave enough to talk to me, and I enjoyed how we'd overcome our communication challenges together.

THE BACK SEAT

Our delayed flight turned into a canceled flight. Fortunately, the airline put us up in a nice hotel, and we used the gift of extra time in Qatar to sign up for a tour.

An Arab monarchy, Qatar has the highest per capita income in the world, and the capital city reflects the population's riches in jaw-dropping ways. Located on the coast of the Persian Gulf, Doha has a cool, futuristic feel. It boasts a playground of stunning architecture with modernist marvels of engineering. Even our hotel seemed wildly extravagant, with exotic floral displays, fifty-foot buffets offering lobster and pastries, and high ceilings with opulent light fixtures.

Our tour guide greeted us in the lobby. Tall and sturdy, Amir was dressed formally in a white robe called a *throbe*, and a white *guthra*, a turban tied with a black cord. His impressive presence matched his strong voice. Perhaps to reassure us, he said Muslims believe in a peaceful existence and a simple life.

He had given me an opening. So I asked Amir what made him happy.

Leading us out to the street, he said, "I believe happiness is up to Allah. Family creates happiness—extended family, too—and a closeness to God. I pray five times a day for a few minutes in order to honor God. All Muslims do, and for this reason there are prayer centers all over, even in the airport and at community centers."

We passed uniformed bellmen opening doors of luxury cars and limos dropping off passengers. When we reached Amir's car, he offered the front seat to Pocky. He turned to me and stated forcefully, "Please, madam, sit in the back."

I had never been asked to take the back seat before, and the metaphor didn't escape me. And the tone of his request was that of a command, rather than an invitation.

Sometimes things happening in the present remind me of my past. This was one of those times, and it instantly reminded me of my father. While Dad had been a good father, he was an old-school German man who believed wholeheartedly that he was older and wiser, and I should never challenge or question him. Because of this aspect of our relationship, I was extra sensitive whenever a man treated me in ways that made me feel silenced.

In short, I felt snubbed by Amir's demand.

Pocky didn't miss a beat, however, saying, "I think I'll sit in the back with my wife."

After that initial bump in the road, Amir didn't dismiss me again. He included me in the conversation and answered all my questions.

Pulling out into the street, he told us matter of factly, "In my country, a man can have multiple wives. But he must treat them equally in terms of gifts, living conditions, and quality of life. And love. This is difficult, so the practice of having multiple wives is becoming less popular."

Pocky said, "What about you?"

"I just have one wife, because it's too hard to take care of two. One is more than enough for me, and we have two children. My father had two wives. Men will take two wives if the first wife is unable to have children. Family—a big family—is important."

"Why is it so important to have lots of children?" I asked.

He stared at me in the rearview mirror and said, "The Koran teaches that children take care of their elderly parents. They must do as their parents say."

We were headed to the Museum of Islamic Art. He talked without flinching as he drove, a true art form in a city where tailgating was like a blood sport.

"The man has a responsibility to provide for his family, and the wife has a choice about working. If she does want to work, she keeps any money she makes to spend as she chooses," he said.

We arrived at the building that housed the museum, which seemed a work of art in itself, with its modern design and geometric angles. Built on a peninsula, the building was set in a park and overlooked Doha Bay. It had a kind of modern Taj Mahal vibe. The galleries were amazing, with fourteen centuries of Islamic art that told the story of ancient times. However, I felt that the newness of everything in the city overshadowed the richness of the ancient history and culture.

After that, we toured the Souq Wazif, a bazaar selling all sorts of garments, spices, perfumes and scented oils, precious gems like diamonds, even falcons. Hookah clouds of flavored smoke wafted out of the crowded shisha dens onto the labyrinthine cobblestone walkways. I was tempted to get a hemp tattoo. As I admired the colorful rugs and pillows in the marketplace, I began to get a sense of the long and ancient history of the country.

As I perused the market stalls, I realized I hadn't seen anyone living on the streets or begging. In most American capitals, you always see homeless people in the busy parts of the city.

Both the men and the women in the marketplace wore burkas, with the men in white, the women in black. Some women covered their faces, and others did not. Often the men and children accompanied a couple of women, perhaps multiple wives. Some kids wore burkas, but most had on T-shirts and shorts. One boy wore a Superman T-shirt. Wearing Western dress probably made it easier for the kids to play.

When we sat down for tea, Amir said, "It is very important to accept refreshment whenever it's offered."

Our waiter offered us lemon water and we all accepted.

Amir then advised us, "In Qatar, you always use your right hand for drinking and eating, as the left hand is regarded as unclean because it is used for toilet purposes. Similarly, you should avoid showing the soles of your shoes or your feet, as this implies you think the other person is dirt, and is highly offensive. We always keep our feet flat on the ground and do not cross our legs."

I began to think I needed a body language guide to the Middle East in addition to a translation app.

We asked him how his country had changed over the last few decades.

He said, "Qatar changed after the discovery of natural gas in the Gulf in the mid-1990s. Since that time, there's been an enormous expansion. This accounts for the many new buildings, each one in competition with the last for the most beautiful and unique design."

We sat for a while to enjoy our tea. Around us, the people moved in and out of the merchant stalls. The merchants weren't pushy; they seemed laid back. Since they didn't have the financial pressures merchants face in poorer countries, it made sense they would be more relaxed. This provided the market with an ambiance we hadn't experienced elsewhere in the world.

When I asked Amir about the government, he said, "Qatar has an emir who appoints all the ministers of the government. The royal family rules the country with the help of the ministers and experts in various areas, like commerce. The new emir is the thirty-five-year-old son of the old emir. He has two wives and his own airport."

"And what do you think of the new emir?" Pocky asked.

Amir smiled. "I like him. Our people receive free education and free health care. Everyone lives in a home with electricity. There's assistance provided for those who cannot work due to disability, but no assistance is provided to those who are able but refuse to work. I like the emir because he shares the country's wealth with the people. Because of this, we have a nice lifestyle. We all have enough, so we don't have to worry about food, shelter, education, or health care. Our families are taken care of."

Qatar managed to provide for the basic needs of the entire populace. This meant the people would not suffer financial burdens in times of hardship or sickness. For these people, the country's money bought them security. And security contributes to happiness.

"Do you think becoming the richest country in the world has created more happiness for the citizens?" I asked Amir.

He set down his tea cup and nodded emphatically. "Yes, I believe it has. However, some of the simplicity of life has been lost. The old traditions are fading, and families are less reliant on each other. Those are the downsides to the wealth."

A colorful minstrel and a snake charmer carrying a large snake walked by our table. I lifted my camera to take their picture, but Amir stopped me. "The locals don't like to have their photos taken." I set my camera on the table again. "It's not good to take pictures of the police, either. Please be careful," he said with a frown.

When we finished our tea, Amir drove us to the Corniche, a waterfront promenade. Pocky and I got out to walk, and strolled along with the other families. Then Amir drove us to a new coliseum where the people gathered for music and entertainment. As we wandered the majestic grounds, I thought about how Qatar was ranked lower than I expected for happiness, listed at number thirty-two in the most recent World Happiness Report. Obviously, more than money was required for people to be happy with their lives. This reminded me of a quote I liked by the geographer Yi-Fu Tuan: "The good life . . . cannot be mere indulgence. It must contain a measure of grit and truth."

Qatar takes care of the basic needs of its people, which relieves their stress and contributes to greater emotional well-being. However, research shows that once people have enough money to cover their basic needs, their happiness doesn't increase incrementally as they make more money. In fact, making more money comes with its own set of headaches. For example, increased workloads and less time off can get in the way of positive experiences.

Many studies show that spending money on experiences makes us happier than spending money on material goods. The pleasure brought by material things passes quickly, while our experiences create lasting memories. And we often remember our experiences as being happier and better than they actually were.

MIRAGE

Back at the hotel, I thought about how Qatar seemed a mirage in the middle of the vast desert, not quite real, with its Dr. Seuss buildings and opulent, everything-new surreality. During our tour of Doha, I hadn't seen any signs of poverty, which gave the city a too-good-to-be-true vibe. The incredible extravagance felt overwhelming, especially after spending time observing people in the most destitute circumstances due to Africa's special brand of extreme poverty.

A study conducted in 1978 by psychologist Philip Brickman looked at a group of people who had just won the lottery. Although the winners were happier shortly after their big win, they soon lost that elation. Eventually, the lottery winners returned to their former levels of happiness. People adapt to new pleasures, then we crave something else, something more. This tendency is known as the hedonic treadmill, or hedonic adaptation. Thus, in time, the emotional aftermath of winning the lottery will make little difference to a person's overall level of happiness. But so will a life calamity like becoming paralyzed. The study showed that those who underwent devastation were able in time to rebound to previous levels of happiness.

The next day we returned to the airport. As we walked through the terminals, I looked at the women in burkas. I thought about the people I'd met during my brief stay in Qatar. They all had a generosity of spirit I would never forget. I understood the world in a new way now, and I looked forward to spending more time with the people of the Middle East to learn about their strikingly different way of life.

Chapter 12

ISRAEL: HOLY KINDNESS

When I talked with people around the world, I often found God played a central role in their lives—and in their happiness. It occurred to me that the ultimate relationship in life for many people the world over is a relationship with God. I wondered if the pursuit of true and lasting happiness actually stemmed from seeking God and cultivating a relationship with him.

The spiritual scriptures have a great deal to say about this.

From the Bible: "Delight yourself in the Lord, and he will give you the desire of your heart" (Psalm 37:4 English Standard Version).

The Koran states, "Do not strain your eyes in longing for the things that we have given to some groups of them to enjoy, the splendor of the life of this world through which we test them. The provision of your Lord is better and more lasting." (Koran 20:131)

In the Talmud, it says, "The best preacher is the heart; the best teacher is time; the best book is the world; the best friend is God."

Wanting to learn more about how God is recognized in other cultures, I booked a trip to Israel. It was on this particular adventure on the blue dot that I began to rethink my own relationship with God. The Bible stories I'd heard as a child could come to life in Israel. I wanted to walk the shores of the Sea of Galilee, where Jesus met his friends at the water's edge after death and resurrection. I wanted to see Tabgha, where the miracle of the loaves and fishes was said to have occurred. I wanted to experience Nazareth, where Jesus spent much of his life.

On the flight over, Pocky and I immersed ourselves in travel books to read about the fascinating history of Israel. The country shares its borders with Egypt, Jordan, Lebanon, and Syria. Parts of Israel lie on the Mediterranean Sea, parts on the Red Sea. Regarded by Jews, Christians, and Muslims as their Holy Land, Israel declared independence in 1948. After the United Nations Partition Plan, the Palestinians lost their land to Israel, and they've lost even more land over the years. At this point, the Palestinians live only in the West Bank and on the Gaza Strip.

WATER, WINE, AND THE IDF

We arrived in Tel Aviv and enjoyed a scenic coastal drive to Caesarea, an ancient Roman capital. The weather was perfect, in the seventies and sunny, and the Mediterranean was gorgeous, the water impossibly blue.

Caesarea was a classical city, constructed by Herod with an artificial harbor, which was revolutionary at the time. We explored the ancient harbor ruins and the Roman amphitheater before continuing our tour.

After brief stops at the charming seaside cities of Haifa and Acre, we arrived at the Scots Hotel on the Sea of Galilee. The sixty-four-square-mile freshwater lake was surrounded by thriving farms and lush green hillsides. The cliffs of the Golan Heights overlooked the rocky beaches and the sky blue water. We found a cozy bar and enjoyed a glass of wine.

I was pleasantly surprised to find that, of all the wine I'd sampled on my travels around the world, this varietal was one of the most delicious. Our host Tamir had suggested the full-bodied black tulip wine, and it was delightful.

Sipping the fruity wine, I had trouble taking in the enormity of the setting; how the history of the events that had taken place around me had forever changed the world. In a way, it was the perfect place for a wine tasting, as Jesus's first miracle was the transformation of water into wine.

When I asked Tamir if he would speak with me about happiness, he agreed to do so. He joined me downstairs in the breezeway of the hotel lobby. The hotel had once been a Scottish hospital, and dated back more than a hundred years. Palm trees stood near the arched doorways that overlooked the lake, colorful gardens, and iron sculptures. We sat in silk chairs across from one another to talk.

Tamir was twenty-eight years old, he told me. Tall, dark, and quite handsome, he was part of a family that had arrived in Israel from Romania. "My family has lived in Israel for 130 years," he said.

I asked him about his background.

"All Israelis must serve in the Israeli Army, which is called the Israel Defense Forces, or the IDF, so all citizens must join at age eighteen. Boys are committed for three years and girls for two, although most of the battalions are all men. I was in the infantry, then I became a photographer for the army."

I asked him, "How did you use your skills as a photographer for the military?"

"Mostly, I took photographs of infantry training. The soldiers practiced their shooting skills with a laser that's kind of like the ones used in laser paintball. I photographed these exercises to be analyzed later. Kind of like football videos."

"That sounds interesting," I said.

He nodded. "Yes, it was interesting, but I would have rather had my freedom to explore photography the way I wanted to. While I understand the mandate of the Army to protect the people and the borders, being in the IDF took away from my youth. From eighteen to twenty-one, all I knew was the serious business of war."

I could only imagine the experiences he'd gone through after being conscripted as a young man. As he spoke, his free-spirited nature rose to the surface, and it became clear to me the structure and discipline of the army had taken a toll on him.

"Do you believe in God?" I asked him.

"I am a secular Jew."

"What is a secular Jew?" I asked.

"Well, Judaism is the religion of the Jewish people. And the word 'secular' means the absence of religious orientation. For some, Jewishness—or Yiddishkeit—is inconceivable without the Torah, which was inspired by the Divine and the worship of the deity who bestowed it. For others, one can be Jewish but not religious. We have choices."

I nodded.

He sat forward in his chair and said, "I think this is why we've had so many technological innovations here. We have choices, and this leads to the entrepreneurial spirit we have in my country."

"What kinds of inventions are you referring to?"

"The cell phone, voice mail, antivirus computers, the USB flash drive. I am a nerd," Tamir said with a smile. "So I have a love of our inventions. I'm happy our enterprising spirits have not only made this land full of energy, but brought much-needed technological solutions to the world."

I asked, "What has made you happiest since you got out of the army?"

He brightened. "So many things make me happy—parties, music, going to the beach and feeling the sun on my skin, eating watermelon with Bulgarian cheese and a good wine. But the happiest day of my life was when I got discharged from the IDF."

"What did you do when you left?"

"I traveled throughout Europe and Asia. It gave me a chance to take my skills as a photographer and use them for something other than battle plans and troop diagnostics. That began my love affair with taking gorgeous landscape shots."

I could relate to that. I asked, "What were some of your favorite locations?"

"I enjoyed many pilgrimages, and found them to be transformative for my life as well as my art. I believe some of the most beautiful transformations occurred when I trekked El Camino de Santiago in Spain, a five-hundred-mile walk. But I also enjoyed the West Highland Way in Scotland. And I completed the 620-mile Israel National Trail."

I was impressed. The boy had stamina. I could have talked with him forever because of the captivating way he spoke. I found his objective way of seeing the world to be refreshing and insightful. I like to observe a young person's enthusiasm for knowledge and facts. Maybe because I remember being young and exploring new things. Maybe because I revel in the hope that youth brings.

When a tight knot of beautiful young women passed through the breezeway, I watched Tamir as he rubbernecked a bit. He flashed them his dashing smile, and the women seemed to approve.

I asked, "How's dating here in Israel?"

"JDate is the most popular dating app. I use it and it works well. I'm looking for a wife who is openminded and good-looking. But I know lots of people who are in marriage-like relationships. We call them *known-in-public* couples," he said.

"I like that expression. We have a lot of that in the US, too," I said.

"Divorce in Israel is easy for most men, but not for women. This is because the husband can refuse the divorce. Women have to have a good reason, like abuse, in order to get a divorce. I don't feel this is fair. It's one of the many reasons I decided to choose to be a secular Jew instead of an Orthodox Jew. I celebrate holidays with my family, but I don't follow the commandments."

I could understand that.

"I hope to get married and have a family one day, but people here are getting married later than they used to. Honestly, prices are so high in Israel now, it's almost impossible for a guy like me to buy a home here—no matter how hard I work. Besides, with all the walls between the Palestinians and us, and all the rules, our stability is uncertain," he said with a frown.

"What do you think needs to be done for Israel to find peace?"

He shook his head. "There won't be peace until both sides talk to each other and understand that there are two sides to the story."

FULL CIRCLE FAITH

The next day, Pocky and I took a tour that began with a cruise on the Sea of Galilee. The sailboat had a huge white sail and held a dozen people. We sat in the shaded area in the middle of the boat. The sea was the exact same shade of blue as the nearly cloudless sky.

At one point, Pocky and I stood at the bow and he recreated the Titanic pose to make me laugh. Then he threatened to try to walk on water because he had found a pair of tennis shoes with "JC" written on them.

We stopped at Capermaum, the village at the center of Jesus's teaching in Galilee. Jesus had moved from Nazareth to Capermaum in order to preach to a wider audience. The town was also home to future apostles Peter, James, Andrew, and John, and the tax collector Matthew.

After we enjoyed panoramic views of the Golan Heights, we made our way to the Mount of Olives, named for the olive groves that once covered the slopes. While we took in the view of the Old City of Jerusalem below, I thought about how this was where Jesus gave the Sermon on the Mount, including the eight blessings of the Beatitudes.

In each of these holy and historic places, a sense of peace washed over me as I called to mind happy childhood memories of going to church with my family on Sundays. Attending church had grounded me.

I had experienced a beautiful childhood, in general. Even though this was something about my life I deeply cherished, I thought about how I hadn't taken nearly enough time to reflect on and feel gratitude for this blessing.

The Church of the Beatitudes was small, with a dome on top. The blessings were carved on stones along the path to the entryway. When we stepped inside the Church of the Beatitudes, I looked up at the gold dome with a blue dot in the center. I suddenly felt an overwhelming sense of comfort and joy. The strong feeling took me by surprise and brought tears to my eyes. This pure joy filled me completely.

It had been quite some time since I had attended church. My sister and I stopped attending after my parents died when we were in college. Church had been a family ritual, but without our parents around, it just didn't feel the same.

As I stood before the altar with its single gold cross, I realized I had been searching for something during my travels. I had been seeking some kind of connection to something all-encompassing, a connection that would bring me comfort, love, and joy—inside and outside myself. The exact feeling I was experiencing in the Church of the Beatitudes.

All the people I spoke with in the Middle East had made God central to their happiness. I began to think they were onto something. I felt my own connection to God strengthening, and deepening.

Pocky pointed to a nun standing by herself outside the church. Short with a round face and warm brown eyes, the Catholic sister held pamphlets with information for visitors. Pocky had grown up with nuns, and he suggested I speak with her about happiness.

I approached her and introduced myself. A Filipina, Sister Rea was dressed in the old-fashioned black-and-white habit. She smiled at me when I asked what made her happy.

"I am happy to have this life, to meet new people from all over the world. I look forward to prayer," she said. Her angelic face radiated peace.

"I believe that happiness is experiencing God, to be in relationship with Him and the Holy Spirit, and to remember to give gratitude for life itself."

These simple words penetrated my heart. I wanted to hear more. I wanted to hang out with her longer, to soak in her radiant peacefulness. But the tour moved on, and Pocky signaled that we had to go.

Her wise words lingered in my mind as I hurried to catch up with the others.

As we walked through the grounds of the church, I kept stopping to read the quotes from the Beatitudes carved into rocks and displayed on plaques. I snapped a photo of one of my favorite Bible verses: "Blessed are those who mourn, for they will be comforted." I would send the photo to a dear friend who had just lost her husband to liver cancer. As I lined up the shot, I wondered, *Does God want us to be happy?*

Yes, I thought, he does.

ACROSS THE WALL

The next day, we traveled to the history-rich Old City of Jerusalem, which had been built by King David in 1004 BC. A most unlikely king, David had reigned over Israel and Judah. The Dome of the Rock, the synagogues and churches, and mosques of pink and white stone, everything felt ancient and filled with meaning.

Traffic was light, and we decided to grab lunch. Pocky and I ate hummus with chicken and beef kabobs, served family-style at a large wooden picnic table. As I shared some thoughts with him about my book project, a man seated next to us said he wished to join our conversation about happiness. I said we'd be glad to hear his thoughts.

He introduced himself as Adham and said he was fifty-one years old. "I live in Bethlehem. I live across the wall, in Palestine." He told us he identified himself as a Palestinian Arab and a citizen of Israel.

"And what makes you happy?" I asked.

The small man smiled. "I love animals and people, and I am curious about everything. That's one of the reasons I became a truck driver, so that I could see everything firsthand and meet lots of different people. Even though there is a split and much anger between the Israelis and the Palestinians, my best friend is an Orthodox Jew," he said with a little laugh.

"Can you tell me about the differences that exist between Israel and Palestine?" I asked him, finishing my last kabob.

"You ask a question that is the most serious," he said. His mood darkened. "I believe that there is one God for all people, and our rights should reflect that. My biggest dream is for us to be one state, but I believe it will take much more bloodshed before that happens. I am allowed to be a citizen of Israel, but not a resident. And because of this, every day I must cross the wall to go to my home."

His eyes were dark and hollow, his sadness deep and penetrating. I said how sorry I was for this situation that must be so difficult for him to endure.

"I believe people are like five fingers." He held up his right hand and wiggled each finger, one at a time. "We are all different, you see, but each is needed."

"What a beautiful way to see the world," I said with a smile.

He nodded. "I think in order to have a good life you need two things: a good mother and a good education. I work really hard so my family will never have to work as hard as I do."

Working hard to make life better for future generations seemed to be a common theme, one I had heard echoed around the world. I remembered how my dad used to say he hoped my sister and I would have a better life than he did. And, in many ways, we did.

"With two daughters in college," Adham continued, "I have made my lifelong dream of provision for them come true. But this comes at great cost."

I wiped my lips with a napkin. "What kind of cost?"

He shook his head. "I must work away from home five days a week. I miss them. But I think this is good for the marriage, because after five days, my wife misses me, but after two days home, she's ready for me to leave again." He had a playful look in his eyes, then the spark quickly faded. "But she is sick now and her medications make her an angry woman."

"How are you handling that?" I asked him.

He shrugged. "I accept that nothing is perfect. And I think it is best in marriage if you set things up the right way in the beginning, so that you have each other's backs for the duration."

I nodded. So true. "How do you celebrate marriages in your culture?" I asked.

He smiled. "Wedding festivities are a big deal and can go on for as long as a week. There are henna nights for the women, and shaving the groom in public, with lots of dancing, lots of people with their extended families and everyone who lives in the town in attendance." He grew serious again. "It's important for us to keep our traditions alive."

I nodded. I loved the idea of henna nights and celebrating the union of two lives for a whole week. Weddings that lasted for days and days had been something I'd discovered on my adventures around the world. People in many countries put a lot of energy into these ceremonies.

I agreed with him about the importance of preparing for marriage and setting the relationship up properly at the start. It seemed to me that, in the United States, too many people rushed into marriage without making sure they would be there for each other. Adham's sentiments about time apart from his wife also seemed wise. Sometimes the best marriages are those in which the couple spends considerable time apart.

As Pocky and I wandered through the historic city, I thought about Adham's calm acceptance of his wife's situation. I thought about the wisdom of letting the little things slide, rather than allowing differences to get in the way of seeing the bigger picture—that is, the beautiful fact that a partnership is working. Sometimes in marriage it is best to agree to disagree.

That night, I reviewed in my mind Adham's five-finger analogy. I wanted to remember it so that I could keep it in my pocket and pull it out when I got home.

FAITH, HOPE, AND LOVE

The next day was sunny and mild. Pocky and I walked to the Western Wall. As we approached, we listened to church bells and the sounds of chanting in Arabic, Hebrew, English, and other languages. The air smelled of spices and my heart raced.

I had prepared beforehand so that I could slip a prayer inside one of the cracks in the Western Wall. One of Judaism's most sacred sites, the 1,600-foot limestone wall is divided into two sections; the men go to the bigger section, separated by a low wall from the women's smaller section. I guessed the men had more to pray about.

I peeked over the divider to look for Pocky. He was easy to spot in his neon-green golf shirt.

Next we went to the Church of the Nativity, which had been built on the spot where Jesus was said to have been born. It was cool and dark inside, and mosaic covered the floors and some of the walls. I expected to experience a sense of peace as I had at the Church of the Beatitudes, but this was not the case.

People from all over the world stood in long lines that led down stone steps to the manger where Jesus was born. The huge crowd wasn't pretty. People pushed and shoved, yelling at each other as, one by one, they climbed into the small opening of the grotto underneath the church. I even saw a nun shove somebody! I don't think Jesus would have approved of such behavior.

When I finally slithered through to the grotto, I stood staring at the floor. A beautiful, silver fourteen-point star had been embedded in the marble to mark the exact location of Jesus's birth. It was stunning. But people were throwing themselves on top of the star, snapping selfies and pushing others aside. It was total chaos.

I had lost Pocky in the madness, so I hurried out of the grotto. When we met up again at the exit to the church, I gave him a big hug.

That night we stayed home. We decided to have dinner and drinks at our hotel. We followed the red carpet into the bar, which was modern and stylish, with thick drapes and clustered chairs in chocolate and ruby hues. The wine list featured lots of award-winning selections from Israel. We ordered a flight of Israeli wine.

After he served us, our bartender told us how he had come to Israel at age nineteen because there were more opportunities than in his homeland. Dawit was an Ethiopian Jew.

"I love my job, and plan to be here as long as I can," he said. "I even got to mix drinks for Obama and Tony Blair!"

Pocky asked, "How did they take their martinis?"

"Shaken, not stirred," he answered with a laugh.

As Pocky and I sampled the first wine, a Golan Heights syrah, I asked Dawit what made him happy.

He said, "I think happiness is having a job I love."

I asked, "What do you want to see happen between the Jews and the Palestinians?"

After he poured the second wine, he leaned on the bar and said, "You know, I feel happy to see Jews and Palestinians living in separate regions because I think things are safer that way. It seems more peaceful now. Happiness *is* peace," he said, before excusing himself to tend to a party of young professionals.

The boisterous bar became still for me in this moment. Dawit saying that happiness is peace in this part of the world had such dramatic meaning for me. I'd heard other people express similar sentiments during my travels around the world, but not in this particular context. And not in the very place the entire world viewed as an impossible place for peace.

During our time in Israel, it seemed like war could happen at any moment. But it gave me hope to know that Adham and Tamir had friends on both sides of the ongoing conflict.

In Israel, I felt history in a different way than I had anywhere else in the world. Apparently, so did Pocky. We had passed by the Stations of the Cross on Via Dolorosa on our way through the bazaars of the Old City of Jerusalem. When we arrived at the Church of the Holy Sepulcher—believed to be the site of Jesus's crucifixion, burial, and resurrection—Pocky's heart had started to race. He told me about this later, saying he had no idea why this happened.

He told me he didn't try to understand it. I guess some things don't need an explanation.

Chapter 13

EGYPT: LARGER THAN LIFE

It had taken months to talk Pocky into going to Egypt. He was worried about safety. Some of our friends and family were also concerned and discouraged us from going. I tried to convince him how amazing it would be to see the iconic sights, the temples, the pyramids, the camels. Finally, after talking to some people who said their Egypt experience had felt perfectly safe and had been the trip of a lifetime, Pocky was on board.

We added a flight to Cairo to our Middle East itinerary.

When we left Tel Aviv for Cairo, we had to make a stop in Jordan. We couldn't fly direct. Egyptian politics required the Israeli passport stamp be issued on a separate sheet of paper. According to *Rough Guides,* the strict passport policy between Israel and some Arab nations set such limitations as the following: "Visas issued in Israel and flight itineraries that specify Tel Aviv (or TLV) may also bar you, as will anything in Hebrew discovered in your belongings."

We arrived in Cairo during rush hour. The traffic was as complicated as the passport politics. The rubber hit the road in a small van as we drove beneath a sea of huge, lit-up, Vegas-like billboards in a streaming river of cars. The cars swerved in and out of clogged lanes while pedestrians randomly walked across the highway. I watched out the window anxiously.

We were booked in a hotel in Giza in a room with a view of the pyramids. At first we thought they were cool new buildings, like the Luxor in Vegas. Eventually, we realized they were real pyramids, and the city and been built around them. Needless to say, the view from our hotel room was surreal.

The hotel had been a royal hunting lodge, and there were manicured gardens, harem windows, and marble mosaics. The lobby was vast, the high ceiling laced with dark wood beams. As we entered the lobby on our way to dinner, a photographer was in the midst of a shoot with a beautiful bride. Later, while Pocky and I ate dinner on the hotel's outdoor veranda, we watched as the wedding took place in front of the panoramic view of the pyramids. We could see the pageantry from our dinner table, and observed the reception start up in an open grassy area featuring a big screen and a stage. A live band played a combination of local music and American oldies, including lots of Tom Jones, like "What's New, Pussycat?" and "It's Not Unusual." Not exactly the playlist I would have expected at the pyramids, but fun. The reception menu included exotic foods and ice cream bars. People ate and laughed. Elegant women in colorful, flowing burkas danced beneath the palm trees.

The happiness of the people at the wedding lit up my senses, my mood as bright as the pyramids in their golden spotlights. Under a night sky filled with stars, romance came alive. Our front-row seats gave us a sort of unofficial invitation to participate in the celebration. So we drank wine and feasted on fresh vegetables, grilled meat, flat bread called *baladi,* and rice pudding. I thought about how Pocky and I began our own journey together so long ago in the snow of Colorado at a much smaller gathering, but every bit as magical.

IN THE SHADOW OF THE SPHINX

Our tour guide was Omar. Originally from Cairo, he had been an Egyptologist for thirty-four years. A short and husky man, Omar gave us the lowdown on all things ancient Egyptian. He liked to laugh and had an infectious smile that made his intelligent eyes sparkle.

We started out at the Great Pyramid of Giza, which had been built around 2500 BC for the pharaoh Khufu. The oldest of the Seven Wonders of the Ancient World, the massive pyramid was estimated to weigh 5.9 million tons.

How the heck did they build this thing? I thought as we neared the entrance. Omar told us about the incredible innovations the Egyptians had made in mathematics and the written language in order to construct the massive tombs.

We had to get low, crawling on our hands and knees through a narrow tunnel. Claustrophobia nearly got the best of me in the dark, closed-in chamber. But I soldiered through while calming myself by counting back from a hundred by threes.

Then I experienced the thrill of being inside a pyramid. I stood up to observe the king's burial chamber. It was dark and hot, empty except for the stone walls and slabs. All of the priceless contents had been stolen by grave robbers long ago.

I breathed in the moment, imagining when the mummified bodies of pharaohs in gilded sarcophaguses were there, along with all their treasured possessions, the things they believed they would need in the afterlife. The ancient Egyptians believed the king was chosen by the gods to serve as a mediator between them and the people on Earth.

After our tour of the pyramids, Pocky and I decided to ride camels. This was one of the most memorable parts of the trip for me. To be seated high up on a majestic camel with the pyramids behind me made me feel glorious, and I reveled in the moments spent in a surreal timeless bubble.

We trotted over to the Great Sphinx, the camel ride much smoother than I'd expected. An off-duty guide looked up at me as I passed. He was lying on the sand, relaxing in the shadow of the Sphinx. I laughed. No matter how sensational the backdrop of your life, you will eventually get used to it. This is how we overlook opulence and poverty, even when they exist side by side.

I reflected on how so many lives had been lived in the shadow of the Sphinx. How many people had stretched out in this shade over the millennia? How many had marveled at this wonder over thousands of years? In the searing afternoon heat, I imagined what it must have been like to see these monuments when they were brand new.

The next day, we flew to Luxor. We toured Thebes on the east bank of the Nile River. The former capital city of ancient Egypt, Thebes has both old ruins and modern buildings. We explored Karnak, a compound of decaying temples, chapels, and other ancient buildings. Construction had begun about four thousand years ago to honor the Thebian creator-god Amun, and was altered over the centuries by dozens of pharaohs who added to its splendor.

Karnak was once known as the "most select of places" by the ancient Egyptians. The Great Hypostyle Hall held perfectly aligned columns, the largest of which was eighty feet high, with a thirty-three-foot circumference. The enormity of the space bestowed a sense of timeless power. The walls and columns were covered with inscriptions like ancient graffiti. Omar told us these were writings from Rameses III, Rameses IV, and Rameses VI.

Omar continued to intrigue us with stories of ancient Egypt as we traveled to the west bank of the Nile to see the iconic sites there. We stopped at the Valley of the Kings, a burial ground of the pharaohs and a UNESCO World Heritage site. Sometimes called the Gateway to the Afterlife, it contained both monuments and underground tombs hidden in the sandy hills. We walked through them, examining the graphics and carvings on the walls. All the treasures that had been buried there with the pharaohs were gone.

We ended the day with a storybook sunset sail on the Nile's historic waters. I loved seeing Egypt in this ancient way. The winds alone determined where we would go. Nature would take us where it would, filling the sails with wind. I longed for that kind of surrender in my life at home, and was so happy to encounter it here.

On the sail back to Luxor, I had an opportunity to interview Omar. We were enjoying afternoon tea in a cozy corner of the ship's dining room. When I told Omar about my book on happiness, he immediately agreed to participate.

He said, "I have spent time sharing my knowledge with Sean Connery and Joan Collins, and now with Pocky and Lisa."

We all laughed.

"How did you become an Egyptologist?" I asked him.

"Like most meaningful things in life, it came to me in a roundabout way," he said with a sparkle in his eye. "Most of it involved working too much," he added with a laugh. "Life was hectic. I married young and we quickly had a girl and a boy. Fifteen years into my marriage, however, my wife asked me for a divorce. She no longer wanted to eat my bread and butter."

I looked at Pocky and he nodded. I'd never heard that expression before.

Omar said, "I worked eighteen hours a day, and neglected my relationship with my wife. When she told me it was over, she spit in my face. At that point, it was too late to repair the marriage. This was the lowest point in my life." He looked grave. "I learned a lot after losing my family. The downslides after my divorce and the kidnapping brought me closer to God and taught me to live and let live, which is one of my mottos."

Pocky stopped him. "What do you mean, *the kidnapping?*"

"Ah, that is another story. One story at a time," he said with a wink. "But as a result of my losses, I try not to judge others. I try to be tolerant and accepting, and to laugh as much as possible. Egyptians are a very humorous people, and that's one reason they like Americans," he said, then placed a hand on Pocky's shoulder. They both laughed.

I asked, "How did the experience of losing your wife bring you closer to God?"

He sipped his tea. "The struggle I endured strengthened my relationship with God because I began to nurture my spirituality in daily prayer. I prayed about everything and trusted that as long as I worked toward good, God's will would be done. I continue to believe this. My trust in God makes me feel invincible, so I have much less anxiety than when I didn't have a strong relationship with God. And those prayers led me to my second wife, and we are very happy." He grinned. "Our first date was to the Egyptian Museum, and the second date was for coffee. On our third date, I told her everything good and bad about myself, and asked her to marry me. We've been happily married ever since, and we have a daughter together."

I smiled at him. "What do you think is the key to your happy marriage?"

He grew serious. "Not just accepting my wife's flaws, but loving them. I think there is too much emphasis on trying to fix the symptoms of problems in a relationship instead of focusing on the reason for the problems."

"I like what you said about loving your wife's flaws," I said, giving Pocky the elbow.

Pocky and Omar exchanged a knowing look.

"What about happiness, in general?" I asked. "What do you think are the keys to a life of happiness?"

"As a married man, I must say that if my wife isn't happy, then I am not happy," he said.

"That's for sure," Pocky said with a grin.

Omar said, "I believe it is the job of the husband to provide a sense of security. I do this for my wife, and I give her the time with me that she needs, which I didn't do in my first marriage. In return for this, my wife loves me and my self-esteem now is in Seventh Heaven."

I finished my tea and set down the cup. "Is there anything else you do to keep the romance alive in your marriage?"

He leaned forward. "I believe the language of love involves roses. I like to think that three roses meant 'I love you,' and one rose meant 'I love you only.' I learned the language of love the hard way, of course."

He shared a laugh with Pocky, then became serious again. "You know, the only thing on my mind while I was kidnapped was seeing my beautiful wife again. I longed for her, and this kept me going. It seemed it had taken me a lifetime to find her. After the bitter divorce with my first wife, I'd finally met her. It only took three weeks to know she was the one for me. Then the kidnapping happened. Everything happened so close together."

"Would now be a good time to talk about your kidnapping?" I asked him gently.

"I don't know if there's ever a good time, but I guess now is as good a time as any." He paused, looking away. "I remember the day like it was yesterday. Life is learning, and I'm afraid I got my most serious lesson on December 12, 2012, which, if you recall, was soon after the Arab Spring uprising. The uprising became the catalyst for a lot of lawlessness and restlessness in the Middle East."

I nodded. "Yes, I remember the news. The Arab Spring seemed to happen so quickly."

He agreed. "It seemed that way to me, too. On that day, I was digging a well on my family-owned farm where my mother and I were staying. When I went inside our farmhouse, five men armed with machine guns appeared out of nowhere. They followed me inside. They said they belonged to the Muslim Brotherhood, so I knew they were there to kidnap me and hold me for ransom."

How horrifying! I asked, "What did you do?"

"I said, 'I believe in one God and Mohammed is my messenger.' As soon as I spoke those words, a calm came over me. It seemed that after I spoke those words, my odds were a hundred to one on my side, so confident was I in the will of God." He looked at me. "I told my kidnappers I would go with them, but if they touched my mother, who was asleep in a nearby room, then I'd try to kill one of them. This would mean they would have to kill me, so they would receive no ransom."

"How much ransom did they want?" I asked him.

"They wanted two million Egyptian pounds. Which, at that time, was around three hundred thousand US dollars."

I sat back and Pocky whistled. I said, "That's so shocking! How did you deal with that?"

He shrugged. "Honestly. I said that two million would be impossibly high for my family to pay. They blindfolded me with a torn blanket and took me away anyway. My blindfold remained on until eleven o'clock that evening. All the while, I told my kidnappers that if they treated me well, we would figure something out."

I was nervous just hearing his story. "How did you keep so calm?" I asked.

He cocked his head. "It was the only way forward. If I panicked, I'd lose my edge, which was my ability to use reasoning. And reasoning needs a clear mind. Fear muddies the mind."

I nodded, impressed by his bravery. "What did you do next?"

"They tried to intimidate me by saying there were people who hated me and had offered them a big price for my head. But I know a lie when I hear one, so I was sure they were bluffing. I had a friend who was connected with the police. So I told the kidnappers this friend would pay the ransom. They had no idea of my friend's connections, so they agreed. And they went along with me when I said I could only afford a hundred thousand pounds. When they contacted my friend, he knew what to do. He worked out a meeting place and a way to transfer the money."

Pocky asked him, "Did you have an idea who the kidnappers were?"

Omar shook his head. "They were foulmouthed, and they all smoked a lot of hashish. But because they were young and naive, I had an easier time reasoning and negotiating with them. I told them if they wanted more than a hundred thousand pounds, they might as well kill me now, and that would be fine, because I was good with God. If my time had come, I'd be prepared to die—and I really meant it."

Pocky and I exchanged glances. Would we feel the same way? I doubted it.

"While they waited for my friend to get the money together, I asked my kidnappers if I could pray. They told me I could, as long as I didn't pray to God against them. This helped my cause with the kidnappers as they saw I was a religious man. I was eventually exchanged for a hundred thousand Egyptian pounds. Then my friend and I went straight home to see my family and friends, and we all celebrated my safe return."

"And what happened to your kidnappers?" Pocky asked.

"They made off with the hundred thousand pounds. But I made off with my life! Three weeks after that, I became a life coach." He grinned.

We all laughed.

I said, "Can you talk about the happiness your religion brings into your life?"

He nodded. "I believe there is one God over all. All the world's religions teach morals, manners, and ethics to guide the way we live our lives. Essentially, we are not that different—Muslims, Christians, Jews. God looks at our hearts, so with right thoughts and good deeds, we will be okay."

I leaned toward him. "And what about the bad deeds done in the name of God?"

He grimaced. "With many religions and cultures, extremists are the problem. People who feel they are the only ones who are right, and have a sole intent of destroying all those in opposition. Extremists are not of God. Unfortunately, although they are the minority, they get a lot of press with their chaotic actions and violent behaviors. This is why so many people believe the extremists are in the mainstream of Islam."

I said, "That belief seems counter to what I know of the people I've met here in the Middle East."

He nodded. "Yes. This is because the extremist point of view is so loud. That view is out of balance with the rest of the believers. And balance is a very important part of happiness. I love to play squash and horseback ride, and I enjoy reading biographies about celebrities. These things bring me happiness of a kind. But my true happiness lies in my spiritual life. I pray to God at the five calls to prayer each day. I believe this form of obedience and devotion to be an important part of worship, important for my happiness."

I said, "The call to prayer is a beautiful part of your religion."

He smiled. "One of the truly beautiful aspects of faith is that if you want to achieve something and you walk to it, God will help you get there. If God wills it, and you've worked hard for it, you will achieve it," he said with certainty.

AN INSIDE JOB

The following morning, we were waiting to board a small motorboat that would take us to the island of Agilkia. Omar walked up and stood next to me. In a low voice, he said, "I have someone I'd like you to meet later on. I think she will be a great interview for your book."

"Wonderful," I said. I wanted another female perspective on the Middle East, and I gave him a grateful smile.

The boat would take us to the Philae Temple, which had been dedicated to Isis, the Egyptian goddess of marriage, fertility, motherhood, magic, and medicine, among other things. No wonder Isis was known as the goddess with ten thousand names! The ancient temple had also been a pilgrimage center for the cult of Isis. The cult's initiates included female priests who shaved their heads and played the sistrum, a percussion instrument that produced a rattling sound rumored to carry magical, protective qualities.

As we cruised up to the island, I was impressed by the stunning beauty of the setting. Bougainvillea in bright coral and pink hues covered the huge stones, the obelisks, and columns. This ancient temple had dazzled travelers for centuries. The sacred site had been highly respected by the ancient Greeks, Romans, and Byzantines.

We disembarked and toured the site, with Omar filling in the historical details. He told us the temple had been dismantled block by block and saved from a watery grave, moved from the original island to the present location in the 1960s. We marveled at all the carvings and the statues depicting Isis, Horus, Osiris, and other honored figures from the ancient past.

On the return trip, we enjoyed an incredible rose and gold sunset. From our seats on the deck, I watched the vivid sky colors fade to the rich purples and blues of evening. The light was impossibly lovely, so I didn't want it to end, nor did I want the beauty before my eyes to fade.

Endings were on my mind as this night was the last of our time in Egypt, and it marked the end of my adventures in happiness around the world.

"How you feeling, honey?" Pocky asked me, rubbing my arm.

A bit choked up, I said, "Happy."

"Then I've done my job," he said.

I smiled at him through my tears. Indeed, he certainly had.

Suddenly, there was loud music and a tall, dark, very lean man in a white turban and a double-layered skirt began to dance around the deck. Spinning, spinning, spinning, his skirt spun wildly as he whirled in circles around us. As I watched him, the dance had a hypnotic effect on me.

"Are you Mrs. Marranzino?" someone asked me.

I turned to face the woman, still in a daze. "Yes," I said.

"Hello, I am Samaa. Omar told you about me?" she asked with a smile.

I smiled back and invited her to sit with us.

A fifty-four-year-old business travel coordinator from Cairo, Samaa was short and sturdy, and she exuded confidence. "This dance we are watching is called Sufi whirling, or what Egyptians call Tanoura. It is a form of meditation in which the spinner aims to discover the source of all perfection. In doing so, we abandon our nafs—or what you call ego—our personal desires. In tuning in to the music, focusing on God, and spinning in circles, one performs a kind of prayer."

As the spinning slowed and the music stopped, I began to shake the hold the dance had on me. Pocky pointed to a table away from the action, and Samaa and I moved to this quieter spot on the deck. We took our seats and ordered iced tea while the last rays of my last sunset in Egypt hovered over the gently rippling water.

Samaa said, "It is so nice to meet an American woman. Egyptians love Americans for their sense of humor, but we stay clear of your politics," she said, taking a sip of her tea. "I will teach you a little Arabic. Marhba means 'hello.' Marhba, Lisa," she said with a wide smile.

"Marhba," I repeated, then said, "Thank you for taking the time to speak with me today. I really enjoy hearing the female perspective on the Middle East."

"Omar told me you are writing a book," she said. "I find that fascinating."

"Yes, I am, and I wonder if we could talk about *your* life, and how you find happiness."

"Well, I am a single woman, divorced many years ago now, and I have an adult son," she said, then sighed. "Deception by loved ones was the most painful part of my life. I was deceived by my husband, and by a couple of my sisters who I believe are jealous of my lively personality and life of freedom. Their behavior deeply hurt me, but now I realize that their jealousy, which is a part of human nature, was really to blame. So I learned not to take their actions against me personally."

I sipped my iced tea. "And your life now?"

"I have chosen to remain single and independent because I believe it will protect my heart and cause me less disappointment," she said. "The more educated a woman is in Egypt, the more acceptable it is for her to be independent and equal, or even *more* successful than men. But in the villages, the old way still holds and women must be subservient to men."

"Have you been able to find happiness in spite of your heartache?" I asked her.

"Well, I have had a lot of pain in my life so I've thought about happiness extensively. I came to the realization that happiness is an inside job. If you want to own your happiness, you must investigate your life in order to know what makes you happy. I mean happy outside of any relationship. If you do this, I believe hardship will not befall you. Happiness needs a lot of work. A lot of attention."

An interesting perspective. I asked her, "How did you begin the process of your inside job?"

She thought about this for a moment. "I learned how to love myself better. How to take care of myself. I began to see the value in advocating for my own wants and needs. For example, if you have a chance to travel and that makes you happy, take it! Whatever experience makes you happy, focus on accomplishing it and doing more of it."

This made me smile. "I like that idea, especially as it relates to travel, since that's what inspires me right now," I said.

"Exactly! So you are finding pleasure in the journey, and that is all any of us can do. After I was hurt, I lost all my confidence. But through my connection to and trust in God, I found it again."

"Can you talk about that process?"

She smiled at me. "Whenever a challenging person or situation tries my patience, I de-personalize it. I stop focusing on whatever is bad or uncomfortable in the experience. Instead, I come up with six things I like about the person or the experience. Six is just a random number, but it works for me. You can use whatever amount you desire," she said.

"Thank you, that's a great tip," I said.

"Shukran," she said. "Shukran means 'thank you' in Arabic," she said with a wink.

"Shukran," I said.

She continued, "I gained most of my confidence when I decided to have a deeper relationship with God. In Islam, Allah has given us many phrases to help us have a better life. I repeat these words over and over again every day and they stay with me always," she said. "I also pray at least five times a day for a few minutes."

"Are there other rituals you observe to help you have a close relationship with Allah?" I asked her.

She nodded. "Yes. I follow our tenets by never, ever drinking alcohol. I also try to be a good person, and make it a point to express my thoughts face to face with people whenever I have problems with them. A lot of people have walked out of my life because of my frankness, but that's okay. I leave them and my fate to God."

I liked her attitude; it was refreshingly honest. "What do you focus on when trying to be a good person?" I asked.

She smiled and said, "Recently I've become very focused on charity. In Islam we are encouraged to donate 2.5 percent of our earnings. I try to do more than that. We are encouraged to take care of our loved ones first, then spread any extra resources we may have to others in need. Islam stipulates that charity takes place in secret so the beneficiaries don't know who their benefactor is. It is my belief I am a messenger of God and I am here to help others."

I liked the idea of anonymous charity. It seemed honorable. This reminded me of a Chinese saying, "If you want happiness for an hour, take a nap. If you want happiness for a day, go fishing. If you want happiness for a year, inherit a fortune. If you want happiness for a lifetime, help somebody."

Samaa said, "We believe in one God, and in the angels of Heaven that can help us here on Earth. We believe in Judgment Day, and that our lives are predestined. I try not to judge others, leaving that to God. It is God who will take care of things in the afterlife of either Paradise or Hell."

I remarked on how so much of what she was saying reminded me of what I had learned in church many years ago.

"I think the biggest similarity is the doctrine we share about love, or ahebk," she said.

I smiled. "Ahebk." I liked the sound of the word.

The stars had come out over the Nile and they were bright in the black sky above us. Samaa's cell phone rang, and she excused herself to take the call.

I finished my iced tea while I watched the reflection of the stars dancing across the ripples of the slow-moving river. I thought about Samaa's commitment to helping others, and how kindness creates a ripple effect in the world. I had learned through my work that lifting the burdens of others can make us happy. Studies indicate this occurs because our bodies release neurochemicals that promote the feeling of well-being in a process known as the "helper's high." Research shows that when we give to others, the part of our brain that is activated is the same area that responds when we're having sex or eating chocolate.

Confident and wise, Samaa had found the happiness that is all encompassing-—physical, emotional, and spiritual. And she had chosen to live a life of giving to others and love for God.

DROPPING THEIR ABAYAS

On our last day in Egypt, Omar took us to see the Mosque and Madrasa of Sultan Hassan. Located in the center of bustling Cairo, the massive mosque had a huge dome. As we were waiting in line to go inside the ancient mosque, I noticed a big group of schoolchildren. They appeared to be around thirteen or fourteen years old. They were whispering to each other and seemed to be staring at me. I had no idea why.

When I smiled at them, one of the kids came over to us. "Can I take a picture with you?" the boy asked me.

"Sure," I said, flattered but confused.

"They are fascinated by your blonde hair and blue eyes," Omar whispered. "They so rarely see this combination."

Suddenly, all the kids rushed toward me, dozens of them, pushing and shoving like paparazzi, cameras in hand. Then the selfie snaps began. I have to admit, it was kind of thrilling. It was like experiencing the fifteen minutes of fame Andy Warhol once said everyone would have.

"Nice work, Marilyn," Pocky said, giving me quick hug. I laughed at him as he fake-fawned over me.

Omar shepherded us inside the mosque.

Built in 1356 AD, the mosque had elaborate architecture with high ornate ceilings, carved marble, and carpeted prayer rooms. As we moved into the expansive foyer, the men and women separated to go to their different worship areas.

A bearded man dressed in a brown robe with beads wrapped around his wrist entered the foyer. He took center stage and began to sing the call to prayer. His deep, melodic voice took my breath away. The lyrics vibrated around the massive space and penetrated my heart, filling it with the ultimate feeling of peace.

This was the same feeling I'd had as I watched the elephants gather at sunset in the African bush. The same deep feeling I'd experienced at the Church of the Beatitudes. It felt intensely spiritual, as if God had just showed up.

I closed my eyes, bathing in the resonant sounds of call and the exotic voice.

When I opened my eyes, I noticed how the burka-clad women all looked at me on their way to worship. My eyes met Pocky's, and he nodded, as if he knew I'd experienced something strong during the call to prayer. We often didn't need to speak because we knew what the other was thinking or feeling, and I loved that.

After we left the mosque, I told Pocky we needed to do some shopping. He agreed, but as usual, he lasted maybe ten minutes. Then he ducked into a hookah coffee bar in the market while I continued browsing. After finding a few treasures to bring home to friends and family, I caught up with him.

The coffee bar had been decorated in blacks, whites, and gold. Pillows were scattered on the chairs and benches. Framed black-and-white photos covered all the walls. Only a few people were in the bar. Pocky sat next to two women dressed in gray slacks. They were smoking hookah together.

"They'd love to talk to you about the book, honey," Pocky said from the middle of a purple smoke cloud.

His chest kind of puffed out with pride. One of the women had given him her fez, which sat at an awkward angle on top of his head. He looked hilarious wearing the tiny hat and a huge smile.

I thought about how far we had traveled on our adventures in happiness. Now Pocky was totally comfortable talking about happiness to complete strangers in faraway places. What a long way we both had come since our first foray in Thailand.

Practice makes perfect.

Pocky and I were different from many of the people we had met around the world. But these people had embraced us and welcomed conversation with us. I marveled at how free we all felt to express ourselves. This made me understand how important, even vital, the business of self-expression is. If we don't encourage people different from ourselves to express themselves in conversation, do we really believe in freedom?

I scooted my packages to one side and joined Pocky and his new friends at the low table.

The women told me they were litigators from Oman. Both in their late thirties, they had long dark hair and sparkling eyes. Khawla wore a soft blue shirt, while Ameer was dressed in a forest-green jacket. They looked quite modern.

They said they had come to Egypt in order to take classes. This was something they did three or four times a year, and these were trips they really looked forward to, they said.

When I asked what they thought about happiness, Khawla said, "Happiness is freedom." She pulled out her cell phone and showed me a picture of herself with her family in Oman. All the women were dressed in burkas, or abayas, as they called them in Oman. "I like to be free from my traditional clothes," she said.

Ameer agreed that happiness was freedom, then added, "But happiness is also love. I love my family and my work."

They asked if I cared to smoke some hookah with them. Not wanting to be rude, I decided to indulge. The fruity cloud filled my lungs and I coughed, and this left me a little light-headed.

The women spoke about their lives in Oman. They explained how they had to limit their activities to work and home because of the cultural expectations of their society.

Khawla said, "This is why we enjoy our time in Cairo, when we travel here for school. We are able to drop our abayas and let our hair down."

Ameer added, "We can wear what we want, put on makeup, go out to eat, dance to music, and smoke lots of hookah, which lightens our spirits. This is happiness," she said with a wide smile.

Quite a contrast with the two women from Oman I had met in the airport in Qatar. Such different experiences with happiness.

Granted, the women before me were older than the young women I'd spoken with in Qatar. But this new encounter seemed to underscore what I had suspected: Women who knew about the freedoms allowed to them in other parts of the world wanted to have them, too. Once they'd experienced such freedoms, they desired a lifting of the restrictions on women in their own culture. They would seek to be free themselves.

Of course, this is true for all of us. Everyone longs for a life without restraint, a life free of judgment, tight schedules, and unpleasant duties—a life in which we are free to ride the current of our own lives, exploring our strengths and desires.

HAPPY MICROCOSMS

On the long flight home, I thought about my experiences in the Middle East, and I realized just how much I loved being on the water. This was because I found such peace there. In Egypt, most of my conversations about happiness had taken place overlooking the Nile River.

On my last moments in Egypt, I had sought out the best view of the river and put my feet up, thinking how unbelievable it was to be there, pondering happiness along the shores of the Nile. So many memories called to me, so much had been stirred up in my heart. The Nile was filled with boat traffic, each ship so very different than another. Each on its own track. While watching the ships sail, I thought about how much we could learn from each other. And it's lucky that we do, because it is this kind of understanding that allows us to bust out of our routines and open up to fresh possibilities—which is the only way to really live.

As the plane dipped and then smoothed out, I thought about how we are all microcosms of the earth's chemistry. And microcosms of each other. Microcosms made up of love and heartache, pain and joy. Maybe not in the same proportions, but underneath our superficial differences lie deep, organic similarities. We are all connected by what it means to be human, and this includes the pursuit of happiness.

In my experiences in the Middle East, I had found most of the people I met were god-loving and family-oriented, with good values. I still feared the extremists, there and in my own country, but I no longer worried about visiting that part of the world or speaking with its people. I realized it was my naiveté that had made me fearful.

Because it isn't our differences that divide us, but our inability to accept and find value in them. After all, our differences are the spice of life.

Pocky slept deeply beside me, so I tucked him in with the airline blanket. He'd proven to be the perfect traveling companion. I knew how lucky I was and this made me happy.

With my eyes closed, I thought about how my travels had opened my heart to difficult chapters in my past, but also brought healing and understanding. I'd deepened my curiosity about people through experiences I could not have had anywhere else in the world. Breaking out of my comfort zone had allowed me to create new bonds with strangers and build friendships with people from all walks of life.

In that moment, I decided that even if happiness was an inside job, the promotion of world peace would happen. But it would have to happen one back-seat, hookah-smoking, Google-translation encounter at a time.

Epilogue

INSIGHTS ON HAPPINESS

I embarked on my adventures in happiness on the blue dot when I found myself slipping into a classic midlife malaise—which I felt guilty about because it seemed so unfounded. Part of what I was experiencing was due to an empty nest and, quite frankly, a hysterectomy. But at the core of the unsettling feelings was an intense urge coming from deep within, an urge that was pressuring me to expand in some way. I knew if I continued to ignore this urge, the pressure and the feelings of emptiness would just get worse. Joining the ranks of the walking dead would be in my immediate future.

To avoid this fate, I decided to explore the world in order to discover how other people found happiness.

As a therapist, I shared strategies all day long with clients who wanted to live a better, happier life. Yet I knew I had more to learn. With seven billion people on Earth, the opinions on how to achieve happiness would be endless. I needed fresh ideas, and I knew the odds were good that others living on the blue dot would have them.

Venturing out into the unknown and speaking to people with beliefs very different than my own has expanded my thinking. The experience has revitalized the way I live and changed the way I look at life.

NOW THAT THE ADVENTURE
IS OVER, AM I HAPPIER?

In many ways, I am. But in an odd twist of fate, my happiness was rigorously tested recently, only a couple months after our trip to the Middle East. Because of this, I had to put into practice all the wisdom I had gained on my adventures. I was required to rely on what I had learned from people all over the world in ways I would never have imagined.

It began a few days after recovering from a particularly nasty bout with the flu. I woke up one morning with a weakness in both legs. It felt as if the connection between my brain and my legs wasn't working right. When I tried to stand up, I went into a free-fall. In an attempt to catch myself against a nearby wall, I discovered my arms were weak, too.

A few hours later, I was in a hospital bed in the ICU, unable to move my legs, feet, arms, or hands. As the creeping paralysis continued to move up my body, the doctors became concerned my respiratory system would be affected and I would need to be intubated.

That afternoon, the doctors told me the diagnosis: Guillain-Barré Syndrome (GBS), a rare but serious condition in which the immune system goes haywire and attacks the body's healthy nerves. The syndrome can be triggered by a virus or vaccine. Apparently, my immune system had begun to attack my peripheral nervous system, interfering with the ability of my brain to send messages to parts of my body. This was prohibiting my body from functioning properly. GBS can affect individuals of all ages, but only about one out of a hundred thousand people ever experience this syndrome.

The grim news came hard and fast: Most people recovered, but there were no guarantees. And recovery could be a slow process, usually taking several months to a couple of years.

I spent twenty-three days in the hospital. I am now four months into my recovery. I walk like a drunken sailor, but at least I can walk. My fingers are typing this awkwardly, but my physical therapists say typing is good for my recovery. The act of writing this story is healing me beyond an emotional level into the physical realm, helping to restore my normal movement.

But there will be no more wandering for me for a while. Instead of conversing with people in Arabic on Google Translate, I am mastering the new language of GBS. This involves new-to-me things like infusion therapies, pain thresholds, medical billing, and insurance glitches.

I thank God for Pocky, who has been steadfast throughout. When I was hospitalized, he brought me Starbucks lattes every morning, fed me, carried me around, and bathed me. He brought bowls of soup, home-made pasta, and plenty of cookies to the nursing staff, too. Although he called himself Nurse Ratched, the nasty character from the movie *One Flew Over the Cuckoo's Nest*, he was my saving grace.

This experience has taught me that happiness isn't possible all of the time, but it *is* possible some of the time, even in the most trying of circumstances. When I couldn't move and was in pain, I found happiness in certain moments. One day I laid motionless in my hospital bed, watching a beautiful snowstorm outside the window. I was able to fully appreciate the mesmerizing dance of the huge white flakes falling gracefully from the white sky, coating every tree branch perfectly. I had not noticed before the way snowflakes move because I'd been living my life in fast motion.

Without the ability to move around and with the luxury of time, I had new insights. I could appreciate the way the world moved around me in new ways. I found that joy and pain were not mutually exclusive and I realized how some of the worst experiences can plant fresh perspectives deep in our brains, becoming the best catalysts for positive change.

I'm so grateful now that Pocky and I didn't do the practical thing and wait until after retirement to embark on our adventures in happiness. Time and good health are not guaranteed.

During my recovery, I read *The Red Notebook* by Antoine Laurain. The following passage moved me, as it so beautifully describes how easily life can pass us by. If something makes me happy now and I can do it, then I'm going to do it—right now!

> We can pass right by something very important: love, a job, moving to another city or another country. Or another life. "Pass by" and at the same time be "so close" that sometimes, while in that state of melancholy that is akin to hypnosis, we can, in spite of everything, manage to grab little fragments of what might have been. Like catching snatches of a far-off radio frequency. The message is obscure, yet by listening carefully you can still catch snippets of the soundtrack of the life that never was. You hear sentences that were never actually said, you hear footsteps echoing in places you've never been to, you make out the surf on a beach whose sand you have never touched. You hear the laughter and loving words of a woman though nothing ever happened between you.

WHAT DID I LEARN ALONG THE WAY?

I learned so much on my many adventures on the blue dot, but certain lessons stuck with me. These range from the simple to the profound. Here are nine of them:

1. I appreciate the power of a warm smile.
2. I am willing to bathe my husband Pocky whenever he asks, and I will probably flirt with him until the

end of our days to show how much I delight in him.

3. I've made peace with the idea of death, and in light of my newfound comfort with loss, I've begun to integrate items that remind me of my departed loved ones into my home and my life.

4. I have learned how to quiet my mind, finding peace in the present moment.

5. I believe God speaks many languages, and can be found in churches, temples, mosques, and the African bush.

6. I've found relief in letting go of first-world problems, and I surrender to life's twists and turns more easily.

7. I relish more in the simple pleasures—like a great meal shared with family and friends, or sipping a blue cheese-stuffed-olive martini while watching the sun set.

8. I've learned that people from every culture in the world are inherently good, and generously wise. Infinite potential lies in listening to one another.

9. I have learned that happiness is a choice, an ongoing venture, something that must be nurtured every day. Like with so many other things in life, the more we practice happiness, the better we get at it.

I wish you well on this, your great adventure in happiness. I'll be rooting for you from the sidelines, hoping your journey includes lively conversations and frequent pleasures shared with others. The appendices offer some helpful tips to assist you along the way. If you wish, you can reach out to me and let me know how your happiness adventure is coming along. Bon voyage, and good luck!

ACKNOWLEDGMENTS

Whew! As it turns out, writing a book was harder than I ever imagined it would be. Hats off to authors everywhere who have completed one. I'm grateful to every family member, friend, and stranger who listened to my stories, offered great suggestions, and provided words of encouragement along the way.

As a therapist, I think about and talk about happiness every day. The clients I've worked with over the years have been an inspiration in writing this book, and in other areas of my life as well. I am grateful to them for trusting me enough share their innermost thoughts and feelings. I'm pretty sure I've learned at least as much from them on the subject of happiness as they've learned from me.

Talking to clients about life is one thing, but asking strangers in faraway places to do the same seemed iffy at best. But I discovered that everyone has a story to tell, or an idea to share, about happiness and life. It's amazing how quickly people engage when they know you are genuinely interested in them. I'm forever grateful to those who took time out of their lives to chat for a while. I'll never forget the lessons and feelings of connection that grew out of our conversations together.

As a new author, I needed lots of professional support to help navigate the winding roads of the writing, editing, and publishing worlds. Thanks to Virginia Aronson, Laura Elliott, Kristi Fisher, and the team at Palmetto Publishing Group for their valuable guidance. It also a meant a great deal to me when my stepson and talented designer, Nick Marranzino, agreed to create the book's cover.

When all is said and done, there's no place like home. I sure didn't need to travel very far to see that my greatest source of happiness is my family. Kaylee inspires me with her courage and zest for life; Cara, with her sweet and caring ways; and Nick, with the ability to look at the world through a creative lens. And finally there is Pocky, my husband, best friend, and travel partner in the journey of life. I am grateful beyond words for all the love and support he provided during the course of this project. This book is dedicated to him.

Appendix A

HAPPINESS DISCOVERIES CHECKLIST

Happiness is a universal quest that unites us all. I've found that sharing ideas over a cup of tea, a glass of wine, after a tango, or even around the skeletal remains of dead ancestors, provides more insight for me than any textbook or well-researched study.

Happiness is infinite, and the sources of happiness are all around us. There are as many paths to happiness as there are people on the blue dot. In writing this book, I had conversations with people all over the world. Some of the names and identifying details were changed to protect the privacy of individuals. I took copious notes, and I conveyed the truth of what they were telling me as I heard it from them. I often wonder how they would tell their own stories about our conversations, because we all absorb information and experiences in different ways; your takeaways from the stories in this book will be unique to you. The fact that we all see things differently makes life more interesting.

I've collected a list of the insights that inspired me on my journey, and the ones I keep in my pocket now. I share them here with you in the hope that they will encourage you and help you breathe more happiness into your own life. If you are not sure where to begin, consider picking the ones that resonate with you, then commit to putting them into practice a few at a time. There is an asterisk next to the ten happiness practices I concluded made the most difference in the lives of the people I met on my adventures. You could also start with these practices first.

Happiness is:
- spending time with friends and family;⋆
- seeking face-to-face connections;
- deeply committing to those who lift you up and encourage your dreams;
- securing the basics (food, clothing, shelter), and helping others to do so;⋆
- letting go of judgment;
- understanding that we all need to be forgiven from time to time;
- bestowing random acts of kindness;
- flirting with your lover (complimenting, kissing, listening, playful teasing).

"Love is not just something that happens to you, it is a special way of being alive."

—Thomas Merton

Happiness is:
- approaching life with an open mind;⋆
- being open to new-and-improved ways of thinking and acting;
- developing optimism;
- choosing to view things with a positive but realistic mindset.⋆

"If you change the way you look at things, the things you look at change."
—Wayne Dyer

Happiness is:

- finding ways to clear the mind (meditation, nature, warm baths);
- releasing overblown fears and living life boldly;
- making peace with the past;
- appreciating the beauty and power of the present;★
- finding hope in the future.

"Let go of all that is no longer serving you, and realize that an infinite power lies in your present moment."
—Mateo Tabatabai

Happiness is:

- making peace with death, the greatest adventure into the unknown;
- finding purpose in suffering (without adding any needless suffering);
- letting go of things that won't matter in a week, month, year;
- building on strengths that lead to resilience.★

"If you're going through hell, keep going."
—Winston Churchill

Happiness is:

- seeking novelty and variety, what's new and fresh in every day;
- embracing life's constantly changing nature;

- creating experiences;
- breathing in precious moments before they drift away;
- replaying positive memories in your mind;
- holding on to curiosity and wonder;
- playing like a child (dancing, skipping, climbing a tree, playing in the dirt).

"Time is a game played beautifully by children."

—Heraclitus

Happiness is:

- finding abundance in simplicity;
- savoring the simple sweetness of life;
- smiling more;
- performing acts of kindness;★
- finding humor in almost everything;
- living a healthy life by moving your body, getting good sleep;
- connecting with the awe of something greater than yourself;★
- feeling full of love and inspiration;
- expressing yourself;★
- following your instincts, passions, and callings;
- wandering;
- sharing good food and wine;
- recounting what you are grateful for in every day.★

"Acknowledging the good that you already have in your life is the foundation for all abundance."

—Eckhart Tolle

Appendix B

HOW TO CHANGE YOUR BELIEFS

Seeing is not believing; believing is seeing. You see things not as they are, but as you are.

—Eric Butterworth

Everything we hear is an opinion, not a fact. Everything we see is a perspective, not the truth.

—Marcus Aurelius

A belief is the understanding we have around a concept or situation. Our level of happiness is determined by our beliefs, which are simply the stories we tell ourselves. Since we are the authors of our own stories, we might as well make them good ones!

Unfortunately, most of us run on remote control, unaware of our beliefs and how they impact our lives and happiness. While we can't always choose what happens to us in life, we *can* choose what we believe about those events and how we respond to them. In order to find the happiest ways to look at life, we need to be willing to free ourselves from worn out mindsets and make room for fresh ideas.

It's been estimated that up to 90 percent of what we think, say, and do today will be the same as what we did yesterday. We're running on old fuel. Our old thoughts and habits can make life feel dim and repetitive. We get stuck in the mud of unhappiness. Our minds can heal us or harm us. The choice is ours.

Here are seven pointers for pulling out of the mud and creating new and improved beliefs on your road to happiness:

1. **Accept that your beliefs are your own subjective interpretations of the world.** They were created by how you were brought up, what you've been exposed to, and what you've been focused on.

2. **Be open to your thoughts and beliefs, and look at them as if you're seeing them—and the experiences around them—for the first time**. Such curiosity will help you begin to notice the stories you are telling yourself about the world around you. Take note of your reactions to these stories.

3. **Make a list of the areas in your life that are not working well, and examine the beliefs you've attached to them.** Limiting beliefs might include: "Love hurts"; "Work is a four-letter word"; "Life isn't fair"; "I'm never enough." Such beliefs reinforce unhappiness and do not improve the quality of your life. Instead, start reframing your beliefs one or two at a time.

4. **Create new beliefs that make you feel empowered—but don't sugarcoat them; your beliefs need to be believable enough that your mind will accept them.** For example, replace the limiting belief "Love hurts" with "Better to have loved

and lost, than never to have loved at all." Replace "Work is a four-letter word" with "My work is a means to an end."

5. **Focus on the new beliefs, and link them in your mind with positive experiences and feelings.** Look everywhere for evidence to support your new beliefs. For example: For "Better to have loved and lost, than never to have loved at all," look for happy people in love. For "My work is a means to an end," watch for people enjoying the fruits of their hard labor. Look for examples in your own life that reinforce your new beliefs.

6. **Absorb each new belief.** Beliefs are stored in the brain *and* the body; allow yourself to feel the new positive emotions coming from your empowering beliefs by breathing them in. Whenever possible, find ways to use all your senses, your voice, and your body language to reinforce the new beliefs until they are installed in your brain and body. Feel them in your muscles and mind; the power of love, the reward of a well-deserved vacation.

7. **Engage in the process of changing your beliefs over and over again**. It may feel challenging at first, so tell yourself you can exercise tenacity. The good news is, if you continuously replace an old negative belief with a healthier one, through repetition your brain will lock into the new belief. Your new positive way of thinking will become a habit that invites more happiness into your life.

"Repetition of the same thought or physical action develops into a habit, which repeated frequently enough, becomes an automatic reflex."

—Norman Vincent Peale

Appendix C
HOW TO CONVERSE WITH A STRANGER

Due to my adventures in happiness on the blue dot, I've become a huge fan of initiating conversations with people who have beliefs vastly different from my own. These discussions can be stimulating for all involved. Talking with others reduces boredom and serves as one of the best antidotes to becoming one of the walking dead.

While I've been working on this book, a number of people have told me they would like to be able to talk to strangers as they journey through life but aren't certain about approaching them. I understand the hesitation. My own approach to strangers around the world went against everything I had learned as a child. I can still hear my mom's voice saying, "Don't talk to strangers." But this was one of the many old beliefs I decided to let go of and replace with a belief that could enhance my adventures in happiness.

So I replaced "Don't talk to strangers" with "Remember that every good friend was once a stranger." Both of these concepts are valid, but adopting the new one made my life more dynamic. This new belief allowed me to meet people who would grant me the kind of wisdom I could never gain on my own.

Here are a few simple tips on how you can make conversing with a stranger a little easier:

- Know that you may learn more from a single conversation with a wise person than through years of studying.

- Go into conversations with a curious mindset. You are inviting someone to tell you who they are and what they think. Many people will be flattered to know you are interested in what they have to say.

- Don't let fear of rejection stop you. People have their own reasons for saying no. A stranger's response to you is usually not personal. Everyone I asked to talk with me not only agreed to discuss the topic of happiness, but also provided me with fascinating social interactions I could learn from while they encouraged me on my project. Only one woman—a survivor of the 9/11 attack on the Twin Towers—asked me to keep her story private, and not include it in the book. She had been heavily pursued by the media at that time, and longed for privacy.

- Understand that timing is everything. When approaching strangers, select people who look like they are not in a rush and seem to have time on their hands. These kinds of opportunities may arise anywhere, such as when you are waiting for and receiving a haircut, a manicure or pedicure, or sitting at a bar or in an airport terminal.

- Be sure to state your intention up front. For example: "I am studying/curious about different cultures"; "I am gathering ideas/finding out what people think about life/fun places to visit in this area." You will discover most people are as interested in talking to you as you are with them.

- Ask for a designated number of minutes of each person's time, and stick to this unless they say they want to talk more. With the prostitute in Amsterdam, after I showed respect for her time, she opened up even more about her story.
- Watch your body language. Proper body language can help you gain the trust and respect of the people you choose to interview. Make eye contact and nod as the person you are speaking with makes their points. Watch the other person's body language, too. Take note of their eyes, smile, and posture. These visual clues will help you understand more clearly what someone is trying to say, and can cue you in to boundaries you might be crossing.
- Ask open-ended questions that start with who, what, when, where, why, or how. Avoid asking simple yes-or-no questions, as these allow for brief answers that can quickly curtail the conversation.
- Comment on the other person's statements so they know you are listening. You can paraphrase their comments as well. This builds trust in the relationship and will help you find ways to go deeper into the information they provide that you are trying to understand.
- Remember, conversation is built on listening to others' opinions and ideas, not on trying to change them.
- Share information about yourself so the conversation feels like a friendly chat rather than an interro-

gation. Be sure to thank them for their time, and let them know how much it has helped you.

- Some people might say no, they don't wish to talk to you. Thank them anyway. And remember, if at first you don't succeed, try, try again.

SUGGESTED READINGS

Cicero, Marcus Tullius. *On the Good Life*, translated by Michael Grant. London: Penguin, 1971.

Corrigan, Kelly. *Tell Me More: Stories About the 12 Hardest Things I'm Learning to Say.* New York: Random House, 2018.

Csikszentmihalyi, Mihaly. *Finding Flow: The Psychology of Engagement with Everyday Life.* New York: Basic Books, 1997.

Dalai Lama and Desmond Tutu. *The Book of Joy: Lasting Happiness in a Changing World.* New York: Avery, 2016.

Dalai Lama and Howard C. Cutler. *The Art of Happiness: A Handbook for Living.* New York: Riverhead Books, 1998.

Demaris, Ann, and Valerie White. *First Impressions: What You Don't Know About How Others See You.* New York: Bantam Books, 2005.

Dyer, Wayne. *Change Your Thoughts, Change Your Life: Living the Wisdom of the Tao.* Carlsbad, California: Hay House, 2007.

Easterbrook, Gregg. *The Progress Paradox: How Life Gets Better While People Feel Worse.* New York: Random House, 2003.

Fisher, Helen. *Why We Love: The Nature and Chemistry of Romantic Love.* New York: Henry Holt, 2004.

Frankl, Viktor E. *Man's Search for Meaning.* Boston: Beacon Press, 2006.

Gilbert, Daniel. *Stumbling on Happiness.* New York: Knopf, 2006.

Gilbert, Elizabeth. *Eat, Pray, Love: One Woman's Search for Everything Across Italy, India, and Indonesia.* New York: Riverhead Books, 2007.

Gladwell, Malcolm. *Blink: The Power of Thinking Without Thinking.* New York: Little, Brown, 2005.

Haidt, Jonathan. *The Happiness Hypothesis: Finding Modern Truth in Ancient Wisdom.* New York: Basic Books, 2006.

Hanson, Rick. *Hardwiring Happiness: The New Brain Science of Contentment, Calm, and Confidence.* New York: Harmony Books, 2013.

Hornby, Nick. *How to Be Good.* New York: Riverhead Books, 2002.

Krakauer, Jon. *Into the Wild.* New York: Villard, 1996.

Lamott, Anne. *Operating Instructions: A Journal of My Son's First Year.* New York: Random House, 1997.

Laurain, Antoine. *The Red Notebook.* London: Gallic Books, 2015.

Lyubomirsky, Sonja. *The How of Happiness: A New Approach to Getting the Life You Want.* London: Penguin, 2008.

Nettle, Daniel. *Happiness: The Science Behind Your Smile.* Oxford, UK: Oxford University Press, 2005.

Rauch, Jonathan. *The Happiness Curve: Why Life Gets Better After 50.* New York: Thomas Dunne Books, 2018.

Rubin, Gretchen. *The Happiness Project: Or, Why I Spent a Year Trying to Sing in the Morning, Clean My Closets, Fight Right, Read Aristotle, and Generally Have More Fun.* New York: HarperCollins, 2009.

Seligman, Martin E. P. *Authentic Happiness: Using the New Positive Psychology to Realize Your Potential for Lasting Fulfillment.* New York: Atria Books, 2004.

Seligman, Martin E.P. *Learned Optimism: How to Change Your Mind and Your Life.* New York: Knopf, 1991.

Tabatabai, Mateo. *The Mind-Made Prison.* Scotts Valley, California: CreateSpace, 2014.

Thich Nhat Hanh. *The Miracle of Mindfulness*, translated by Mobi Ho. Boston: Beacon Press, 1975.

Tolle, Eckhart. *The Power of Now: A Guide to Spiritual Enlightenment.* Vancouver, Canada: Namaste Publishing, 1997.

Weiner, Eric. *The Geography of Bliss: One Grump's Search for the Happiest Places in the World.* New York: Twelve Books, 2009.

ABOUT THE AUTHOR

Lisa Marranzino is a licensed professional counselor with a private practice in Denver, Colorado. She works with individuals, couples, and families, and specializes in relationships, transitions, personal growth, and developing resilience in challenging times. She also provides coaching and training for business organizations.

Before becoming a therapist, Lisa worked with non-profits, advertising agencies, and in public relations, helping to market everything from Procter & Gamble-sponsored race cars to McDonald's hamburgers. She has a bachelor's degree in technical journalism and a graduate degree in psychology.

With an adventurous spirit stronger than her fear of flying, Lisa has traveled to more than forty countries, and has gone skydiving and hang gliding. When she's not working, she enjoys time with her husband Pocky and their three grown children, exploring new places, or hanging out in the kitchen.

Happiness on the Pale Blue Dot is her first book.